ADVANCE PRAISE FOR *The Last Letter*

"*The Last Letter* is a compellii
how individual family stories
process of Holocaust rememb
by the children of the victims, about those
who perished and those who su...ved, but also about the continuing
impact on their descendants."

WILLIAM H. WEITZER | John H. Slade Executive Director, Leo Baeck Institute—New York and Berlin

"Both a very private account and a general outline of the German Jewish experience of the twentieth century, *The Last Letter* comprises the story of a family that contributed so much and lost so much. Allowing herself intimacy and trepidation in her reflections, Karen Baum Gordon offers one of the central intellectual challenges of Jewish existence in the aftermath of the Holocaust—the question of how to comprehend the ruptures that the Shoah denotes. This book names the ghosts of the past that haunt us, and it charges us to change our world for the better."

RABBI PROF. DR. WALTER HOMOLKA | Rector, Abraham Geiger College, Potsdam, Germany

"In this haunting and remarkable book, Karen Baum Gordon reminds us that the Holocaust is a story that remains with us, and that storytellers like her are essential in passing the story on from generation to generation."

MICHAEL SHAPIRO | Professor of Journalism, Columbia University

"Having had the privilege of knowing Rudy Baum during the last decades of his life, I am deeply moved to read the extraordinary story of his years growing up in Germany, then fleeing the Nazis, finding refuge in the United States, and finally learning of the murder of his parents, friends, and extended family in the Holocaust. Rudy and his family come to life in vivid letters and photographs, giving us a window into daily life for Jews in Nazi Germany."

SUSANNAH HESCHEL | author of *The Aryan Jesus: Christian Theologians and the Bible in Nazi Germany*

The Last Letter

Drawing from the past, living in the present, shaping the future!

RABBI ABRAHAM GEIGER, my great-great-great uncle

LEGACIES OF WAR | *G. Kurt Piehler, Series Editor*

Karen Baum Gordon

THE LAST LETTER

A Father's Struggle, a Daughter's Quest, and the Long Shadow of the Holocaust

The University of Tennessee Press / Knoxville

The Legacies of War series presents a variety of works—from scholarly monographs to memoirs—that examine the impact of war on society, both in the United States and globally. The wide scope of the series might include war's effects on civilian populations, its lingering consequences for veterans, and the role of individual nations and the international community in confronting genocide and other injustices born of war.

Manufactured in the United States of America. First Edition.

Photographs are courtesy of the author and her family except where noted. Letters, autobiographies, and other documents are held in the archives of the Leo Baeck Institute.

LBI Archives AR10440 | https://links.cjh.org/primo/lbi/CJH_ALEPH000199153

Author site: karenbaumgordon.com

Library of Congress Cataloging-in-Publication Data

Names: Gordon, Karen Baum, 1956- author.

Title: The last letter : a father's struggle, a daughter's quest, and the long shadow of the Holocaust / Karen Baum Gordon.

Other titles: Father's struggle, a daughter's quest, and the long shadow of the Holocaust

Description: Knoxville : The University of Tennessee, 2021. | Series: Legacies of war | Includes bibliographical references. | Summary: "Part of the Legacies of War series, *The Last Letter* is a family memoir that spans events from the 1930s and Hitler's rise to power, through World War II and the Holocaust, to the present-day United States. Karen Baum Gordon's gripping narrative opens on her father Rudy Baum's attempted suicide in 2002 at the age of eight-six and unfolds in an investigation of generational trauma within her extensive German Jewish family. Gordon grounds her research in eighty-eight letters written mostly by Julie Baum, Rudy's mother and Gordon's grandmother, to Rudy between November 1936 and October 1941. Gordon examines pieces of these worn, handwritten letters and other archival documents in order to recreate the fatal journeys of her grandparents in the camps and ghettos of the Third Reich and trace her father's efforts to save them an ocean away in America. Doing so, Gordon discovers the forgotten fragments of her family's history and a vivid sense of her own Jewish identity"—Provided by publisher.

Identifiers: LCCN 2021033644 (print) | LCCN 2021033645 (ebook) | ISBN 9781621907039 (paperback) | ISBN 9781621907046 (kindle edition) | ISBN 9781621907053 (pdf)

Subjects: LCSH: Baum, Rudolf Berthold, 1915–2009. | Baum, Rudolf Berthold, 1915–2009—Family. | Baum family. | Jews—Texas—Dallas—Biography. | German Americans—Texas—Dallas—Biography. | Holocaust, Jewish (1939–1945)—Germany—Frankfurt. | United States. Army. Corps, XX—Biography. | Children of Holocaust survivors—United States. | Gordon, Karen Baum, 1956- | Frankfurt (Germany)—Biography.

Classification: LCC F394.D219 J54 2021 (print) | LCC F394.D219 (ebook) | DDC 940.53/18092 [B]—dc23

LC record available at https://lccn.loc.gov/2021033644

LC ebook record available at https://lccn.loc.gov/2021033645

TO MY FATHER AND HIS PARENTS;

MY SONS, Matthew and Adam;

MY HUSBAND, Bob, and future generations of our family;

and to all those touched by the long shadow of the Holocaust.

Contents

Part 4: The War and the Peace

Part 5: The Stumbling Stones

Illustrations

Foreword

What are the enduring legacies of war? At the outset of this series, I intended scholars to explore the myriad effects war had on society, from economic and geographical impacts to personal accounts of tragedy and loss. And while countless books have been published on World War II, the Holocaust, and the enduring tragedies born of that conflict and genocide, scholars, researchers, and students are still examining what is commonly referred to as the long shadow of the Holocaust, or the longsuffering generational effects that ripple through the families of veterans and Jews alike. The serious study of the Holocaust's lasting consequences has produced fascinating questions as to whether severe trauma born from war and genocide can be passed down to subsequent generations. Though medical studies are not definitive toward this end, in terms of the cultural impact on family units there is no question that generational trauma is a very real issue and that Holocaust victims and their extended families live with continual reminders of the worst genocide the world has ever seen. Karen Baum Gordon's beautiful exploration of her own family's search for answers amid a personal tragedy presents this near-universal testament among Jewish survivors in stark and honest detail.

In *The Last Letter*, Karen Baum Gordon recounts the impact of the Holocaust and World War II on four generations of her family. She seeks to understand the lives and deaths of her paternal grandparents, Norbert and Julie Baum, German Jews, who went from a comfortable life in Frankfurt, Germany, to exile and death in a Polish ghetto. She remembers her own experiences growing up with her father, Rudy Baum, who managed to escape Germany and appeared over the years to have successfully embraced his American identity. But deep down, her father could not escape the trauma he endured from his inability to save his parents from the clutches of the Nazis. At eighty-six years old Rudy Baum attempted suicide. This would not only shock his daughter, but also sparked her quest to understand his reasons. This led her to reconstruct her grandparents' and father's stories through family letters and related archival sources, numerous trips and interviews, and existing scholarship on the Holocaust.

This is a story of how individuals grapple with their identity. Karen Baum Gordon recounts the assimilation of her grandparents into German society in the opening decades of the twentieth century. While the Baums remained observant Jews, they rejected Zionism and they viewed themselves as Germans first. Like many other German Jews, her grandfather had fought bravely in the German army during World War I. Within a few short years of the Nazi's seizure of power, her grandparents faced betrayal as the Germany they had loved deprived them of their freedom of movement, property, and citizenship. Although the majority of German Jews managed to leave Germany by 1941, her grandparents would be unable to escape and were deported to a Polish ghetto.

Rudy Baum would be fortunate to leave Germany before the door slammed shut. Not only did Rudy embrace his new country and its customs, but he also joined the ranks of the US Army during the war and ultimately took part in the liberation of the concentration camp Buchenwald. After the war ended, Rudy served in the occupation government of the American zone in Germany and played an important role in reestablishing one historical German town's free press. *The Last Letter* offers insights into one channel supporting Germany to make the transition from fascism to a stable democratic nation.

Equal parts biography, personal memoir, and anthology of family correspondence, Karen Baum Gordon eschews simple analysis and is brutally honest. She offers a compelling portrait of a good son, husband, father, and citizen who struggled with demons that haunted him for decades. She is honest about what she views her father grappled with, about what she grapples with, and about what she sees in her sons' emerging identities.

As this work will underscore, the legacies of war can endure for decades after the fighting stopped.

G. Kurt Piehler

FLORIDA STATE UNIVERSITY

Preface

The letter was written on onionskin paper in *Sütterlin*, an ornate early twentieth-century form of German handwriting, nearly eight decades ago. It was written by my grandmother, a woman I never knew. The yellowed paper was brittle and ready to crumble to the touch. It must remain intact, I thought, as it is, as it has been for these many years. A corner can't tear; a word can't be lost. It is just one letter in a stack of many, and I begin to wonder about the journey of my grandparents' lives, some of it surely revealed in these letters.

This is a story of three journeys, the first being that of my grandparents Julie and Norbert Baum, who lived in Frankfurt, Germany, under Adolf Hitler. They believed that the worst would not come to pass. They believed this until it was too late.

The second journey was that of my father, Rudy, Julie and Norbert's son, who escaped the Nazis for America and built a life here, but who was unable to save his parents. He would return to Germany after the war to help liberate Buchenwald, but despite Rudy's achievements as a soldier, he paid a great personal price for that failure.

The third journey is my own, as I worked to understand my father's late-in-life attempt to kill himself, and that event's connection to his parents and their fate; and to come to terms with my own German Jewish heritage.

The book is informed by, and in fact quotes at length, eighty-eight letters written by my grandparents (primarily my grandmother) to their son (my father) between November 1936 and October 1941—letters to America full of everything from gossip and laundry instructions to portents of the unspeakable. It also draws upon my father's writing and speeches about his experience, including his autobiography; on documentary research; on multiple interviews; on the work of great historians like Saul Friedländer and Marion Kaplan.

I discovered numerous documents through the hours of research on the internet in the quiet of my own office. Tracking down documents and people through sources such as ancestry.com, the Red Cross International Tracing Service, and the websites of various Holocaust museums. After I learned that the "older" Frankfurt archives are housed in the Hessian State Archives in Hesse's capital, Wiesbaden, I requested the complete document files of my grandparents. Those files, for the years 1935–1961, had more than two hundred pages, almost all tax-related, many with official stamps and signatures; included were tax returns, records of furniture sales, financial office notes of suspicion about my grandfather, employment verification for my father, restitution papers. Reading through the pages chronologically, I felt the gradually increasing scrutiny and restrictions tightening the financial noose that slowly limited my grandparents' lives. Lives with virtually no choice. Small living quarters. Almost no money and no assets. No work. Little food.

Meanwhile, I have expandable file folders bursting with documents and artifacts from my father's life. These treasure troves of history offered me tangible connections to what would otherwise have been a "reading about" or "description of." I can hold in my hand the very bits of history that my father touched, that he chose to save for these oh-so-many years. A tiny newspaper clipping from 1941 recounting my father's naturalization proceeding. A postcard with a picture of the ship my father took when he left Germany, leaving his parents behind, with the ship's scheduled to-the-minute itinerary of its port arrivals and departures. Picture albums with photos of everyday lives in "normal times" just before and after the turn to the twentieth century, and then albums full of photos during World War II.

I also directly traced and retraced elements of my father's and grandparents' past on several trips to Frankfurt and one to Lodz, Poland, where my grandparents died in the ghetto.

In Frankfurt, I met with an archivist of the Jewish Museum. In his large office with floor-to-ceiling piles of historical materials and barely a place to sit, together we pored over telephone books from the 1930s, in search of addresses and occupations. He clicked through his familiar databases in focused search of answers to one or another of my several questions.

I spent time with a historian at the *Institut für Stadtgeschichte Frankfurt am Main*, the Institute for Frankfurt City Archives. We solved the mystery of the location of my grandfather's office, as its street address no longer existed. We thumbed through scores of 2' x 3' maps piled upright to find those that could tell us the story of the street changes overtime. Then, with a few short taps on his computer, the historian sent me on my way with a CD that held the answer to my question, fitting neatly in my small bag.

I had the privilege to work with and befriend the late Monica Kingreen, a researcher at the Fritz Bauer Institut, who was one of the foremost experts on the deportations in the 1940s from Germany. Her research provided detailed accounts of the deportations, the kind my grandparents endured, beginning with the moment people were forcibly pulled from their homes.

I walked through cemeteries in Frankfurt and Lodz with cemetery administrators who, for decades, have taken care not only of the gravesites, but also of people like me in search of loved ones' burial sites and tombstones. The administrators were deeply knowledgeable about Jewish burial and grieving customs, though they were not Jewish themselves. They were full of stories about the lives of the people whose tombstones they guard.

The weaving together of the threads of my search resulted in this big history as seen through ordinary lives. As I recreated the journeys of my grandparents and my father and confronted my own, William Faulkner's words about history became a guiding truth: "The past is never dead. It's not even past."

Geiger Family Tree

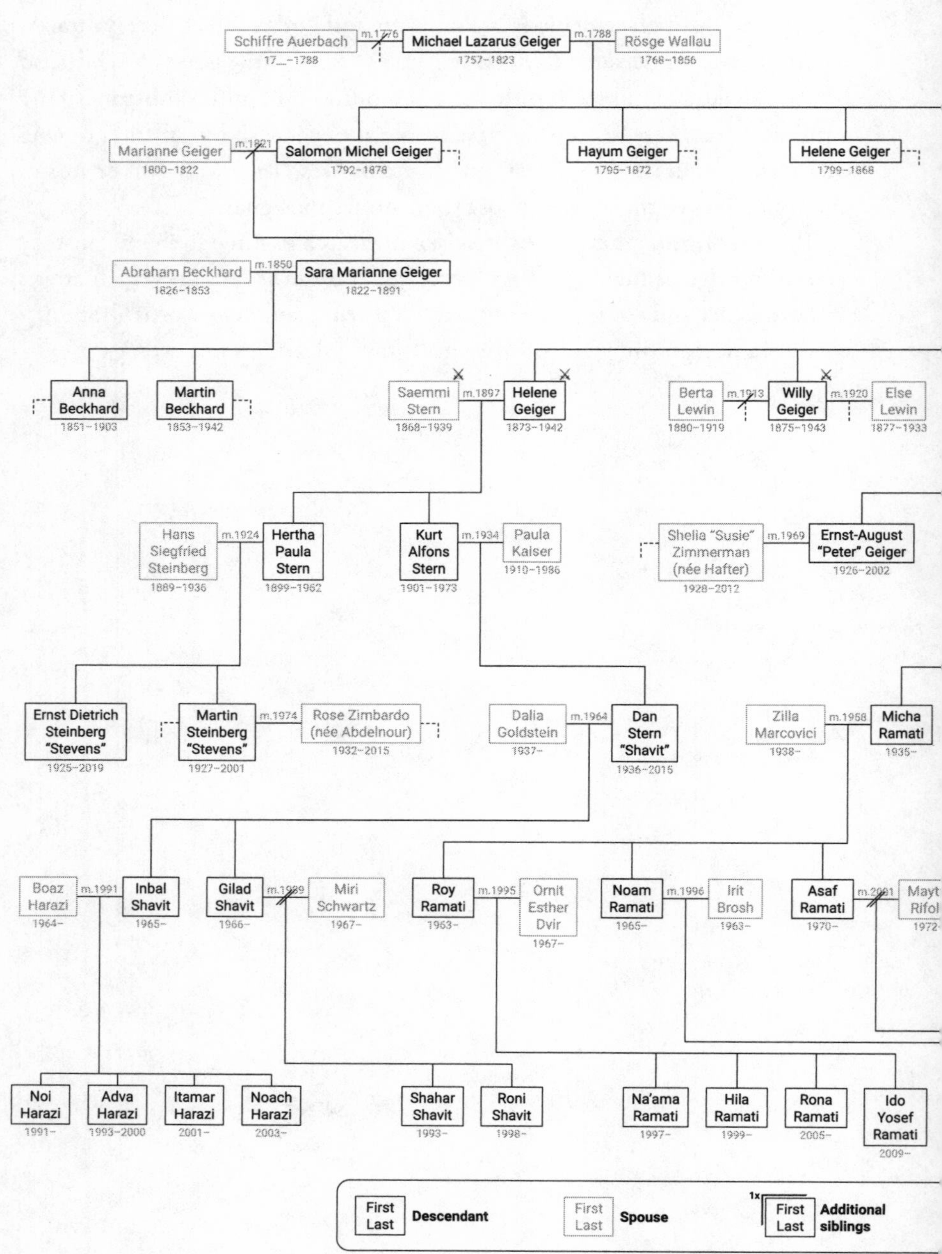

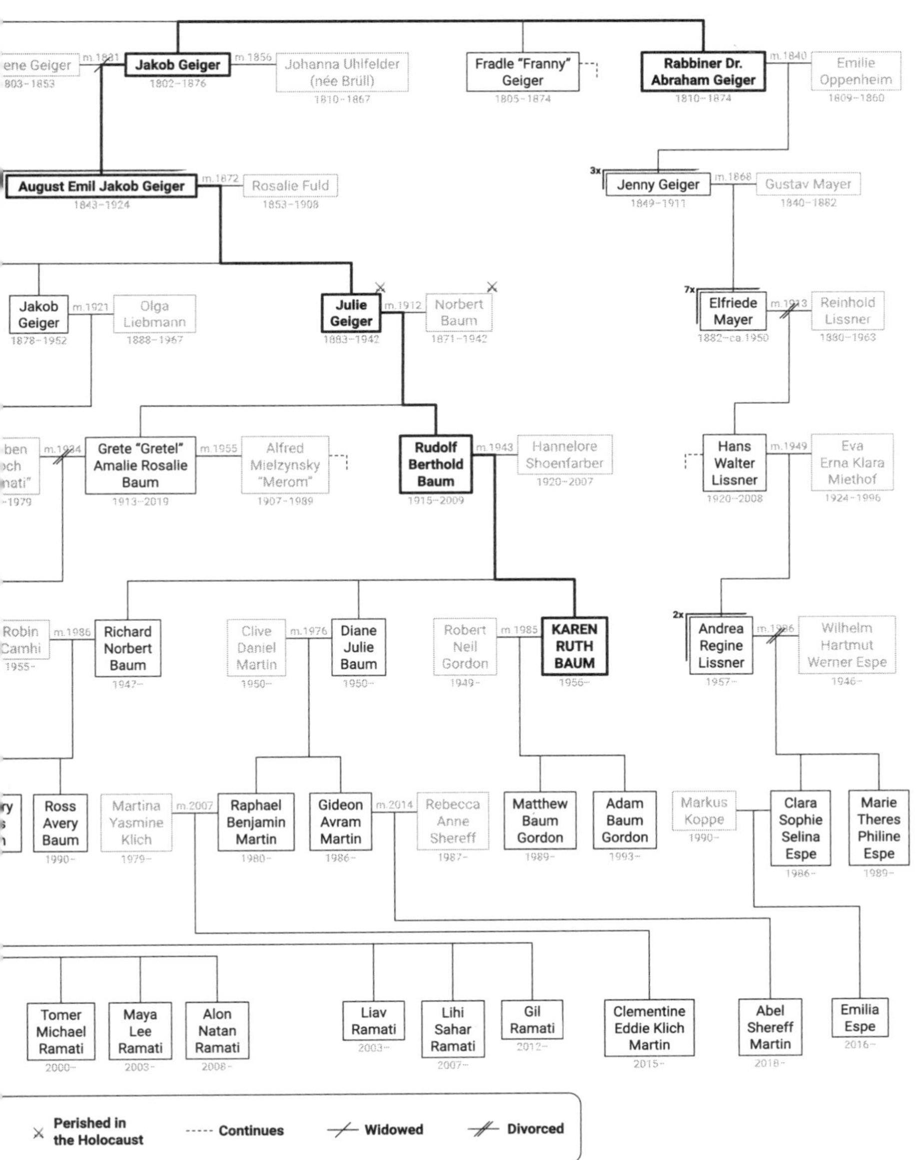

Jakob Geiger
1802–1876
m.1831
m.1856
Johanna Uhlfelder (née Brüll)
1810–1867
Fradle "Franny" Geiger
1805–1874
Rabbiner Dr. Abraham Geiger
1810–1874
m.1840
Emilie Oppenheim
1809–1860
August Emil Jakob Geiger
1843–1924
m.1872
Rosalie Fuld
1853–1908
3x
Jenny Geiger
1849–1911
m.1868
Gustav Mayer
1840–1882
Jakob Geiger
1878–1952
m.1921
Olga Liebmann
1888–1967
Julie Geiger
1883–1942
m.1912
Norbert Baum
1871–1942
7x
Elfriede Mayer
1882–ca.1950
m.1913
Reinhold Lissner
1880–1963
m.1934
Grete "Gretel" Amalie Rosalie Baum
1913–2019
m.1955
Alfred Mielzynsky "Merom"
1907–1989
Rudolf Berthold Baum
1915–2009
m.1943
Hannelore Shoenfarber
1920–2007
Hans Walter Lissner
1920–2008
m.1949
Eva Erna Klara Miethof
1924–1996
m.1986
Richard Norbert Baum
1947–
Clive Daniel Martin
1950–
m.1976
Diane Julie Baum
1950–
Robert Neil Gordon
1949–
m.1985
KAREN RUTH BAUM
1956–
2x
Andrea Regine Lissner
1957–
m.1986
Wilhelm Hartmut Werner Espe
1946–
Ross Avery Baum
1990–
Martina Yasmine Klich
1979–
m.2007
Raphael Benjamin Martin
1980–
Gideon Avram Martin
1986–
m.2014
Rebecca Anne Shereff
1987–
Matthew Baum Gordon
1989–
Adam Baum Gordon
1993–
Markus Koppe
1990–
Clara Sophie Selina Espe
1986–
Marie Theres Philine Espe
1989–
Tomer Michael Ramati
2000–
Maya Lee Ramati
2003–
Alon Natan Ramati
2008–
Liav Ramati
2003–
Lihi Sahar Ramati
2007–
Gil Ramati
2012–
Clementine Eddie Klich Martin
2015–
Abel Shereff Martin
2018–
Emilia Espe
2016–
Perished in the Holocaust
Continues
Widowed
Divorced

Part One

A TORTURED SOUL

May God forgive me.

RUDY BAUM

1

Dallas, 2002

My father tried to kill himself when he was eighty-six years old. My mother, his wife of fifty-eight years, was still alive, and needed him. He enjoyed spending time with his three children and their families, including his six grandsons. The small tent calendar on his desk had, until not long before his suicide attempt, something scribbled in it for almost every day—lunches, dinners, panel discussions, cultural events. He had seemed so full of life.

He was rather slight, at five-foot-seven and a steady weight of 127 pounds. He kept in shape by walking vigorously two miles most days. He had a full head of silvery gray hair with a touch of waviness, hinting of once even wavier hair. He was usually dressed sharply in slacks coordinated with a collared shirt, often relatively new purchases. But in his later years, he somehow wore his belt closer to his armpits than his waist.

My friends, who found my father to be charismatic, would have to book a month in advance to have lunch with him. He was a good conversationalist and usually had an informed point of view about all sorts of topics, such as Dallas mayoral candidates or Texas gubernatorial candidates, the Dallas Cowboys, the stock market's ups and downs, retailers that were expanding, companies filing for bankruptcy, the dot-com bubble, world leaders, global summits.

I had a strong relationship with him. I always felt his unconditional love and support. As a little girl, I ran down the driveway on Friday afternoons to greet my father, a traveling salesman, when I heard his big Buick pulling up as he returned from his five-day road trip. I was eager to download in one breath all of the seemingly major events of the week—how I did on my most recent math test, why Mom yelled at me, how my sister's friend was mean to me. And then I couldn't wait to see if he had brought home any delicious treats, such as *kolaches*, the Czech filled-pastries, from the tiny town of West, Texas; or sausages from New Braunfels, a town with German heritage in the heart of Texas Hill Country. My father appreciated a wide range of foods—from authentic grub found in hole-in-the wall spots to fine French cuisine offered in fancy restaurants. No surprise: I grew to have a love of food. I even trained as a chef and managed several restaurants.

My father and I were similar. Both extroverts. Both people connectors. Both early birds energized by jam-packed days. Both interested in family history, in the past.

I never thought my father would ever do something that would hurt those he loved, including me.

Still, he tried to kill himself. On February 11, 2002, a Monday, I was in my kitchen in Brooklyn, making dinner, when the phone rang. I recognized the 214 area code—Dallas—but not the number. My husband, Bob, answered upstairs. After a few minutes, he called to me, "Can you come up here for a minute? It's Don Cole." Don and Judy Cole were my parents' neighbors.

The previous months, December and January, had been particularly trying for my parents. My mother's congestive heart failure and lymphoma had left her ever more compromised, though she could still drive to the grocery store and to her water aerobics class. So my father had assumed a more active caregiver role, well beyond merely covering for my mother's early-stage dementia. He would sit on a stool in the humid bathroom when my mother showered, watchful that she didn't fall, ready with her towel. He did the cooking, the grocery shopping, the pharmacy runs. In charge. Dependable.

My brother, Dick, my sister, Diane, and I had gathered with our parents that January in Dallas to discuss their situation. Do they stay in their house with help from caregivers? Do they move to a senior residence in Dallas? Do they move to a senior residence on the East Coast, where all three of their children and six grandchildren live?

There had been another reason for such questions, however, beyond our mother's frailty. At the time, we also had a family session with our father's psychiatrist. Upon our urging, my father had recently started seeing him again. For the last several weeks, my father's small tent calendar no longer showed a busy schedule, but blank days, one after the other. His affect had become dull and quiet. His mood seemed one of resignation. He had lost weight. Twelve years earlier, this psychiatrist had helped him get through a deep depression with therapy and medicine after triple bypass surgery, a period that lasted months but then seemed to dissipate. So we encouraged my father to try him again during this stressful period.

In the course of that family session, I said that I was "afraid of Dad doing something stupid," an indirect allusion to suicide. The psychiatrist had turned to my dad and said, "You hear her, Rudy?" My dad nodded sheepishly. "Rudy," the psychiatrist said, "that's not the legacy I think you want to leave your kids. Right?" Again, my father nodded.

Soon after that, my parents came to New York to sign a lease at a senior independent living residence in Manhattan. But my father was passive and withdrawn, and the day after he and my mother signed the lease, they broke it and returned to Dallas.

Now, a few weeks later, my husband was handing me the phone and telling me that my father was in an intensive care unit. My father was in a coma.

I was standing in our bedroom. Time stopped. I shook uncontrollably. Don Cole's deep voice, with its strong Southern accent, was usually so calming. He was telling me that my mother, Hanne, had found my father on the floor of the garage. As he told the story, she had thought it strange, and said to herself: "He doesn't know a thing about fixin' cars. What's he doin'?'"

Still shaking, I held on to Don's every word. It seemed that my father had turned on the car, shut the garage, and lain down by the exhaust pipe.

Gas? He tried to gas himself? He tried to create his own gas chamber?

And now he could die. The doctors weren't sure.

Don explained that his wife, Judy, had brought my mother to their house, and that, although my mother seemed to be OK, he wasn't sure how much she understood. She might be in shock.

There was more: my father had apparently taken a number of sleeping pills, too. My mother had found them in the bathroom, all over the counter.

"Oh, my God," I said. We told our sons, Matthew and Adam, twelve and nine years old at the time, that "Grandpa was very sick." We called my brother and sister and their spouses and told them the full story. My brother and I booked a morning flight to Dallas. I began to pack. I took my black suit off its hanger, the one I would wear to a funeral. I carefully folded it and laid it in my suitcase.

But my father lived.

He was moved from the ICU to the inpatient psychiatric ward. When we brought his personal effects and clothing there, we were told of the many stipulations—no shoes with shoelaces, no regular razors (only electric), no scissors.

As my brother, sister, and I searched for a suicide note, we stumbled upon a gray metal box containing his will, along with an envelope with the words "Letter to My Children to be opened upon my death." But that was an envelope we had seen a glimpse of in years past, and not what we were looking for now. Our search continued. My father, indeed, had left a suicide note. It was scrawled in shaky print across several pages in the middle of a small pad, behind and between pages of other random notes, and next to the small tent calendar.

As though he momentarily engaged with life again, one of the pages with random notes had four lines of instructional information: "Be sure and take" the money out of a closed bank account; "We never went back to [the attorney] to sign the new papers, my ethical will is in the gray box"; and "You all have access to the safe" and bank account.

My father spent several weeks in the psychiatric ward. He initially seemed drained of vitality. Flat. He underwent seven sessions of electroshock treatment, his hair cut short on the left side of his head for the electrodes. He spent time in art therapy with drug addicts in their twenties.

Over the course of those weeks, I went to Dallas frequently and always stayed with my mother. One morning the phone rang at 7 a.m. I jumped out of bed and ran from my childhood bedroom to answer it.

"Karen?" It was my father. His voice was trembling.

"Come and get me out of here," he said. "This place is a prison."

I raced to the hospital, my mother in tow, though she agreed to stay in the waiting room. I found my way to my father's room. He was sitting on the edge of his bed, waiting, with his frail frame and sullen face. His eyes expressed helplessness.

We walked in silence to the end of the hallway and sat on a wide windowsill, with a view of Dallas skyscrapers in the early morning light.

My father again demanded that I get him out.

I didn't know what I could say to convince him, but I knew he had to remain there. I found myself trying to be compassionate, agreeing that it must be difficult. Then I heard myself saying words that came from a place unknown to me in connection to my father: a deep anger. "In some ways, Dad, you committed a crime," I said. "You attempted suicide." I bluntly reminded him of the history of suicide in our family and then continued, "If you don't want this to happen with any of your children or grandchildren, you have to get better. You have to stay here for a little while longer and get better."

Silence for a few moments. The slow blinking of his eyes, as though my words were sinking in. And then he just repeated how much he disliked the place, shaking his head from side to side, his lips tightly pressed together. I

LOOK FOR MY BODY

IN THE GARAGE

SORRY BUT I

COULD NOT GO ON

MY HEALTH IS GONE!
MY MIND IS GONE!
HEARING, EYESIGHT, CONSTIPATION
INCONTINENCE - WEAKNESS

SORRY
I COULD NOT GO ON
I'VE LOST MY HEALTH
I'VE LOST MY MIND
A TORTURED SOUL
HAS COME TO REST
MAY GOD FORGIVE ME

again pleaded with him to consider staying, and to do it for his children and grandchildren. After forty-five minutes or so, he finally calmed down.

But in the weeks and months and years that followed, I was left to consider my words: "You committed a crime. If you don't want this to happen with any of your children or grandchildren, you have to get better." I was left to consider my anger at my father and maybe a fear of suicide in future generations of our family. And perhaps more than that, I was left to ponder the roots of his despair.

I did not want to feel this anger toward my father—not now, not ever. And yet I did, deeply. My father was, at eighty-six, "a tortured soul" whom I needed to forgive for wanting to abandon us all. For wanting to abandon me.

But to forgive him, I would need to understand him. And to understand him, I would have to learn his story, and how he came to be the man who, after so many years, with so many people who loved and needed him, no longer wished to live. It would take me back through the years, to Germany before and during the Second World War, to his own parents and what happened to them, to what he was able and unable to do for them, to things he never articulated, maybe not even to himself.

2

Frankfurt before 1933

My story begins on April 11, 1915: I was born . . . during World War I
as the younger of two children of a middle-class, German Jewish family. . . .
I began life in a fourth floor walk-up apartment located on the fringes
of the Westend, the home of the Reformed, well-to-do Jewish population.

RUDY BAUM | "A Son of a Respectable Family"

My grandparents on my father Rudy's side, Norbert and Julie (née Geiger) Baum, lived in Frankfurt, sometimes referred to as Frankfurt am Main, or Frankfurt on the river Main.

My grandmother's Frankfurt roots date back to 1632, from a long line of well-educated professionals, including lawyers, physicians, linguists, philosophers, authors, and rabbis. Her great uncle was the renowned scholar and theologian Rabbi Abraham Geiger, a founder of Reform Judaism, born in 1810 in Frankfurt. His legacy was his challenge to and reform of traditional Jewish thinking, rituals, and customs such that an entirely new branch of Judaism emerged and thrived.

Julie was born only two generations after Rabbi Abraham Geiger, in 1883, into a middle-class family. She had three siblings—Helene, Willy, and Jacob.

Julie had chestnut brown hair, somewhat frizzy and often pulled back in a loose bun. Her piercing chocolate brown eyes were set beneath thick brown eyebrows. She wore glasses for reading, little or no makeup, and simple, moderately valuable jewelry: a diamond brooch, a diamond pendant and earrings, a gold bracelet studded with tiny pearls and diamond chips. Her "smile lines" were the Geiger-family type, running from each side of her nose to the corners of her mouth, distinctively separating her cheeks from her upper lip. Those smile lines were passed down to my father and his sister. Julie dressed elegantly, wearing custom-made suits and jackets.

In 1912, at the age of twenty-eight, she married my grandfather, who was forty, twelve years her senior. He was from a family of butchers in the nearby

Rabbi Abraham Geiger, circa 1869.

village of Hasselbach. His given name was Norbert Nathan Baum, and he went by Norbert.

My father knew little else about his parents' lives before their marriage. He never knew what level of education either of his parents had achieved or what brought his father to Frankfurt—or even how his parents met. But they did indeed meet, and then married and had a daughter, Grete (also known as Gretel), in 1913, and a son, Rudolf (also known as Rudy)—my father—in 1915.

My grandfather, shorter than my grandmother, was a stern man of few words. He conveyed to his children an attitude of "Don't speak unless spoken to." My father rarely spoke about his parents in personal ways, but he did tell me that he didn't dare contradict his father. Norbert usually wore such a serious expression that it bordered on a frown. He wore rimless eyeglasses in front of his heavily lidded eyes, and often furrowed his brows in photos. He had a red moustache, graying temples, and thinning dark hair outlined by a prominent receding hairline.

Norbert was one of two owners of the Norbert Harff Company, a wholesale tailor supply business, selling items such as silk linings, buttons, and thread. His partner was also Jewish and named Norbert (Norbert Plaut); Norbert was a common German name. Together, the two Norberts bought the Harff

TOP LEFT Julie and Norbert Baum, 1918.
TOP RIGHT Julie with Rudy and Gretel, 1918.
BOTTOM Rudy and Gretel, 1924.

Company and changed the name to the Norbert Harff Company. The company's two employees were Mr. Plapper, who helped draw up the sales contracts, and a female secretary, whose name I do not know. Because my grandfather traveled frequently for business, much of the childrearing was left to my grandmother. She was the disciplinarian, and delivered punishment, sometimes slaps.

Although my grandmother was somewhat tough and judgmental, she had a gentle side, and a fragile core. She was a high-strung woman who smoked cigarettes throughout the day, and she was prone to bouts of depression. My father recalled her suffering a couple of nervous breakdowns, for which she spent up to six weeks at a time in a sanatorium. The nanny would take care of Gretel and him.

According to my father, my grandmother was an accomplished pianist and singer, a member of the choir of one of the local amateur symphony orchestras. She also had a talent for poetry. My father guessed that she had completed high school. As a young girl, Julie attended a finishing school, *Pension Heinemann* in Frankfurt, for daughters of "good Jewish families." There she learned manners and cooking. She was social and cultured, playing bridge, going to coffee circles, and attending lectures and concerts. She was an avid reader and a member of a women's literary circle led by Dr. Martha Wertheimer, who studied history, philosophy, and English philology and received a doctorate in philosophy and was the editor of the most popular Jewish newspaper, the Sunday weekly *Israelitisches Familienblatt*, and a journalist for the *Offenbacher Zeitung*, the newspaper of Offenbach, a suburb of Frankfurt. Dr. Wertheimer later became an anti-Nazi activist.[1]

My grandparents lived in Frankfurt's largely Reform Jewish Westend, on a main thoroughfare, Reuterweg. They rented a five-room apartment on the fourth floor of an attached row house, number 73. It had a living room with a gramophone for the family's approximately one hundred records as well as a piano that Julie played. A copy of Rembrandt's painting *Man in a Golden Helmut* adorned the walls. Connected to the living room was a "smoke room," where my grandfather enjoyed his nightly cigars, often after returning from his skat card game. In the smoke room was a bookcase with glass doors that held close to six hundred books.

The dining room had a table with eight leather-upholstered chairs and an original Max Beckmann oil painting, the acquisition of which I know nothing about. The room also had a sideboard and a hutch—filled not only with hidden tins of my grandmother's homemade cookies, but also with a complete set of china for eighteen and another for twelve, a Japanese tea set for twelve, a silver tea service, a complete set of silverware for twenty-four, three dozen crystal glasses, several silver and crystal bowls, and silver vases. Also in the dining room was a chair with a well-worn leather cover, a symbol of my grandfather's pride in his two-and-a-half-year military service in the German Army during World War I. He had sat in that chair in uniform in the military headquarters.

In addition to the dining room and living room, the geranium-decorated balcony provided a venue where the family, and sometimes a few friends, gathered for coffee and conversation on sunny Sunday springtime afternoons.

Engravings hung on many of the walls and Persian carpets covered much of the dining room and living room floors. Each room had its own stove for heating, and the eat-in kitchen had a large cooking stove. Bedroom space was minimal. My grandparents' bedroom had two twin beds pushed together and an armoire, given that built-in closets were rare. My aunt slept in the living room. My father slept in the bathroom—an oversized bathroom by American standards.

The Baum family was considered well situated in Frankfurt's middle class, and comfortable. Like other middle-class Germans, they had extensive household help, often hired from what would have been considered the poorer working class. Beyond their live-in maid, who had a private room in the attic, there was someone to do the laundry, someone to iron, another to sew, another to do the heavy cleaning, another to cook, and a nanny for the two children. Family excursions included strolling through the Palmengarten, the expansive botanical garden twelve blocks away, or attending symphonies, operas, or the theater. All the necessary stores were a short stroll from their row house—a bakery, a butcher, a fish store, a vegetable store, and the seasonal stands like the ones for white asparagus. The small grocer Schade & Füllgrabe was on the southwest corner of Reuterweg and Grüneburgweg.

Norbert's office was at Große Kornmarkt 18, near *Paulskirche* (St. Paul's Church) and not far from the River Main. As it was only a mile from their apartment on Reuterweg, he came home in the middle of the day for lunch and a nap. It was also only eight-tenths of a mile from Frankfurt's central train station, which was convenient for the business travel that took him throughout Germany, Luxembourg, and beyond.

Norbert had been raised in an Orthodox home, but his wife and children considered themselves Reform Jews, although they were members of both the nearby Reform Westend Synagogue and the Orthodox Unterlindau Synagogue.

Altogether there were some thirty thousand Jews among Frankfurt's population of six hundred thousand, and the city had five synagogues. Many of the Orthodox Jews lived in the Eastend. In 1924, the city elected a Jewish mayor and a Jewish treasurer. And Frankfurt had been home to many prominent Jews: Paul Ehrlich, the Nobel Prize–winning physician and scientist; Martin Buber, the philosopher; and the Rothschilds, the European banking dynasty.

My grandparents, with my father and my aunt, attended Friday night services at the grand Westend Synagogue, resplendent with its tiled dome, marble courtyard, and its two lion statues, protective of those coming and going through the portal. They were Jews and they were German. As my father would later put it, in a speech in 1995, "We were Jewish, went to services, but highly assimilated. We were Germans first and Jews second." And, as the historian Saul Friedländer wrote in his Pulitzer Prize–winning 2007 book, *The Years of Extermination: Nazi Germany and the Jews, 1939–1945,* "For many Jews in Western Europe, the main goal was social and cultural assimilation into surrounding society, while maintaining some elements of 'Jewish identity,' whatever that meant."[2]

Occasionally on Friday nights, my father dined with his maternal grandfather, August Geiger, who lived within walking distance from Reuterweg. Rudy recalled those evenings fondly, although he didn't always like the menu at his grandfather's house.

Sometimes, on Saturdays, Rudy walked hand-in-hand with Norbert to the Orthodox synagogue across town. My grandfather wore a black top hat or a derby for these walks, which offered Rudy rare moments to be alone with his father, though he never felt he had a close relationship with him. He would later write about early memories of attending high holiday services with his father, particularly the evening service ushering in the Day of Atonement. "Of all the *Kol Nidre* services I have gone to since my childhood," he would write, "none can approach the holy feeling I got from those services of seventy years ago."[3]

Rudy's *bar mitzvah* at the Orthodox synagogue was the final large gathering of the extended Geiger-Baum family. My grandmother not only prepared an elaborate dinner, but also wrote, and set to music, a poem, to celebrate my father and the family.

Passover was my father's favorite holiday, with its extensive and varied foods, from gefilte fish to matzo ball soup to matzo charlotte. When my aunt Gretel had a Zionist boyfriend in the early 1930s, she would emphasize the concluding words of the Passover Seder, "Next year in Jerusalem." That would incite a volatile family discussion, year after year, as my grandparents opposed her talk of emigrating to Palestine.

My father attended kindergarten just across the street from Reuterweg 73. Years later he wrote that "I always lived in the fear that I might come home to an empty apartment, with nobody there to look after me." His closest group of five or six friends, only two of whom were Jewish, often played with lead soldiers, steam engines, and construction sets. He particularly enjoyed the soldiers.

For primary school, he attended the century-old Jewish day school, the Philantropin, in the Northend of Frankfurt. He then attended the Musterschule, a boys' *Gymnasium* (grades 5–13), which was a middle and high school focused on math and physics and modern languages, rather than Latin and Greek. There, my father pursued what proved to be his favorite subjects—math, English, and French, which he studied for seven years. Each grade had approximately twenty-five students, with only five or six Jewish students in his grade. He was one of the shortest boys, with the nickname of *Baumchen* (little Baum), and was not inclined toward physical fitness. He didn't do well in gym class. His major challenge in his middle school years was that he developed a stutter, which he did not overcome until his late teens, after years of working with a speech therapist.

In 1930, the Depression hit. My grandfather, in all his pragmatism and sternness, told my father that he would not be able to send him to college after high school. My father, only fifteen years old at the time and with two remaining years of high school, decided to drop out of school. Without college in his future and with his dream of becoming a lawyer dashed, finishing high school seemed pointless. It remains something of a mystery to me that my father chose, and was seemingly encouraged, to drop out. My father's sister, Gretel, matriculated in 1932. Furthermore, my grandmother was from a highly educated family and presumably placed great value on education.

After pursuing many empty promises for employment, Rudy finally got a job, on April 1, 1931, as an apprentice at Ada-Ada, a fine children's and ladies' shoe manufacturer owned by two Jewish brothers, Richard and Wilhelm "Willy" Nathan. The Nathans were members of my grandfather's *B'nai B'rith* Lodge. My father commuted to work by train to Höchst, six miles outside of Frankfurt. He worked part-time during his apprenticeship, and attended a vocational school, where he learned basic business skills.

Rudy,
Summer 1933.

After two-and-a-half years, he was promoted from apprentice to the position of "young man"—one of the people responsible for the sample department. He was assured that he would become a traveling salesman within two or three years. My father assumed that he had a job for life, and would continue to work his way up the company ladder. Life seemed good.

But then Hitler came to power in January 1933.

3

Germany and America, 1933–1936

In Jan 1933 everything changed. . . . Signs appeared like "Jews and Dogs Not Allowed," "Jews stay out," or "Not for Jews" (on park benches). So it became clear quickly that things would change, though we felt Hitler was a crazy man and would last only six months.

RUDY BAUM SPEECH | March 9, 1997

Overnight, in January 1933, my father's experience at Ada-Ada shifted—from one of enjoying the workplace camaraderie and loose banter to one of extreme wariness. He had to be careful about what he said and to whom. One of the Nathans' sons fled to Spain, after being denounced, or reported to authorities (in all likelihood by an ordinary citizen), for having a relationship with a non-Jewish girl. As my father would write in a brief essay years later:

> I was working in a Jewish owned factory . . . and the day after the Nazi takeover the covert party members and sympathizers came out of the closet. Swastika armbands and lapel buttons made their mass appearance. The atmosphere in the workplace had changed forever. The close camaraderie, which had existed amongst a group of teenage apprentices of both sexes, Jewish and gentile, began to unravel. I suddenly found myself in a situation where I had to look over my shoulders and watch what I was saying and who might be listening.[1]

The groundwork for all of this had been in place for some time. The intensity of German anti-Semitism in the early part of the twentieth century was largely rooted in three major factors, one feeding into the other.

First, Friedländer explains, the period between the late nineteenth century and the end of World War II saw the rise of the revolutionary far right (Nazis and fascists) and the revolutionary far left (socialists and communists)—and the two detested each other. What's more, the far right saw Jews as the promoters and carriers of socialism as well as promoters of liberalism, which they also hated. Thus, they blamed and hated the Jews.[2]

Secondly, Eastern European Jews steadily migrated into Western Europe between World War I and World War II—due to the extreme nationalism of countries such as Poland, Romania, and Hungary. That nationalism devised state measures to drive Jews out of the economy. So more Jews were coming into countries such as Germany that were already building a case about Jewish aspirations for power and dominance.[3]

As early as 1920, Hitler had publicly stated his goal to separate Jews from Aryan society and to abolish the civil, legal, and political rights of Jews. This intention was documented in the twenty-five-point Party Program of the National Socialist German Workers' Party.

Some of the points in the Party Program that explicitly separated the Jews were:

> Only members of the nation may be citizens of the State. Only those of German blood, whatever their creed, may be members of the nation. Accordingly, no Jew may be a member of the nation.
>
> Non-citizens may live in Germany only as guests and must be subject to laws for aliens.
>
> We demand that the State shall make its primary duty to provide a livelihood for its citizens. If it should prove impossible to feed the entire population, foreign nationals (non-citizens) must be deported from the Reich.[4]

Finally, during the 1930s, powerful Jews in stable democracies such as the United States and Great Britain chose not to advocate on behalf of Jews threatened in Europe, in part because of the rise of anti-Semitism in their own countries and a belief that little could be done, according to Friedländer's *The Years of Extermination*.[5]

One such powerful Jew was the publisher of the *New York Times* from 1904 to 1935, Adolph Ochs, who was the son of German Jewish immigrants. Married to Iphigenia Wise, a daughter of Isaac Mayer Wise, a rabbi renowned as one of the foremost leaders of the Reform Jewish movement in the United States, Ochs believed that Judaism was a religion. Period. Not a race. So he would not support the American Jewish Committee's efforts to help Jews in European war zones in World War I.

Adolph Ochs was succeeded by his like-minded son-in-law, Arthur Hays Sulzberger. Like his father-in-law, he believed that Judaism was a religion, not a race or ethnicity, so therefore carried no obligation to helping fellow

Jews. He viewed European Jews as part of a broader refugee problem and was anti-Zionist. Jews should neither be persecuted because they were Jewish, he thought, nor helped because they were Jewish.[6]

As Laurel Leff documents in *Buried by The Times*, her searing account of the *New York Times*'s coverage of the Holocaust, Sulzberger was concerned about inciting anti-Semitism in the United States, and thus was not publicly sympathetic to the Jewish plight and was intent to act in ways to disprove Hitler's insistence that Jews were a race.

Sulzberger felt that helping European Jews because they were Jews could undermine perceptions of his American identity. "Sulzberger would use his position to persuade both Jews and non-Jews," she writes, "that no matter what Adolf Hitler said, Jews were exactly like everybody else."[7]

"If Judaism was his faith, however, assimilation was Sulzberger's religion," Leff writes.[8] Sulzberger philosophized that "In doing what I can to help distressed German and Austrian Jews, I must act as an American and not as a Jew. . . . As a Jew, in my judgment, I have no right to cross national boundary lines in a manner which may involve nationalism."[9] As such, he insisted that Jews not be treated as a group either in the writings of the *Times*, nor in public policy.[10] According to Leff, he permitted very few editorials about Jews and the current situation and ensured that articles about the Nazi atrocities were kept short and given no prominence. That was the tone for other US opinion makers and journalists, too, as the *New York Times* was considered the "newspaper of record." As Leff writes, if the owners of the *Times*, who were Jews of German descent, treated the persecution and murder of millions of Jews as relatively unimportant, then so, too, would others.[11]

Meanwhile, approximately one-third of German Jews would emigrate from 1933 to 1938.[12] During the first six years of Hitler's reign, beginning in 1933, more than four hundred rules and decrees regulated the private and public lives of Jews. These included national laws as well as state, regional, and municipal regulations. Thus, many people at all levels of government were involved in the persecution of Jews early on.

And it is during this period—in 1935—that the Nuremberg Laws were created, a set of laws building on the twenty-five-point Party Program, including stripping Jews of their citizenship. But Jews tended to believe in the rule of law, especially the rule of German law, and felt that such a set of laws finally provided clarity and relief. As Friedländer notes, "Many German Jews still hoped that the crisis could be weathered *in* Germany and the new laws would create a recognized framework for a segregated but nonetheless manageable Jewish life."[13] He continues by quoting David Bankier, the Holocaust historian, who says in his article *Jewish Society Through Nazi Eyes: 1933–1936* that "the Jews were relieved precisely because the laws, even though they established a permanent framework of discrimination, ended the reign of arbitrary terror. There was a measure of similarity in the way average Germans and average Jews reacted. The Germans expressed satisfaction while the Jews saw ground for hope."[14]

My father did not talk to me much about these days until very late in life, but he must have sensed Germany's terrible shift. Things began to change in ways that my grandparents surely saw and worried deeply about as well: My grandmother no longer permitted to sing in the choir for one of the Frankfurt symphonies; the signs forbidding Jews in many public places; the banning of Jews from public swimming pools;[15] many parks and restaurants made off limits to Jews; the establishment of the Nazi-approved *Kulturbund*, an organization of Jewish artists, musicians, and actors who performed for other Jews.[16] While Frankfurt's branch of the *Kulturbund* was a philharmonic orchestra, other cities had choruses, cabarets, theater ensembles, and opera societies.[17] Although the *Kulturbund*—albeit directly supervised by the Nazi regime—could be viewed as a lifeline for Jews by providing a continuing cultural life, as Friedländer writes, it also "foreshadowed the Nazi ghetto, in which a pretense of internal autonomy camouflaged the subordination of an appointed Jewish Leadership to the dictates of its masters."[18]

It was also in the 1930s that attendance at the Jewish lodges, or religious fraternal groups, such as *B'nai B'rith*, grew even more robust. These lodges provided a lively alternative for Jews to spend time together. Meanwhile, the *Reichsbund Jüdischer Frontsoldaten* (National Union of Jewish War Veterans) created gatherings for women.[19]

* * *

Later that same year, 1933, the artist Max Beckmann—the painter whose work hung in my grandparents' dining room—was dismissed from his post as professor at the *Städelsches Kunstinstitut* in Frankfurt. His paintings were no longer allowed in exhibitions.[20]

Then on Saturday, April 1, the usually busy shopping Saturday only eight days before Easter Sunday, my father witnessed the first organized boycott of Jewish businesses. Members of the black-shirted SS (initially Hitler's bodyguards) and brown-shirted SA (Nazi street fighters or storm troopers) painted swastikas and wrote "Jewish Pigs" on storefront windows. They shouted, "Do not do business with Jewish swine, but only with your Aryan friends." They threatened anyone attempting to enter Jewish establishments.

After the boycott, the Jewish retailers met to discuss how to respond. But the SS broke up the meeting and chased nearly one hundred of those participating through the streets of Frankfurt and brought them to police headquarters.[21]

On May 10, 1933, my father, along with thousands of onlookers, witnessed the book burning in Römerberg Square, in front of Frankfurt's City Hall. The books were brought in by the truckload from libraries, schools, and universities. The SS, SA—and hundreds of Hitler-sympathetic professors, rectors, and student leaders—were attempting to cleanse Frankfurt of books written by Jews or by those opposed to Nazi doctrine. They chanted rallying cries such as "Garbage! Jewish gutter literature!" against a backdrop of festive band music, as they danced around the bonfire of books—works written by Heinrich Heine, Stefan Zweig, Thomas Mann, Bertolt Brecht, Lion Feuchtwanger, Franz Kafka, and others. Though he rarely spoke of this to us, my father later wrote, "The hysterical frenzy that accompanied that bonfire left me with an indelible scar."[22]

As my father once said:

> During this period, a dreaded new word found its way into our vocabulary—*Konzentrationslager*—concentration camp. It was not long before we received eyewitness accounts of the brutalities and murders at Dachau, the first camp that had been set up in Germany, in 1933. One of my cousins [Albert Baum] who was picked up in a raid and sent there, witnessed tortures and killings, but was finally released with the condition that he leave Germany within thirty days or else be rearrested. He was also warned not to disclose what he had seen.[23]

My father and his family heard many other accounts of Jews being taken away or jailed. At that time, many were released but returned broken in body and spirit.

Given that "any denouncement to the police or the party could get you arrested and put away . . . and everyone was subject to the dreaded knock at the door,"[24] my grandparents, their safe and ordered world crumbling before them, finally relented to my Aunt Gretel's wishes and gave her permission to

Eysseneckstraße 20, circa 1935.

immigrate to Palestine. She left in April 1934, "without regret and without looking back." As she put it years later, "It would be untrue to say that the parting was difficult or painful. . . . I only knew that this final step brought me nearer to realizing my aim"—to live in Palestine and help build a Jewish state. "Everything else," she said, "was unimportant." She traveled with a group of fellow young Zionists, first by train to Munich, then Trieste, and finally on the ship *Gerusalemme* to the port of Jaffa in Palestine.[25]

* * *

Six months later, presumably because my grandfather's business began to decline, Norbert, Julie, and Rudy moved from their home on Reuterweg, where my grandparents had lived since 1913, to a smaller, less expensive apartment at Eysseneckstraße 20, in the Northend.

The front windows offered a view of the street's wide green center strip. While the Westend was home to the upper middle class and upper-class Reformed Jews, the Northend was home to a lower class, and to fewer Jews.

My grandparents retained their household help for a number of years—for 600 Reichsmarks ($1,470 in 1935 US dollars)—and paid their life insurance premiums of 1,100 Reichsmarks ($2,695 in 1935 US dollars) annually. Yet, for the tax year 1935, my grandfather wrote to the Tax Office in 1936: "As you may see from the income tax forms provided by me, an income tax payment for the year 1935 is for me out of the question. I prepaid already in Dec.10, 1935 RM 53—and I ask politely, to book this sum as a prepayment on June 10, or to defer until the tax assessment on June 10."

In 1935, with the enforcement of the Nuremberg Laws—and with the Nathans urging their Jewish employees to leave Germany—my father would recall that, "Taking all of this into account, it became clear that there was no future for any Jews in Germany."[26] What that meant was that my grandparents frantically searched for someone to give my father an affidavit to immigrate to America, the place to which he desired to flee.

And it was not easy.

Those seeking asylum in America in the 1930s needed an Affidavit of Support and Sponsorship and an entry visa. The affidavit was a government document stating that a visa applicant had the support of a sponsor—an American citizen or permanent resident, preferably a close relative of the applicant—and would not become a public charge of the United States.

In 1930, in an effort to restrict immigration, the Hoover administration had more strictly reinterpreted part of the Immigration Act of 1917. With jobs difficult to secure during the Depression—unless the applicant was independently wealthy—it was very difficult to gain entry.[27] Sponsors were scrutinized carefully. The sponsor was required to provide:

A completed Affidavit of Support and Sponsorship form
(six notarized copies)
A certified copy of their most recent federal tax return
An affidavit from a bank regarding their accounts
An affidavit from any other responsible person regarding other assets
(e.g., an affidavit from the sponsor's employer)

To acquire an entry visa, an applicant was required to provide:

Visa Application (five copies)
Birth certificate (two copies)
Quota number—place on the waiting list
Certificate of Good Conduct from German police authorities, including two copies of each of the following:
Police dossier
Prison record
Military record
Other government records about the individual
Proof that the applicant passed a physical exam at the U.S. Consulate[28]

Connections—either to relatives or friends or friends/relatives of friends—were thus essential for getting an affidavit. My father's maternal grandfather had a cousin who lived in America, visited Frankfurt regularly, and had offered repeatedly to give my father the required Affidavit of Support and Sponsorship, if and when my father would be interested. My father was told that he should write to him as "uncle." He wrote to this man several times, requesting the affidavit, but never received a reply. Deeply disappointed, the family tried many other possibilities, until finally Martin Beckhard, another second cousin of my grandmother, made the commitment. Beckhard moved in prominent circles; for example, he was a pallbearer—along with the law firm partner Paul Cravath, *New York Times* publisher/owner Adolph Ochs, Sears's owner Julius Rosenwald—for the internationally known banker Jacob Schiff, father-in-law

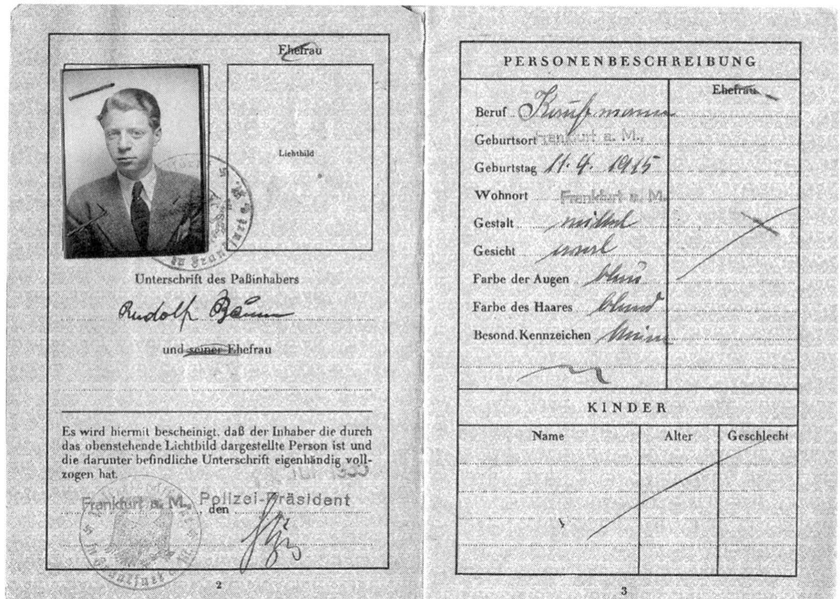
Ehefrau

Lichtbild

Unterschrift des Paßinhabers

und ~~seiner~~ Ehefrau

Es wird hiermit bescheinigt, daß der Inhaber die durch das obenstehende Lichtbild dargestellte Person ist und die darunter befindliche Unterschrift eigenhändig vollzogen hat.

Frankfurt a. M., den

Polizei-Präsident

2

PERSONENBESCHREIBUNG

	Ehefrau
Beruf	
Geburtsort Frankfurt a. M.	
Geburtstag 11. 4. 1915	
Wohnort Frankfurt a. M.	
Gestalt	
Gesicht	
Farbe der Augen	
Farbe des Haares	
Besond. Kennzeichen	

KINDER

Name	Alter	Geschlecht

3

Rudy's passport, 1935.

of the renowned banker Felix Warburg. Both Warburg and Beckhard were executives at Kuhn, Loeb & Co. Beckhard, at eighty-three-years-old, opened the door for my father to begin the journey that would carry him to a new life in America.

The first personal hurdle in the process for my father, now twenty-one, was the required physical examination. He passed.

He already had his passport, but he needed the required visa.

It was not easy to secure the visa given the United States's strict quota on immigrants. The American refugee policy had a slim German-Austrian quota of 27,370 persons per year in FY 1933 (that is, July 1, 1933 to June 30, 1934) and remained the same through FY 1945.[29]

Although many were not so lucky, my father received his visa on September 22, 1936, from the consulate in Stuttgart. That consulate had recently increased its staff to process the overwhelming number of applicants. It was not until December, 1936—*after* my father received his visa—that Franklin D. Roosevelt enabled German immigration to the States to increase significantly by reinstating the more liberal "likely" to become a public charge, rather than the more restrictive "probably."[30] This loosening was new. But luckily my father still got through under the earlier language.

After receiving his visa, my father wrote to the Tax Office in Frankfurt on November 6, 1936, requesting a tax clearance certificate, explaining that he had no taxable property and had financed the 400 Reichsmarks (about $162 in 1936 dollars, or $3,058 in 2021 dollars) required for his emigration from his savings.

> Herewith I ask for a tax clearance certificate.
>
> I enclose a confirmation of my employer, the company R.& W. Nathan, Ffm-Höchst, about the punctual payment of my taxes.
>
> Herewith I declare that I do not own any taxable property. I have financed my emigration from my own savings, which amounted to RM 400. I already received a tax clearance certificate from the Tax Office. I ask for a prompt settlement, because I plan to leave within the next few days.

Only a few days later, my father received approval for the tax clearance certificate from the Tax Office: "The Jew Rudolf Baum, son of Norbert Baum (see enclosed documents) Ffm, Eysseneckstr. 20, intends to emigrate . . . [He] is not in arrears with his taxes. . . . According to his statement RB has not received or is expected to receive any gifts from his parents whatsoever." Copies of this notification were sent to the Gestapo, the Department of Customs Investigation, the Department of Tax Fraud Investigation—all in Frankfurt—and the Central Intelligence Service of the Tax Authority in Berlin. The latter office was in charge of coordinating efforts throughout the Reich to make sure that Jews did not abscond with secret funds when emigrating.

The preparations for his departure thus began. Rudy packed enough clothing for five years. Years later he would write, "I will always carry with me the picture of the big piece of luggage sitting in the hallway, being gradually filled."[31] The family shipped a large trunk to America. In addition, my father would carry with him two suitcases, containing a tuxedo, a few pictures, clothing, shoes, and mementos. His only currency was ten Reichsmarks, the maximum allowed under Nazi regulations, and a Leica camera, worth $125 on the black market—the "refugee currency" as my father would later refer to it in his autobiography. My father made his rounds of obligatory goodbyes, collecting the names and addresses of contacts in the United States.

Then, at last, in November of 1936, the gray, rainy day of his departure arrived. His parents accompanied him to Frankfurt's main railroad station. It was, he would later write, "the most painful memory of my life. I can still see my parents waving. . . . I had the feeling I wouldn't see my parents again."[32]

The train took him to Holland, where he took a ferry to Southampton, England. There, on November 18, 1936, he boarded the Cunard ship *S.S. Berengaria*, to sail to New York via Paris and Cherbourg. The scheduled journey from Southampton to Cherbourg was just under three hours, and then from Cherbourg to New York was five days, twenty-two hours, and twenty-six minutes.[33]

* * *

Why did my grandparents not also seek to leave?

In 1936, it seems that my grandfather's business was providing enough for them to live on. More to the point, my grandparents believed that their relatively old age (my grandmother was fifty-three and my grandfather was sixty-five in 1936) would protect them, that the Nazis would allow the older generation to live out their lives. (This, even though many of their friends had already left, before 1936, and were continuing to leave thereafter.)

They also felt German. Germany was *their* country. After all, my grandfather had been a German soldier. They thought that his military service during World War I would protect them further from the Nazis and enable them to remain safely in Frankfurt.

It wasn't until well into his seventies, that my father began to talk and write about this painful time in his life. In a recording made in 1997 at New York City's Museum of Jewish Heritage, my father can be heard saying his oft-repeated sentiment: that in Germany, "We were Germans first and Jews second." He once cited the photojournalist Edward Serotta, who entitled one of his book chapters "Jewish Was Our Religion—German Is What We Were."

Yet much of Germany did not agree.

According to Friedländer, the year 1936 marked "the beginning of a new phase on the internal German scene. . . . Most immediately three main lines of action dominated the new phase of the anti-Jewish drive: accelerated Aryanization, increasingly coordinated efforts to compel the Jews to leave Germany, and furious propaganda activity to project on a world scale the theme of Jewish conspiracy and threat.[34] Furthermore, the Hitler Youth became the official youth arm of the Reich, as it comprised 60 percent of the country's youth in 1935, and then acquired all the other Nazi youth organizations.[35]

The accelerated Aryanization showed up in 1936 in the many new orders restricting Jews in Germany, controlling them in many dimensions. For example, Jews were denied their right to vote;[36] domestic and foreign assets and property owned by Jews had to be registered, as a prelude to the German authorities severely taxing those possessions or selling them to non-Jewish Germans at well below market value; Jewish doctors could treat only Jewish patients;[37] Jewish-owned employment agencies were ordered to stop their activities;[38] two thousand books of 650 Jewish authors were blacklisted.[39]

By January 1, 1937, the last Jewish department store, Wertheim, was in the process of Aryanization—meaning that all of the shares held by Jewish family members were transferred to non-Jews; Jewish employees were fired; and the name was changed in 1938 to AWAG, an acronym for Allgemeine Warenhandelsgesellschaft A.G. (General Retailing Corporation).[40]

Meanwhile, there was an emerging focus on the "*complete* emigration" of the Jews from Germany. The state secretary in the German Ministry of the Interior, Wilhelm Stuckart, led a conference that prioritized a plan for the total emigration; that is, compulsory emigration—a euphemism for expulsion—of the Jews.[41]

At the same time, the Sachsenhausen concentration camp was opened in Oranienburg, in the northwestern part of the country, some thirty-five kilometers north of Berlin. The only other camps formally called concentration camps at the time were Dachau, near Munich, and Lichtenberg, near Merseberg in Saxony, for female prisoners.[42] In addition, there was a network of 110 camps—detention camps and forced labor camps—that had been created since Hitler's rise to power in 1933, imprisoning approximately ten thousand people, including political opponents. With Germany's expansion of power came the growth of the network of camps and ghettos, according to United States Holocaust Memorial Museum, "to confine and sometimes kill not only Jews but also homosexuals, Gypsies, Poles, Russians, and many other ethnic groups in Eastern Europe. The camps and ghettos varied enormously in their mission, organization and size, depending on the Nazis' needs."[43]

The idea of Aryan superiority won a propaganda victory with the June 19, 1936, triumph of the German heavyweight boxer Max Schmeling over the promising African American heavyweight Joe Louis, at Yankee Stadium. Schmeling knocked out Louis, known as the Brown Bomber, in the twelfth round. Friedländer quotes Goebbels's personal diary: "Schmeling fought and won for Germany. The white defeated the black and the white was German."[44] Hitler himself sent flowers to Schmeling's wife, with a note: "For the wonderful victory of your husband, our greatest German boxer, I must congratulate you with all my heart."[45]

One of the greatest propaganda successes of the Third Reich was the 1936 Summer Olympics, held in Berlin. It was the world's first look inside Nazi Germany, though to many it was not evident just how staged that scene was. Evidence of anti-Semitic sentiment or activity—such as signs that refused access for Jews to shop in selected stores or sit in particular places—were removed from the Olympic area and other areas likely to be visited by tourists. Even FDR believed that stories of persecution of the Jews were overstated. In October of 1936, one month before the presidential election, he chose to meet with Rabbi Stephen Wise, the president of the World Jewish Congress. According to Friedländer, FDR told Wise that the German "synagogues were crowded and apparently there is nothing very wrong in the situation at the present."[46]

One footnote to the propaganda effort: a notable blatantly anti-Semitic action that took place behind the scenes was the Reich's removal of Grete Bergmann, the Jewish high jumper, from the German team only two weeks before the start of the games. Ostensibly, the change was because she had "underperformed," as the Reich had struck from the record Bergmann's June 30, 1936, tie with the national record. Ironically, the Reich wanted to present itself as open-minded and tolerant and so had coerced her to return for the games to Germany from the United Kingdom, where her parents had sent her after she had been expelled from an athletic club in 1933 for being Jewish. But then the Reich changed its mind and removed her, once it was sure that the United States would not boycott the games.[47]

Bergmann was the niece of my grandmother's best friend, Hedwig Hirsch. So presumably my grandmother knew much of this before others did. Yet another incremental event that would chip away at the foundation of their hopes. My father remembers my grandparents trying to reassure him. When he said his final goodbyes to them, he recalls that my grandfather saying, *"If worse comes to worst, we'll take the last train."*

Part Two

MY DEAR RUDOLF

Of course, one worries a lot here;
you can't completely avoid that.

JULIE BAUM | *May 1937*

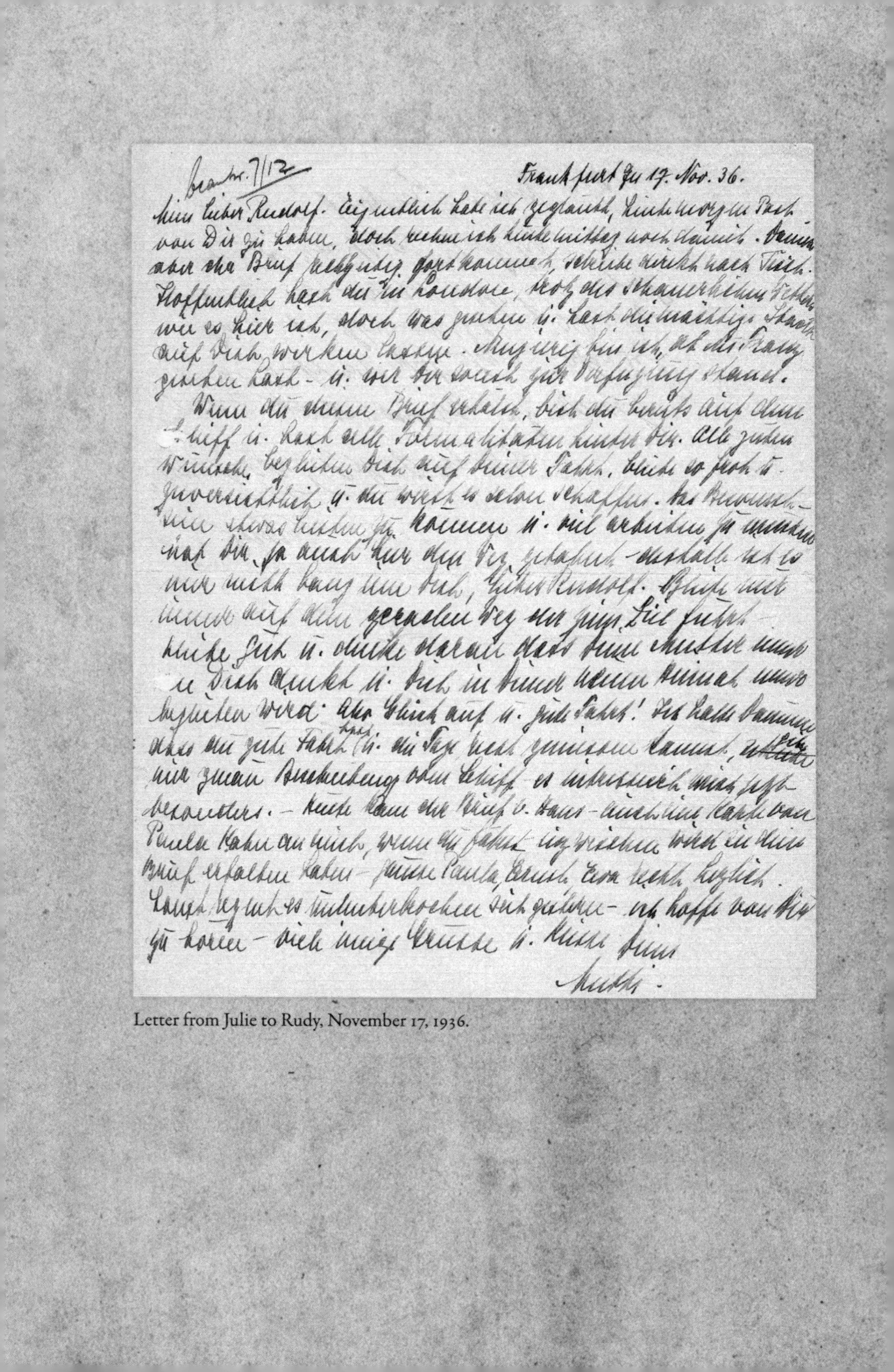

Frankfurt a/M 17. Nov. 36.

Letter from Julie to Rudy, November 17, 1936.

4

Frankfurt and New York, Late 1936

Frankfurt am Main, 17 Nov., 1936

My dear Rudolf.

. . . All good wishes accompany you on your journey, remain cheerful and confident and you will manage it. The awareness of being able to achieve something and having to work a lot has helped you on your way here too—therefore I do not worry about you, dear Rudolf. Just remain on your right way that leads to the goal. Remain well and think about that your mother always thinks about you and will accompany you in your new homeland. Good luck and a good journey! . . . much love and kisses,

Your Mutti

My father was still at sea when my grandmother wrote those words, part of her first letter to him. It was just a few short paragraphs, but they were filled with words of encouragement. She also asked for a detailed description of the ship, perhaps to compare it to the ship she had taken to visit Gretel in Palestine a year earlier.

After nearly three weeks on the *Berengaria*, my father set foot on American soil, arriving in New York City at the end of November 1936. It was only three short weeks after Franklin Delano Roosevelt had been reelected in a landslide election—capturing 85 percent of the Jewish vote.

My father was greeted by a relative of Mr. Beckhard, probably Mr. Beckhard's son-in-law, Sigmund Weiss. Mr. Beckhard had arranged for my father to stay at the Wellington Hotel, on Seventh Avenue at 55th Street—a private room with a bathroom. My father had never known such luxurious accommodations. The expensive $2.50 daily rate—$47.19 per day in 2021 dollars—motivated him to find a furnished room to rent and a job as soon as possible.

Armed with his lengthy list of contacts—friends of his parents, friends and acquaintances of friends—he began his search. He quickly found a furnished room, which he shared with Curt Bier, whose parents in Frankfurt knew my father's parents. The rent was $5 a week for a bedroom in a brownstone at 329

West 89th Street on Manhattan's Upper West Side, a neighborhood with many German Jewish refugees, where, according to my father, it seemed that more people spoke German than English. The brownstone was five stories high with bay windows, reminiscent of the apartment house on Eysseneckstraße, where he last lived with his parents. Around the corner, in the park on Riverside Drive, was the Soldiers' and Sailors' Memorial Monument commemorating the Union Army soldiers and sailors who served in the American Civil War, a war my father probably knew very little about.

Rudolf and Julie, my father and my grandmother, exchanged letters weekly, with great orderliness to their mother-son correspondence. My grandmother initially numbered her letters—*Brief 1, Brief 2*, and so on, though that lasted only four months. My father diligently wrote the date of his reply in the upper left-hand corner of the first page of every letter he received. Sometimes he scribbled notes to himself on the last page about points to include in his response.

Often Norbert, my grandfather, would add a few lines at the bottom of my grandmother's lengthy letters, and a handful of times he wrote a separate letter or postcard. Regardless, he seemed ever present in Julie's letters. My grandmother often explained that Norbert was rushing her to finish writing so that he could post the letter in time for the departure of a particular steamship, although my grandparents soon came to realize that, given schedule changes, it was better not to specify the ship and instead to post the letter for whatever the next departure was.

My grandmother was disappointed to hear that my father had not received letters to him addressed to the ports in Cherbourg and London. Perhaps those letters were lost or maybe they were intercepted due to censoring.

The possibility of censorship, in fact, likely tempered and shaped all of Julie's letters.

Germany's president, Paul von Hindenburg, had issued a censorship decree on February 28, 1933, the day after the *Reichstag* (the German parliament) burned down due to arson. At the urging of Hitler, Hindenburg issued an emergency decree "for the Protection of the People and the State," which stated that

> restrictions on personal liberty, on the right of free expression of opinion, including freedom of the press, on the right of assembly and the right of association, and violations of the privacy of postal, telegraphic, and telephonic

communications, warrants for house searches, orders for confiscations, as well as restrictions on property, are also permissible beyond the legal limits otherwise prescribed.[1]

Censorship must have prevented my grandmother from describing the actual state of affairs in Germany whenever she communicated with her son (and vicariously enjoyed her son's freedom). But her letters were laced with allusions to and harbingers of life becoming more difficult.

In those initial days after my father's departure, my grandmother was relieved to learn that Rudy had landed safely, and she continued to give him encouragement, "At the beginning it certainly won't be easy to find what's needed, but I know that you know what needs to be done and people with whom you can deliberate." She told my father about the many friends and relatives asking about him, and relayed a compliment from his former boss, Willy Nathan, who said, "He'll find his way, such a capable guy."

My father quickly had good news to report: on the third day of his job search, one of his many contacts came through. He had applied for a job at Golo, a ladies shoe importer located at 129 Duane Street, a five-story red brick building in lower Manhattan. Golo—the name had been derived from the Frankfurt business Goldschmidt-Lowenick—was owned by Adolf Heilbronn, a friend of the Ada-Ada owners, the brothers Richard and Willy Nathan. Heilbronn had promised the Nathans that he would always have a job for any of their five sons, if and when they wanted it. The Nathans asked Heilbronn to give the promised job to my father, instead, and wrote a letter of recommendation on my father's behalf. During his second week in New York, my father interviewed with Heilbronn, a short and stout balding man who continually smoked cigars. Rudy explained that he had been an apprentice for two-and-a-half years and most recently had been in the role of "young man," primarily responsible for the sample department. Evidently the interview did not go all that well as, at the end, Heilbronn said that he did not have a job to offer my father.

But as Rudy walked toward the front door to leave, he was stopped by Heilbronn's son-in-law, Arthur Samuels, who had overheard the conversation. Samuels told my father to report on the following Monday in the warehouse, to work as a stock boy, earning $15 for a six-and-a-half-day week.

My grandparents were elated with the news—"the most beautiful birthday gift you could give Papa. . . . Papa and I are so happy; we feel blessed, in ways

I have not known for years." They wanted to know more about the company, the job. My grandmother also wondered how my father was settling in to his apartment—Did he have room for all of his belongings? Did he have a good bed?

My grandmother steadily provided my father with names and addresses of people with whom he should connect. She acknowledged how lucky my father was to have the relationship with Mr. Beckhard, who often invited my father to fancy gatherings at his beautiful Upper West Side brownstone to meet many other German Jewish refugees. My grandparents' friends envied the extensive connections that my father made, a talent that my father had for a lifetime. At the same time, my grandmother advised Rudy to improve his English, and to assimilate. "It is much better to be with Americans—because practice is good for speaking," she wrote. "I wouldn't always sit together with the folks from Frankfurt, no matter how pleasant."

But then she also reminded him whom to call or go visit—usually other refugees from Frankfurt. She wrote, "I would pay a visit to the Dr. Ulrich's; they are both very nice and you don't need to have a special reason. It would be nice for you to be in a family." Two weeks later, she persisted, "Did you visit Ulrich's? I'm sure they're frequented by young people. I'd go under any circumstances—do not feel embarrassed; that's of no use in N.Y." This was part of her way of being in the world, and she continued to teach my father her ways. "That you have people with whom you can always be together is really nice. Not everyone will have that. But you have a long way to go to get through all the acquaintances—Marta Reinemann said that she wrote to her sister-in-law over there who expects you. Otto, too, hopes to see you soon. You are none too eager to make these visits quickly—but the connections are good ones. How do you like the people over there and how are the fetching 'girls'?"

Her commentary on this friend or that acquaintance sometimes reflected her judgmental and gossipy side. She asked if this one "still shoots off his mouth." She reported an engagement "that will knock you flat" of an eighteen-year-old daughter of a friend—to a dentist twenty years her elder. She mused about another friend's son who was engaged in polygyny. And she referred to a fellow in New York as someone who "has always been a big schmoozer, ... has never accomplished any great deeds, but he supposedly has a gorgeous wife ... who must be a character." Julie wondered if the wife could "cook good matzoh balls."

Her letters were full of such news and details. But I would be curious to know how Rudy reconciled his mother's "news" with what he might have read in the American press. In my father's favorite weekly publication, *Time Magazine*, on December 14, 1936, an article was headlined "Germany: Death for Hoarders Reported": "Putting their Nordic heads together to see what could be done to make The Fatherland a still more fit place for Aryan heroes, Der Führer Adolf Hitler and Minister-President Hermann Wilhelm Göring last week launched a new series of laws so super-drastic that even Germans long used to the rigors of Nazidom shuddered with apprehension. The first of these laws, framed by General Göring, imposes the death penalty on any German who 'knowingly and unscrupulously, out of sheer selfishness or for other base motives, sends or leaves his money or other property abroad.'" It also stated that "every German boy and girl, 'without exception,' must join the Hitler Youth 'to be trained physically, spiritually, and morally.'"

My father must have been terrified if he read such news. I imagine he was comforted by my grandmother's letters, meanwhile, which were often upbeat and forward looking, yet he must have been disturbed by some of her words, which at times expressed a continuous ache of a mother missing her son. She ended one of her early letters with: "Sometimes it does seem like a dream to me. You are here again—I keep your things in order and cook your favorite dishes. How I would love to send you something. We do miss you a lot, no matter where we are. I think of you lots and lots and don't let myself realize how long we may be separated. But it makes me happy when I get such good, happy reports from you. I have the feeling that you are coming alive and can breathe as a young, free human."

5

Frankfurt and New York, Early 1937

Frankfurt a.M., 9 March, 1937

My dear Rudolf.

. . . On Sunday afternoon they had a big Bridge and skat tournament at the Lodge for the benefit of the home at Waehlerstr. Forty-five tables—and they raised 450 Mark. Today, Tuesday, is the initiation of 10 ladies and corresponding brothers with elaborate food and drink. I even have to get gussied up . . . .

Last night I went to a special event for Jewish artists. . . .There I was assaulted by a flood of words from Berta Bendheim with the beautiful Irma. She just can't shut up about her Hilde. . . .When you hear the stories people tell about their children, everything is fabulous—well, I just listen quietly. . . .

Your housekeeping appears to be extensive—should I send you a few more recipes—please don't embarrass me—and don't make any pudding with lumps.

I have to finish now. . . . Unfortunately it always gets very late with me, as you know; newspaper, radio, just now a good book, too. Many loving, heartfelt regards and kisses,

Your Mutti

On New Year's Eve, 1937, my grandparents celebrated with their friends the Feitlers—playing cards, and then making three toasts at midnight—with one to my father and his well-being. In her letter describing this event, my grandmother asked my father about his own New Year's celebration—Was it a round of visits? How was the party at the Beckhard's? What kind of food was served? But she knew some of the answers already: "We have heard," she wrote, "that you hung out until 7 a.m. See, word gets around. Be careful, even over there you are not safe."

Indeed. In the letters, she instructed him on everything from darning holes in his socks to how to do laundry. "How about laundering of socks," she wrote. "It's best you wash them yourself in Persil [Germany's most popular detergent], approx. a small tablespoon per bowl; dissolve in cold water and wash lukewarm, and rinse well cold, so no soap remains. Otherwise they become hard and matted. How are your shirts treated? Did you find the right solution? It would be a pity if they weren't delivered looking nice."

She worried out loud about appearance. And, of course, "Did your tuxedo have its premiere yet—These are all matters of great interest to me." If the tux had its "premiere," she wanted to know if the girls liked him in it.

Julie wanted all the details. She was happy to hear that my father's coffee maker was in good working order again. And she simply could not understand his eating habits. "I just don't understand why you eat sandwiches in the evening. When do you have your warm dinner food? I thought you had to work straight through 6 p.m.—please let me know. Because once a day you must have real food."

In between all the unsolicited advice, my grandmother folded in some reports on her own day-to-day events. In a January 1937 letter, she explained that she and Norbert had given notice that they would not renew their apartment lease as of April 1. However, their landlord, Herr Herrmann, did not acknowledge it. I imagine that my grandparents were beginning to struggle financially and that the apartment was too expensive. Or perhaps they were anticipating that Herr Herrmann would not continue to rent to Jews or would significantly raise the rent.

While they quickly found another apartment, the next few letters were filled with anxiety about if and when Herr Herrmann would release them from their lease. My grandmother worried that they would be spending their silver wedding anniversary—their twenty-fifth, on March 29—in a moving van. But then it was official. Herr Herrmann found new tenants for their apartment, much to their relief. In a letter dated January 31, 1937, my grandmother wrote, "Our current apartment has been rented—a couple with children—they greeted us very nicely with the German greeting," the official name for the Hitler *Sieg Heil* salute.

This indirect reference to Hitler was accompanied, in that same letter, by a direct reference: "Yesterday, January 30, was marked by the seizure of power [a reference to the anniversary of Hitler's appointment as chancellor on January 30, 1933]. Big celebrations everywhere, meeting of the Reichstag, and big speech. We went to the movies in the evening to celebrate, a charming film, *Spiel an Bord*" (Play Onboard—a German comedy that premiered November 3, 1936, about a journey on the *Bremen* to America).

In the letters over the next few months, Julie offered multiple descriptions of the new apartment. It was the top floor of a three-story building at

Wolfsgangstraße 132, with a back window looking out to the imposing I.G. Farben Building, the world's largest office building and the ultimate symbol of big business in Germany. After nearly three years on Eysseneckstraße in the Northend, my grandparents would be back in the Westend, not far from their Reuterweg apartment where they had lived for twenty-one years. The Aryan landlord of the Wolfsgangstraße apartment was an acquaintance of my grandfather.

My grandparents' lives were packed into twenty-five baskets and suitcases and crates, including six that were solely glassware and china. Presumably to make some money, my grandmother sold a number of items before moving—the buffet, table and chairs, and Gretel's washstand. "Until now I have found nothing that belongs to you, so there doesn't appear to be anything of value left," she wrote. "Unfortunately one still has too much stuff—all unimportant. Well, I am glad that at least there was no need for a big declutter—that made it significantly simpler. I am sure it'll be very nice and cozy."

My grandparents fixed up the Wolfsgangstraße apartment to their liking. The curtains were hung and the lighting put in place. My grandmother described the new apartment: a vestibule, a small hallway, two beautiful rooms. "The great room without the sideboard/buffet works much better—you remember, of course—for the round table we had a larger top made, and we had the lower shelf removed from the *dressoir*—it looks good. The small room is especially nice: desk at the window with a shelf for plants."

The kitchen featured their old cupboard, freshly painted and in place, though the new kitchen was not as workable as the built-in kitchen in their previous apartment. Their bedroom was large, with a covered veranda. "But everything has drawbacks, the location is not as nice—on the top floor, for example, but it is not so far [from our day-to-day needs]."

And so my father, as much as was possible from thousands of miles away, could picture his parents' new residence.

It happened that on the same day as their move, on March 15, 1937, an anti-Nazi rally was staged in New York, at Madison Square Garden. Some twenty-thousand people attended and heard Mayor Fiorello LaGuardia; CIO chief John L. Lewis; Erika Mann, daughter of exiled author Thomas Mann; General Hugh S. Johnson, former administrator of the NRA; and Rabbi Stephen S. Wise, head of the American Jewish Congress—all condemn Hitler and Nazism. LaGuardia described Nazism at "the gravest menace to peace, civilization, and democracy." The rally was reported prominently on the front page of the *New York Times* the next day.[1] I wonder if my father went to it.

In March, in honor of Julie and Norbert's silver wedding anniversary, my father and Gretel sent my grandparents a wonderful present—a radio. Did my father ship a 220–240 volt radio from the States or arrange for someone in Germany to purchase and send it? It was a wooden tabletop model and, based on pictures, likely a Deltrola or Fairbanks Morse, if sent from the States. Receiving that radio was one of the most joyous occasions recounted in my grandmother's letters.

> And now I have to express my great gratitude to you—what a joy and surprise you created for us. Just when I wasn't home a large crate was dropped off on your order—You know, I was so touched and filled with nostalgia. How did you manage that? My joy has no limits (Papa, too), but I did cry—that we are so apart and had to celebrate our wedding anniversary so alone—But our thoughts are always with you children. Nothing else is left to us other than the knowledge that one's dear children are out of here, for whom one perseveres.

Thanks to their new radio, my grandparents' connection to the outside world suddenly became broader, deeper, more palpable. They listened to music—Wilhelm Furtwangler conducting in Berlin; Gustav Jacoby in the Cologne Cabaret; to the audio of movies, such as *Tango Notturno,* with Pola Negri; to sports events, such as boxing. They heard news directly.

The next correspondence from my grandfather had an edge of anxiety. It was written from Luxembourg, outside the reach of German censors, in April 1937. "With us everything is as usual," he wrote. "It hasn't gotten noticeably worse but not better either. Businesswise one leaves us alone. What happens later no one knows. The emigration continues. Recently one hears of many departures."

How did the tone of that letter and the news of the anti-Nazi rally in New York City influence my father's efforts to get his parents out? Did he begin to feel a sense of urgency, or did he adapt to his parents' ambivalence and apparent resignation to the unknown?

The following month, in May 1937, the *Hindenburg*, a German airship, was destroyed by fire as it attempted to land in New Jersey. My grandmother wrote: "I forgot to write in the last letter about the catastrophe of the dirigible/airship—which of course caused horrible dismay here. How must it have been for you in N.Y. I am very curious to hear from you about that—for what excitement and horror to see this beautiful, wonderful ship happily at its destination—and then this horrendous end. Did you see anything or could one hear the explosion?" She was innocently curious. At the same time, theories abounded outside of Germany that the catastrophe could have been the result of sabotage by a passenger with anti-Nazi sentiments.

The quotidian details of my grandparents' lives unfolded throughout the letters: Who came over for dinner, what they ate, how my grandmother kept busy, sewing and crocheting. She also was knitting—a dress for her, a scarf for my father. She played bridge, attended lectures, and joined afternoon coffee klatches. She asked my father about his bridge playing, pleading, again, "Don't embarrass me."

The letters are all of a piece. Packages sent. Movies seen. *Kulturbund* events attended. Card games played. Holidays celebrated. Describing the weather in Frankfurt and wondering how the weather was in New York. Expressing curiosity about my father's job and prospects for advancement, his living situation and housekeeping, his learning to socialize in the States. Sending regards to Martin Beckhard or Adolf Keller or Curt Bier (my father's roommate). My grandmother continually sent my father homemade cookies and cakes, as well as small necessities, either through the mail or with friends who were coming to the States.

Mixed in were assurances that Norbert's business was alright. The economic picture of my grandparents' lives must have been troubling for my father, despite my grandmother's continual attempts to minimize their financial difficulties. Just a few months after my father left, my grandmother wrote, "Papa is satisfied thus far with the business; his health is quite decent, too. One muddles on—could use a hundred [marks] now and then—but I am content that I am feeling well when it comes to nerves etc."

Still, between the lines there were signs of struggle. Basic utilities such as the telephone were too costly. "Unfortunately I have to confess to you that the telephone bill is still too high and that Papa continues to be upset for hours. I'm sure you'll laugh about it . . . but I have now set up a kitty, into which you have to put 10 Pfennig every time."

Despite her worries, Julie never failed to remind my father about the proper social graces. Peppered throughout the letters were her reminders to him to send notes for various occasions. "Uncle Emil celebrates his 60th birthday on Feb 1, . . . Write a card to him; that always makes people happy." Or instructing my father to send his sympathies: "This week Herr Sundermann has died, it was a release—the man was very ill and his wife suffered terribly on account of that. You will send your condolences to Lore."

And the letters are interspersed with the unsettling news of people leaving—most immigrating to the States, some going to Palestine, some to Argentina, France, or Holland. Some were trying to get out, "That the Kahns still are not making progress is too bad. . . . Hedwig wants to go in spring . . . Eisenberg's also don't have anything yet. Berta is getting nervous; She's gone to see Eva in Paris; there, too, it's not working out as it should." Others left for brief visits elsewhere and then returned to Germany.

At one point, my grandmother noted, "Nowadays when one gets together with friends, one hears reports from all parts of the globe."

Yet there seemed to be no sense of urgency about my grandparents leaving, neither in their 1937–1938 letters nor in my father's writings. How did he reconcile that lack of urgency with what he heard from those visiting or emigrating from Germany, and also from the news reports here? Had he read the article, "Germany: Hitler v. Everybody" in the May 3, 1937, issue of *Time*?

> Last week armed German police smashed their way into Berlin's B'nai B'rith lodge, arrested the members, cleared out the premises and seized the property. All over Germany other B'nai B'rith lodges were raided, seized and evacuated, as were children's homes, sanatoriums, and homes for the aged supported by the society. Though most of those arrested were later released, the entire organization was ordered dissolved and its funds seized, on the pretext that one of the 14,000 German members of the B'nai B'rith had 'engaged in Communistic propaganda.' . . . Three weeks ago an order was issued forbidding Jewish organizations of any sort to hold any meetings whatever for 60 days. So stringent was this rule that if so many as five Jews should meet over a herring in a public cafe they might be liable to arrest.

6

Frankfurt and New York, Late Spring and Summer 1937

Frankfurt a.M., 11 May, 1937
My dear Rudolf,

. . . So it has turned really summer over there. . . . Be careful; hopefully you won't have any unpleasant aftereffects from your first sunburn. I have been thinking about your wardrobe. . . . I hope the frock is not too big a purchase and doesn't constitute too great a burden. I heard that clothes over there are made much better and more suitable. That you are so dissatisfied with the laundry is very sad, but perhaps you will find somewhat better opportunities. . . . Here there are other things that are difficult; by now you will have talked with Hedwig. . . .

White asparagus season is starting here. Do they have that over there, too, or do they have other delicacies? They must put on quite a spread for the Friday evenings at the Keller's. . . . Of course, one worries a lot here, you can't completely avoid that. You know that I take things a bit hard—it takes time, then it gets better. Don't worry about it—but I have to write to you about it, then I feel better. . . . there's not much new to report from here. . . .

Now with the nice weather I am hoping for pictures from you. Many affectionate regards and heartfelt kisses,
Your Mutti

[A facsimile and complete translation of the original letter is in the Appendix]

In the late spring and early summer of 1937, Julie's melancholy became much more pronounced. Her letters had only the rare mention of movies, lectures, walks, socializing, entertaining.

Julie and Norbert spent a few days away for their silver wedding anniversary—staying at the Hotel Schwarzer Bock in Wiesbaden, spending time outdoors and enjoying good food and drink. But my grandmother bemoaned, "Particularly on such a special day, one thinks only of one's children and that puts me at times in a melancholy mood, that one can't be together especially for hours such as these. But one must get over it, because it's about your future."

My grandfather occasionally referred to my grandmother's depression, hoping that the *Nervenarzt* (neurologist) could help her. My grandmother often related her emotional state to her separation from her children, her overwhelming sense of loneliness, and the overall state of affairs in Nazi Germany, although she tended to be vague about that. She wrote:

> I have been overcome again by loneliness and the longing for you and Grete and Micha (Grete's one-and-a-half-year old son). I don't know whether it is the new environment. Papa has been gone a week. This time it is awfully hard for me. Until now I have not felt quite at home here—I actually looked forward to the apartment so much, but it hasn't had much effect on my mood. I hope that I get over it again—but the situation/location at times weighs more heavily—I have suffered from it over the last years enough. You can't begin to know how much I think of you—that many things are not easy and that it takes a lot of strong will and energy to prevail.

"That's why one regards everything here as meaningless," she wrote at one point, "because one no longer is present with one's thoughts. It is for all of us parents a hard fate—to live so separated from one's children. This week Frau Bier called me, because Curt's letter had not arrived on time—it's the same everywhere, one waits from one mail delivery to the next."

Julie yearned to participate in my father's life challenges. He was only twenty-two. Yet she strained not to be *too* involved. Rudy entertained switching jobs because his boss broke a promise for a promotion, rendering him uncertain about his future. Julie offered her opinion, but then stepped back, encouraging my father to consult with his connections in the States to help him make his all-important job decisions. While she initially wrote, "I don't want to issue any prescriptions regarding the job; I can't judge that from here," she later said, "Let us participate fully and completely in your life over there." And she expressed unwavering confidence in my father's ability to make the right decision, ultimately.

Although she tried to be reassuring, her melancholy was ever present. "Unfortunately I am a bit under the weather in terms of nerves, but you need not worry. It's all the circumstances. One lives quietly for oneself, much at home, has one's various people, and thinks of and lives only with one's children.

The separation is, perhaps the longer it goes on, often very difficult after all, and unfortunately the time has once again overcome me."

It is striking that my grandmother never even mentioned the possibility of leaving Germany in these 1937 letters. Was it censorship or was it a false optimism?

A good many German Jews, it seems, did not yet seriously entertain the idea of leaving their homeland. Despite the worsening conditions, friends and acquaintances of my grandparents took short trips to the United States and elsewhere in 1937—and then returned to Germany. And, conversely, some visitors from the United States and elsewhere came to Germany. My grandmother was optimistic that her grandson, Micha, would come visit and that Mr. Beckhard would make plans to come to Germany to visit his many relatives.

Julie's best friend in Frankfurt, Hedwig Hirsch, visited New York. My grandmother mentioned the upcoming trip several times in letters and told my father that Hedwig would bring him birthday greetings. Upon Hedwig's return, my grandmother wrote that Hedwig "gave us a quite content report. You can imagine that I am interested in everything. . . . She is convinced that you will succeed. . . . Hedwig is still quite dazed from the big trip and the impressions, the people she encountered."

"Of course she is not excited by everything," my grandmother wrote. "One needs to be young to integrate oneself. She does not want to live there yet." I suspect that Hedwig's perspective, based on her first-hand experience, supported my grandparents' belief at the time that they were better off staying in Germany in spite of the increasing anti-Semitism.

Yet my grandmother intimated that Hedwig must have shared with my father the realities of their lives—well beyond what my grandmother could write in her letters. What might Hedwig have shared? That the German Ministry of the Interior had issued a new order depriving Jews of municipal citizenship? That Jewish-owned employment agencies had been ordered to stop their activities? That Jewish public meetings, except for synagogue services, were now prohibited?[1] That Jews were prohibited from working in offices? That many Jewish merchants had lost their businesses?[2]

Emigration did come up, albeit obliquely, and in reference to others. Julie wrote that my father's cousin, Albert, and his wife, Irma, were making plans to leave. Albert had been held in Dachau in 1933 and, as noted earlier, had been told to leave Germany when he was released. How he got around that warning for four years, I do not know. The couple received safe passage to Holland, leaving behind a beautiful apartment and Albert's well-paying job. Albert and Irma had visited my grandparents often—for the holidays, for a meal, for *Eintopf* (one-pot stew). Referring to their departure, my grandmother observed that these continual leave-takings were "sad news from all sides" and that, somewhat enigmatically, "one must know why one decides to do this," to emigrate.

But the subject was not developed. The weather continued to be a constant theme, and she often linked the weather to her mental health. My grandmother wrote about how muggy and hot the days were in Frankfurt, how she continually dripped with sweat and wiped her brow. Her nerves were "acting up again, but that's also the Spring, which makes you tired," she wrote. And more dramatically, "We need rain badly, my brain feels quite dried up." She continually inquired about the weather in New York. She thought it wise that my father stayed cool by going to the movie house, as he had reported to her. She was curious about my father's wardrobe for the intolerable heat. How was his linen suit? And his bathing costume?

Though she had reminded him to be careful about sunburn, my father and a few friends, on the Fourth of July, 1937, visited Coney Island and, although my fair-skinned father donned a long beach coat, he was severely sunburned on his ankles and feet. The sunburn was so bad that he was unable to wear proper shoes the next day. When he showed up for work—by this time he had become an office clerk—Mr. Heilbronn proclaimed, "This is no kindergarten. You're fired." Once again, Mr. Heilbronn's son-in-law, Arthur Samuels, rescued my father. He took my father to lunch and explained, "Mr. Heilbronn means well. You can keep your job."

I have often wondered about my father's adventures at Coney Island on that sunny day in America. Did he ride the Thunderbolt 80, the high wooden roller coaster? The Wonder Wheel? The B&B Galloping Horse Carousel? Did he and his friends view the dwarf Tom Thumb, the "130-year-old" Charlie Parcansas, or the Ostrich-Faced Lady?

Meanwhile, back in Frankfurt, my grandmother wrote of Grete Bergmann, the near-Olympian, record-breaking high jumper, and how she stopped in Frankfurt on Pentecost Sunday, presumably on the athlete's way to immigrate to the States.

Another theme for my grandmother was food. Julie was curious about the fruits and vegetables available in the States. And she wrote about enjoying

Kaltschalen und rote Grütze (cold fruit soups and red berry jellied dessert) in the depths of the July heat. I imagine Rudy savoring only the memory of those foods while he tried all sorts of new foods from various venues. Did he try the clams and oysters from the street vendors? The roasted peanuts? Did he eat the clam chowder or hamburger steak at the Horn & Hardart Automat? My father was not raised keeping kosher.

Julie continued to send packages and became quite perturbed when friends or acquaintances visiting the States either refused to take a package or failed to deliver it. "I don't really understand Ella W.—she has a small package for you, did she give it to you? How about Hirschberg, whom I gave the preserves for you and also some cookies?"

She often shifted focus within a single paragraph. She could yearn to travel and ponder what to sell—presumably to earn money—and then abruptly shift to speculate on fashion. "Travel is not so big right now. One has to ponder what to sell. But the children need to be visited. How is the season now at your end? During the heat the stores were very busy (also shoe stores). The wide form has not caught on here—is the fashion there still quite different?"

7

Germany, 1937

Frankfurt a.M., 31 May, 1937

My dear Rudolf!

I hope you continue to do well and that you will have good experiences with Golo. From here it is very difficult for me to give you advice. You will do the right thing. With us everything is unchanged. When I go on the road before long, I'll let Mutti go to the *Sommerfrische* [the countryside]; hopefully that will be good for her.

For today, heartfelt regards and kisses,

Your Papa

What else was happening in 1937 in Germany that was *not* mentioned by my grandmother, who wrote most of the letters?

Jews were forbidden from studying medicine and barred from receiving university degrees. German citizens could see only non-Jewish doctors. German Jewish musicians were forbidden to play Beethoven or Mozart during Jewish cultural concerts. Jews were not allowed to be part of the German film industry. German Jews could only buy books from Jewish booksellers, who could only sell works by non-Aryan authors, as recounted in *A World in Turmoil* by Hershel and Abraham Edelheit.[1]

Munich had hosted two art exhibitions deriding Jews: Goebbels's Propaganda Ministry sponsored one of them, called *Der Ewige Jew* (The Eternal Jew), that highlighted the "Jewish features" of political figures such as Leon Trotsky, and emphasized supposed attempts by Jews to bolshevize Germany. It also depicted the Jews as financial exploiters. The exhibit traveled to Vienna, Berlin, and many other German cities, enabling more than four hundred thousand people to see it.

Another exhibit, *Entartete Kunst* (Degenerate Art), exemplified the Nazi denouncement of art that did not "illustrate the ideas of National Socialism and the glorification of the State"—that is, works of classic modernity, of Jewish artists, and of social criticism. The art featured in these exhibitions had been created by avant-garde artists, such as Beckmann, Chagall, Klee, and Kandinsky. Although they had been recognized and esteemed in the 1920s, these exhibitions aimed to deride and condemn these artists as well as all Jews and other "undesirables." Only a month after the *Entartete Kunst* opened, the Nazis confiscated what they deemed to be degenerate art from museums all across Germany—totaling nearly sixteen thousand works from just over one hundred museums. Some were sold abroad and nearly five thousand works were burned.[2]

Julie and Norbert heard on their radio about Mussolini's visit to Berlin, which came in the last week in September 1937. "It is quite a fabulous reception and is celebrated in style," my grandmother wrote—a short, relatively uninformative comment, likely the product of fear of censorship and far short of illuminating the Hitler-Mussolini grandstanding, including an extensive military parade.[3]

My grandparents must have worried that Hitler's talk of protecting European culture and reconstructing the homeland portended increasingly difficult times for them. On the other hand, were my grandparents aware of the memorial service in Berlin, conducted by the National Union of Jewish War Veterans, honoring the twelve thousand Jewish soldiers killed in World War I?[4] Did such a memorial reinforce their hope that my grandfather's military service in World War I would be instrumental in keeping them safe?

The confinement of Jews in Germany was further enforced with the November 1937 restriction that passports were issued to Jews only for emigration or business travel, no longer for leisure travel. My grandfather had to reapply for an extension of his passport in December of 1936, May of 1937, and December of 1937, which meant requesting a waiver of the taxes imposed on property when fleeing the Reich. In one such request, on December 24, 1936, he wrote: "I ask for the grant of a tax clearance certificate for the purpose of applying for a passport. I am not in arrears with my taxes and I don't own any property which is subject to the law of taxes for fleeing the Reich. I need the passport for business trips abroad, which I intend to start in January, therefore I ask for prompt settlement." Before my grandfather received the tax clearance certificate, the Tax Office conducted its own research.

Tax Office Ffm
December 29, 1936
Re: Suspicion of Intention to Emigrate

The merchant Norbert Baum is under suspicion of emigration.
Reason for above suspicion: Letter dated Dec. 24, 1936
The above mentioned is not in arrears with taxes of the Reich.

a) Last declared income for the calendar year 1935: 9149.-RM
b) Last declared business assets 1.1.1931-1.1.1935: 11949.-RM
less life insurance claims: 5561.- RM
Remaining total assets: 6588.-RM

January 12, 1937
According to the files presented there is no need for a tax for fleeing the Reich, because there have not been assets in excess of Rm 50.000, nor an income of more than 20.000 RM ascertained from Jan 1. 1931 on. At this time this Office does not raise objections against the granting of a tax clearance certificate.

For Jews who did not emigrate, the emergence and expansion of concentration camps became the next level of threat to their existence.

The Buchenwald concentration camp was opened near Weimar in east central Germany, initially for males only—primarily political prisoners. Eventually administering eighty-eight subcamps and detaining women as well, Buchenwald would become one of the largest concentration camps in Germany.[5]

Construction to enlarge the concentration camp Dachau began in early 1937. The SS prisoners were forced to do the hard manual labor to expand the camp, to accommodate nearly ten thousand prisoners by the end of 1938—almost double the 4,800 prisoners in its first year, 1933.

8

Zurich and Frankfurt, August–September 1937

Zurich, 31 August, 1937

My dear Rudolf,

. . . Today I have been already 14 days with Rosenfelds and have very nice days here. . . . I was able to be at the lake a lot. In the afternoon I took nice walks with Alice. . . .

Today I am invited at Frau Abelmann (formerly in Frankfurt) who has a fabulous villa here, so people here are still quite well off and they have a comfortable life. You can imagine how good I feel here now—not to hear always the same things, and to have cheerful people around me. . . .

Alice would like to keep me here over the holidays [the Jewish High Holidays], I don't know yet how it will work out. I don't want to leave Papa alone for all these days, but he wrote that I should enjoy it and four days is a long time—I would feel bad about it. . . .

I live here in the land of plenty. I eat so well and so much—whipped cream, chocolate, cake—wonderful. I sent you a package, chocolate from here. . . .

I kiss you heartily and have good holidays, with heartfelt greetings,

Your *Mutter*

[For a facsimile and complete translation of the original letter, see Appendix, p. 254.]

"Our community is shrinking and that's not nice," wrote my grandmother in August 1937.

With conditions deteriorating in Frankfurt, and after eight months of separation from both of her children, Julie was desperate to get away on vacation, like her friends and relatives who were traveling to Upper Bavaria and Königstein, and beyond Germany to Marienbad, Prague, and Budapest—leaving and returning.

So my grandmother went to Zurich for two weeks to stay with her dear friend Alice Rosenfeld, who had moved to Zurich from Frankfurt. During that time, my grandfather worked in the small scenic town of Oberreifenberg, the highest town in the Taunus mountains that he and my grandmother occasionally visited. Although only twenty miles from Frankfurt, the town offered a welcome break from "the business of the big city."

My grandmother was "glad of course to breathe Swiss air," a wonderful treatment for her melancholy. "Everything is going all right here and it does one good to be out and not to see and hear anything. It is such a pleasant feeling, not to hear always the same things and to be able to move about freely. I was in dire need of a vacation this year and it has not become easier for us in the meantime—but you hear enough about this already."

I picture my grandmother in Switzerland like a caged bird that had been freed. She was able to take walks along the lake and in the mountains, swim in the beach pool, ride a steamboat, shop, and eat in ways she had not known for some time. "I really love the food here, all very plentiful, something which is not the case back home. I hope very much to gain a few pounds and to come back quite recuperated."

Julie and Alice attended the opening performance of *Die Meistersinger von Nürnberg* (The Master Singer from Nürnberg), Wagner's sole comedic opera, at Zurich's *Opernhaus,* which accommodated nearly eight hundred people. *Die Meistersinger* was used frequently as Nazi propaganda, as its main character espoused the need to protect German art from foreign threats. Some argue that anti-Semitic stereotypes were part of the fabric of the opera. Nonetheless, my grandmother must have been thrilled to attend a cultural event that was not part of the restrictive *Kulturbund*, and she knew how fleeting that opportunity was. "For once I have stopped thinking about everything and lived carefree into the day. It will be over for me again."

During my grandmother's stay, the Zionist Organization's Twentieth Congress met in Zurich. The mission of the Zionist Organization, founded in 1897 and later renamed the World Zionist Organization, was to establish a home for the Jewish people in Palestine, secured under public law.[1] At its meeting in 1937, the Twentieth Congress considered a British Royal Commission's proposal for a partition plan to create a Jewish and Arab state in Palestine, given the extreme unrest between the Jews and Arabs.[2]

In the end, Chaim Weizmann and David Ben-Gurion convinced the Twentieth Congress of Zionists to equivocally approve the recommendations—called the Peel Commission Recommendations—as a basis for more negotiation, to support a Jewish state, but to reject the proposed borders. This was the first proposal for a Jewish state in Palestine and, although not accepted, it became an important starting point for partition discussions.[3]

Referring to the Zionist meeting, my grandmother wrote, "All hotels were full. Unfortunately also here were unpleasant incidents against the Jews. This is not very pleasing. I was not there when it happened, the main days were already over, but everybody is very upset about it. A solution has not been found so far."

She extended her stay in Zurich through Rosh Hashanah, the Jewish New Year. Though she felt guilty about not observing the holiday with my grandfather in Frankfurt, she welcomed the opportunity to attend synagogue in Zurich. Still, she wrote, "During such days one always feels it more to be alone. When will we celebrate again together?"

Although Alice urged my grandmother to stay longer, my grandmother returned to Frankfurt after three weeks.

> Now I am also looking forward to be home. I had a very nice time. . . . I was well taken care of and recuperated very well. I only hope that it will last— Zurich is a glorious city, one can live here really well. Also the shops here are very nice, which won't impress you, but I found everything very nice here and I get quite a different feeling about everything. Also very beautiful shoe stores. I was very interested, looked into the shop windows. Very elegant things—many shoes, but all again with narrow shapes.

I long to know why my grandmother was ready to return to Germany and leave behind the freedom she had tasted. And she was hardly the only one.

Upon her return, the harsh realities of life for German Jews pierced her. Although my grandmother had gained four pounds and wrote, "I feel it [improvement] in my nerves," she ached with loneliness. She prepared the evening meal before the fast for Yom Kippur, the High Holiday Day of Atonement, but felt "I cannot get used to the idea that it is just the two of us. These are days which make being alone so hard for us." My grandparents attended synagogue, but with far "fewer people all the time, fewer acquaintances, and the atmosphere was quite melancholy."

* * *

My father, meanwhile, attended synagogue in New York for Rosh Hashanah and Yom Kippur. My grandmother hoped he found the holiday tastes of home, such as chicken and apple cake.

Consistent with his extroverted and social nature, Rudy hosted a large party in his own apartment in New York, perhaps for the Break Fast, perhaps for many from back home. Julie was glad that my father entertained extensively, and wrote, "Who were your guests and who are the girls—from here or already these American girls? You seem to come along well, as the head of a household. Forty sandwiches, one must commend you for this."

My grandmother delighted in hearing, probably on the radio, that Grete Bergmann had won the US women's high jump and shot put competitions, a triumph for a German Jewish woman who had been dismissed by the Nazis.

And she continued to write about various friends and acquaintances who were leaving—going to London, Brazil, Holland, the States. "One sees so many here, where and in which direction they all go. Everybody has the story of a different fate to tell."

She wondered if my father had connected with Frau Dr. Mannheimer or Marta Reinemann, friends from Frankfurt. Had he received the packages of chocolates and sock preservers? She sent my father clippings about the news that the Jewish owners of Ada-Ada had sold their business and came "out ahead." Perhaps, yet again, my grandmother was aware of the censorship of mail. Otherwise, such a sale, much less a profitable sale, is a mystery to me, because by early 1937, Jewish merchants were either being forced to sell their business at a loss or to give up their business. [4]

The letters continued. No matter how melancholic or tired, my grandmother wrote to my father weekly. At the end of one letter she wrote, "I have to go to sleep, because my eyes hurt."

9

Frankfurt, October–December 1937

Frankfurt a.M., 4 November, 1937

My dear Rudolf,

. . . On such a day [Julie's birthday] I think especially of you all out there, the thoughts that we might soon see each other again are my fondest wish. You have been away now for a year and it seems to me to have gone by so quickly, although there were many hard days for me and some months which were not nice. I am glad that I am functioning again and feel equal to the situation again. It just should stay like this. The birthday passed in a very satisfactory way; in the afternoon was the traditional coffee with Geigers, Hedwig, Irma, Alice Ettlinger, etc. It was good and plentiful, among other things a delicious cheesecake—How would you like that? In terms of presents, I got a silk scarf, a handbag, a few handkerchiefs, underwear, a foldable shopping bag, the beautiful chrysanthemums, and chocolates. All things, which I can use very well and I was very happy about them. . . .

Your Mutti

In the fall and winter of 1937, my grandmother's letters frequently mentioned concerns about money. As my grandmother wrote, "I have to spring for a new winter coat this year; fortunately I already have the material for it. We cannot afford big expenditures now; Papa just paid an installment to Josef B. It was quite hard for him and cost him much trouble; I hope eventually we'll be free of that as well." My grandparents were clearly stressed by the pressure of continual loan payments to this fellow called Josef B., likely Josef Baum, who was a distant cousin of Norbert. Perhaps this was a loan for my father's emigration-related expenses to America.

That year, Julie and Norbert did not travel as often as they once had to the neighboring towns; for example, they did not go to Geinsheim for the new crop of apple cider, to be enjoyed with walnuts. Instead, they stayed home to enjoy the fall treat. My grandmother mentioned that she was unsure that she had enough money to buy my grandfather birthday presents of neckties and a hat.

To earn a few extra marks, she began making and selling felt flowers, an enjoyable craft she had learned in a class. She sold the flowers for one or two marks, "not much but it adds up." She even asked my father to explore the potential market in the States for the flowers. Such resourcefulness was common in my grandmother's cohort. As she wrote, "The atmosphere is very depressed, after all—everybody still wants to get some sort of training."

Much of this training was offered through the League of Jewish Women, an organization with feminist roots, founded in 1904, that in the thirties helped German Jewish women cope with the increasing restrictions on their lives, while maintaining Jewish traditions. It also prepared Jewish women for emigration. Among its many offerings, the league taught crafts, sewing, and household work. In 1935, it published a cookbook with many vegetarian entrees, as kosher meat was becoming scarcer. In 1937, its cooking classes focused on apples, potatoes, and cabbage—likely staples of Jewish households.

My grandmother took English classes—reading and writing—for an hour and a half weekly at the *Lehrhaus,* or House of Learning, a Jewish studies school shaped by its founding director, the philosopher Franz Rosenzweig, a renowned Jewish thinker who grappled with the many existential questions emerging from a Jewish identity. For her studies, Julie even asked my father to return to her the pocket German-English dictionary she had given him when he left, assuming that my father's English was well beyond needing the dictionary by then. I have, from my father's possessions, a Langenscheidt's German-English/English-German 3"x 4" pocket dictionary published in Germany in 1930. Well worn: a gap between the fragile spine and the pages, with tiny broken threads visible between, are all that remains of the book's hinge. Is that the one? The one that my father repeatedly pulled out of his pocket for a much-needed word?

At that time in Germany, learning to speak English as an adult was connected to considering living outside of the country. The course at the *Lehrhaus* was "so well attended that the students had to be divided into three groups." Julie yearned to speak English as well as Marta Reinemann, who travelled to the States and England. She wanted to take a conversational English class, but could not afford it, she told Rudy. She observed that my father's former English teacher in Frankfurt had "one of the best jobs," due to the great demand for her services.

My grandmother was yearning. Period.

"These days I am thinking so much of your emigration last year," she wrote.

"So time passes and one has to resign oneself to live with one's children also in letters. But even if life over there also comes with some difficulties, the time is still much too short to get used to everything. . . . If one has the feeling that one will come back, it will make life satisfying."

To bring in more money, beyond the few marks from her felt flowers, and to cope with her loneliness when my grandfather was away, my grandmother rented their second room to a boarder. Renting rooms was not uncommon. After much searching, my grandmother chose a Jewish cellist, who performed with the *Kulturbund,* as a boarder. He paid her thirty-eight marks for rent, higher than the average rent of thirty marks. He practiced one or two hours a day, and his music became a dear companion to her. She served the boarder breakfast, but he polished his own shoes and did his own laundry, which my grandmother implied was an unexpected bonus. The cellist and my grandmother formed a close friendship over the months. He often gave my grandparents advance notice about upcoming events, ensuring their ability to get tickets.

My grandmother continued to "parent" my father from afar. She inquired, "Are you still well supplied with everything for winter—Is everything still all right and without moth holes? Is your winter suit not too hot—Did you wear it last year? And what about your underwear? Can you keep it in good repair and is the underwear still in good shape?"

In one letter, she harshly admonished him for not concluding his letter with a proper ending. But, he "shall be forgiven this once," she said. She also mailed Rudy a letter of complaint from her brother Willy, in Berlin, who said that "his feelings were very hurt" because he had not heard from my father.

The arrival of the letters both to and from Germany, meanwhile, became more erratic. Fewer ships were transporting an increasing volume of mail. And in her less regular notes, my grandmother often wrote that "not much is happening." In fact, one week she wrote my father a postcard, not a letter—because, she said, she had little to report, but wanted to adhere to her weekly correspondence. At this time, she wrote that her brother, Jacob, was struggling. He would be restricted to call on Jewish customers only as of January 1, 1938, and he had lost money. "Of course it was to be expected," she wrote, "but it is just awful."

* * *

"Not much is happening." Yet Jewish market stalls and shops were being picketed by Nazi police. At a Frankfurt museum, *Städel*—officially the *Städelsches Kunstinstitut und Städtische Galerie*, the National Socialists confiscated seventy-seven paintings and seven hundred prints, declaring the works to be "degenerate art." The final Aryanization of the City Administration of Frankfurt occurred, meaning that Jews were no longer allowed to work in the city administration.[1]

Around this time in the States, FDR delivered his famous Quarantine Speech, warning Americans against continued isolationism, saying: "There is a solidarity and interdependence about the modern world, both technically and morally, which makes it impossible for any nation completely to isolate itself from economic and political upheavals in the rest of the world, especially when such upheavals appear to be spreading and not declining."[2] He addressed the need to "quarantine the aggressors," referring to Germany, Italy, and Japan. Americans' intense negative reaction to the speech indicated the strength of the isolationist sentiment in the United States.

In Frankfurt, friends and acquaintances continued to leave. Each of the three families in Julie and Norbert's apartment house had a son who had immigrated or was trying to immigrate to the States. Frau Marx's son was a chemist in Boston, and Frau Löwenstein's son, Erich, left for New York in November 1937. His mother gave a party for his departure, with guests including Erich's girlfriend and other friends. My grandmother wrote that all the parents "have already decided to travel together to America next year. In the meantime we console each other." On behalf of another friend's son, a chef trying to immigrate to the States, my grandmother asked Rudy to "find out if there is an opportunity through the committee for him to come over."

It is difficult to fathom how it is that my grandmother solicited my father's support on behalf of others but not for her and my grandfather. It certainly seems indicative of the depth of their ambivalence about leaving.

Yet, she regularly commended my father on his decision, or perhaps on *their* decision, for him to emigrate. She noted that it had been a shock to leave a job at Ada-Ada, but that his former colleagues and employers there "all to a man are following you [to America]. They themselves don't keep it a secret any more."

She wrote about the outings that she and my grandfather still took. These included strolls at the nearby Rothschild Park, "which is open to the public," meaning open to Jews. She considered attending a culinary exhibition, where she could "eat in the American way." I wonder if the exhibition was especially for Jews, since so many of them were emigrating to the States. Julie and Norbert went to the cinema a few times, seeing such fare as *Kapriolen* (Capers—a comedic love story about a famous male reporter and female pilot) and *Daphne and the Diplomat*. While not welcomed as Jews at the movies, as described in Marian Kaplan's book *Between Dignity and Despair,* they were not officially prohibited from such venues until 1938.[3]

Julie and Norbert went to the *Kulturbund* to hear chamber music and singing, making good use of their membership, which at 2.50 marks per month was "rather expensive, but one must hear something," according to my grandmother. They heard the young baritone Ernst Wolff, the son of cantors, in Frankfurt. She urged my father to attend concerts as well, especially because she had heard that admission is sometimes free in the States. "You never were much for classical music, but one gets something out of listening to such concerts."

Julie praised Rudy for continually making efforts to assimilate, which she gleaned from his photos and letters. "You seem to . . . Americanize yourself and also the language continues to make progress successfully. I am very happy to have such good news from you, because that's essential, if one wants to be successful in that land." She continually inquired about the parties, wanting to know all the details about the dress, the food, the socializing. She even requested menus.

But she sent him reminders of home, too. For Chanukah, my grandmother sent my father *Kaloderma* (a brand of soap and cream made in Berlin), *Lebkuchen* (a traditional ginger spice Christmas cookie), and chocolates. She appreciated my father's gift, apparently money. "Of course I can use it very well. . . . I don't know yet how to best invest it." (How did my father send money? Perhaps through a visitor who returned to Frankfurt? Maybe such a gift enabled my grandparents to comfortably treat themselves to a feast of goose for Chanukah.)

Often in the afternoons, my grandmother played bridge with other women, and sometimes in the evenings with my grandfather and other couples. While the game provided escape, the conversations usually focused on "news" about who intended to emigrate, or who had taken a short trip. Or about those who already had emigrated—what they were doing in the States or elsewhere: how this one got married, how that one can work in the States as a lawyer, how another will work as a housekeeper, and how some parents have joined their children. She wrote of one friend who had visited the States and returned to Germany with full reports: "Frau Dr. Mannheimer was here with me in connection with my round of bridge, which was excellent, by the way. She was very impressed by the life and the way things work there (in America).... Frau Dr. found you looked splendid, gained some weight and have 'arrived' as an American quite well. I am very happy about this."

Indeed, my father had been promised his long-awaited promotion to become a driver for a traveling salesman and had already received a raise of two dollars per week. My grandparents were thrilled that he had progressed so far in only a year, finding this to be, in the words of my grandfather, "a great reassurance" and "emotionally liberating." As typically proud parents, they believed that my father's boss did not yet fully appreciate how great an "asset" my father was. My father told his parents that he took driving lessons to prepare for his new position, and my grandmother cautioned from afar—"I only have one worry: Be very careful while driving. Please take care and don't race around."

In the last week in December 1937, my grandfather's letter ended with a note of foreboding.

"What the New Year will bring for us," he wrote, "cannot be foretold."

Part Three

THE LAST TRAIN

We hope at all cost that you will succeed in helping us, so that we shall finally be relieved of these awful worries. It is neither nice to write such letters, nor is it nice to receive them, but we have no other choice.

JULIE BAUM | *October 1941*

10

Frankfurt, January–March 1938

Frankfurt, 27. February 1938

My dear Rudolf,

For days we have been waiting for your letter, which arrived today, Sunday, by way of exception. I hear, however, that there was no earlier steamer, because nobody in our building received mail until today. We are always happy together and the relationship between the tenants is especially nice. Frau Marx (on the ground floor) named our house *das Dreimäderlhaus* [as in the 'The House of the Three Girls', the title of a Schubert operetta], however a bit elderly, but really cozy. Tonight everybody in the building will come to us and in addition the two young girls, friends of Erich L. The only man is Papa—A great pity, you should be here.

. . . Today I was in a good mood for a change—I saw a wonderful movie last night, with Grete Weiser (Berlin). The fat tears were rolling when I was leaving the cinema.

So many are leaving and one's heart is often quite heavy. I am glad that I am very busy and don't have time to dwell on this. I think I already wrote to you that I am taking a sewing class in addition to my flower fabrication, which gives me much joy. . . . Yesterday we sent off the photos of us; you will have received them in the meantime. They were meant to be part of your birthday present, but we could not wait so long. I am curious how you will like them. . . .

And now for you, many dear cordial greetings and a thousand kisses,

Your Mutti

My dear Rudolf!

We received your letter yesterday. I am sorry that you have this disappointment, but hold your head high, you will prevail. This manner is really terribly mean. . . . Our business here is very quiet. Next week I shall go on a trip for three weeks.

For today, cordial greetings and kisses, Your Papa.

Norbert and Julie Baum celebrated New Year's Eve 1938 with their thirty-two-year-old nephew, Albert Baum, and his wife, Irma, who were visiting after recently immigrating to Holland. It was a quiet celebration at home. They played bridge, ate the traditional New Year's fare of carp, and drank a toast to their children—my father in the United States and his sister Gretel in Palestine.

Friendships meant a great deal at that time, even more than in ordinary times. Marion Kaplan, a scholar of modern Jewish history and a renowned historian of German Jewish women, explains in her book *Between Dignity and Despair*, that in these times Jews often restricted their social life to their own homes or organizations. She quotes a woman who told her: "Those who remained behind, whose circle got increasingly smaller, closed ranks all the more tightly. Friendship once again became the essence of life."[1]

Indeed, *das Dreimäderlhaus* provided tremendous support to Julie, and she treasured her relationships with her apartment neighbors Frau Marx and Frau Löwenstein, both of whom had sons in the States and also yearned for them. Indeed, as Marion Kaplan notes, the expression "children turned into letters" (*aus Kindern wurden Briefe*) captured the excruciating separation.[2]

When my father failed to write, my grandmother chided him on behalf of all: "Whenever the mailman comes with mail from America, the whole house is full of expectation. And what disappointment when the letters don't arrive on time!" The three ladies' worries about their respective sons were one and the same—How were their sons faring? Would their sons be successful? When Frau Löwenstein's son, Erich, had difficulty finding a job in the States, for example, my grandmother solicited my father to help Erich find a job, if not in Erich's field of banking, then in any field.

Julie wrote about how the three ladies were always happy together. They traveled together to Rosenhof Manor, just north of Nauheim, a town about twenty miles from Frankfurt, in the middle of meadows and fields. They lounged in deck chairs, enjoyed the sun, and were cheerful together there. They socialized with acquaintances among some seventy people who were visiting at the manor for afternoon coffee. This must have been a Jewish oasis—owned by Jews for Jewish guests. Once a "big enterprise," it was now only large enough to sleep ten to twelve people. The husband was the cook, and the facility no longer included a large farm.

However, gathering together with fellow Jews—where the conversation often turned to emigration and to dreams of no longer being frightened when the doorbell rang—brought with it the fear of being watched by non-Jews, especially the Gestapo.[3]

In her letters, the weather often served as bookends for my grandmother's descriptions. She wrote of a "glorious Spring Sunday: In the morning I went to the cemetery" to observe *yahrzeit*, the anniversary of the date of death, for her mother, who had died thirty years earlier. It had been fourteen years since Julie's father died, when her son, my father, was "still a little boy." Looking back over those years, Julie wrote that she found it hard to believe "all that has happened in the meantime."

She goes on in that letter to talk about walking in the park, noting that the "snowdrops and crocuses are blooming everywhere already." Music was an ongoing theme as well. Julie listened for hours to her beloved radio, enjoying classical music, the Cologne Cabaret, and Carnival Session—the festivities for eight days before Ash Wednesday. She wrote, "I laughed so hard [listening to the Cologne Cabaret], that I almost felt sick to my stomach, when I went to bed at 1 a.m. . . ."

She continued to attend music performances—a piano soloist playing Mendelsohn; a Mozart symphony; the operetta *Fledermaus*, by Johann Strauss II. Because Mendelsohn was Jewish, his music was restricted to the *Kulturbund* and could not be played in any general public forum or on the radio.

But my grandmother's letters in early 1938 intimated that my grandfather was not doing well—neither his health nor his business. Gretel wrote from Palestine to her parents, concerned that the business climate in Frankfurt was not so good for my grandfather. Julie subsequently explained to my father that, as she put it in a letter, "One lives carefully and nothing can be changed that quickly. Thus far he continues to work as before. Pl[aut, his partner] is traveling and next month Papa will go again, too." My grandfather closed a letter with "our business here is very quiet." Perhaps to keep his sanity, my grandfather continued to play skat with his friends in the evening.

* * *

Up until this point, the letters to my father from his parents gave little, if any, hint, of an urgently ticking clock marking my grandparents' days.

But the clock was there, ticking loudly in the background. The construction to enlarge Dachau continued. The Gestapo was given the power to place prisoners in "protective custody" at its own discretion. Hitler further consolidated his power and authority by taking control of the German Armed Forces, naming himself Supreme Commander of the Armed Forces, with control over the newly created *Oberkommando der Wehrmacht*.[4]

In the United States, meanwhile, on January 28, 1938, FDR asked Congress for increased appropriations to build up the armed forces, saying "that our national defense is, in light of the increasing armaments of other Nations, inadequate for purposes of national security."[5] Yet the US secretary of state, Cordell Hull, had given contrary signals only a few weeks earlier. He declared that the United States cannot intervene in the internal affairs of Romania, where the citizenship of Jews was being revoked—a worrisome declaration in light of the unfolding events on the world stage.[6]

Then, in February 1938, my grandmother began to express a sense of darker, more desperate times.

Her letters were increasingly filled with the plans of other people, and those people were trying to leave Germany—Ludwig B., whose "preparations were not working out yet"; the Rambergs, who "don't have anything yet" but are still packing; the Rambergs' daughter, who is a musician and who will arrive soon in the States; Berta Friedel, who will go somewhere else before going to the States.

She began to express a greater depth of sadness and uncertainty, reporting that "everything is changing, everywhere people are making plans," that she is "always sorry when somebody leaves, for how many more are going to depart?" And that "It is awful what one hears from all sides, saying good-bye again and again."

How did she pass the time at home? In addition to listening to the radio, she sewed three times a week, from 9:30 a.m. to 1 p.m.—fulfilling her commissions for felt flowers, knitting herself dresses, sewing her own underwear, nightgowns, a blouse, and summer shifts. She did the housework. She hired a new cleaning lady, who must have been either Jewish and/or over the age of forty-five, as the Nuremberg Laws prohibited Jews from hiring German housekeepers under that age.[7]

At this time, for the first time in her voluminous correspondence with my father, my grandmother fleetingly indicated that she and my grandfather *might* consider emigration. In response to Gretel being worried, my grandmother wrote on February 1, 1938, "We should give it [emigrating] some thought, but for now the problem is not acute." She made this maddeningly brief reference between commenting on the weather beforehand, and then about a gift for Gretel. She said that that my grandfather only had day trips during the recent miserable weather of heavy rain—"so things are quite alright so far." And she then noted that she had sent Gretel a "delightful silk blouse (pale blue) for her birthday."

Yet while the quotidian details continued to dominate her letters, Julie began to steadily make references to darker elements of life in Frankfurt. In a few short sentences, she embraced the contradictions of listening to a threatening speech and enjoying beautiful weather. On February 20, 1938, she reported: "Today, Saturday, we had invited our boarder and his wife for dinner, because we were listening to the speech on the radio; in the morning we went outside for a bit, it was glorious." "The speech" was Hitler's third Reichstag Speech. Along with assuring the masses that the relationship between Germany and Poland finally had been transformed into one of sincere and friendly cooperation, Hitler derided Jewish intellectualism and Jewish international bolshevism as evil.[8] He also reiterated his supremacy and the power of his government.

Just days after that speech, on March 12, 1938, came the *Anschluß* [union], the occupation and annexation of Austria into Nazi Germany. Germans celebrated this major step toward a greater German Reich. My grandmother wrote, "The last days one has been entirely under the impression of the most recent events; there are flags and enthusiasm everywhere. One keeps hearing the reports on the radio—I am just listening to [the news from] Vienna." I assume that her mood was not one of celebration, but mounting fear, though she gives no hint.

Meanwhile, on March 28, 1938, the Reich issued a law that abrogated legal recognition of Jewish cultural organizations.[9] As a result, my grandparents' prized *Kulturbund* was no longer entitled to any civil rights. Meanwhile J. Dreyfus and Company, a large Jewish-owned investment bank, was Aryanized on March 7, 1938.[10]

And, on March 31, 1938, just after my grandparents' twenty-sixth wedding anniversary, Hitler came to Frankfurt, visited the *Römer*, the medieval building housing city hall, and delivered a speech as though he were the Messiah: "I believe that it was also God's will that from here a boy was to be sent into the Reich, allowed to grow to manhood, and be raised to become the nation's *Führer*, that he might lead his homeland into the Reich. There is a divine will, we are nothing but its tools."[11]

He also referred to Frankfurt as a city polluted by Jews. My grandmother simply wrote, "There was the big speech that day in the *Festhalle* [the Festival Hall] and Papa was home in the afternoon." Despite the times, Julie wrote that their anniversary "was celebrated appropriately." Norbert showered her with his traditional anniversary gifts of flowers, chocolates, and schnapps.

Still, the dangerous uncertainty of the times rang louder in her letters. Referring to my grandfather's business, she wrote, "Of course one cannot make any long-term predictions." Julie also began to plan a trip to Dresden to visit her sister Helene and brother-in-law Saemmi, whom she had not seen in two years, and she noted in passing that "quite a few things have happened, and nowadays it is not worth putting things off."

And yet she continued to give voice to her maternal curiosities about something as light as my father's social life. She had her eyes on his love life, for example, all the way across the ocean. When my grandmother learned that my father had a girlfriend, she wanted to know everything: "Is she pretty, smart, nice? And what does she do for work?" She even wondered what my father gave his girlfriend for her birthday. She continued, "I have already heard bad things about the subject of 'girls' over there. I would be very interested in hearing your opinion about this." But she quickly amended her remark: "I definitely would not count your girlfriend among those, but I would like to hear more about experiences you have made already. One always is thinking of you all out there and wants to stay connected very closely."

With one of the letters came a surprise: Julie had commissioned an aspiring amateur photographer, the son of friends, to take pictures of her and her husband to send to my father and Gretel. My grandfather asserted in the accompanying letter that these photos served as proof that he and my grandmother were well. A half-dozen photos showed my grandparents in their apartment—my grandfather writing, my grandmother writing, smoking, reading in bed, reaching to turn on the radio.

My grandmother was eager for my father's reaction to the photos, inquiring in letter after letter. When he did finally respond, he apparently was not lavish in his praise, and she was deeply disappointed by his observation that her facial expression, "a try-it-on face" in the pictures, as he apparently put it, did not seem sincere. She told him that he was "not correct. That's just what you think." She went on at length about this interpretation, writing that she was "very offended"; that the photos "were all so beautiful"; that "the photos of Papa are great. There have never been such pictures of Papa"; and that the photographer had done the pictures "really nicely." I cannot help but question

Julie and Norbert,
Wolfsgangstraße 132,
January 1938.

if my father saw through an attempt by my grandparents to quell his concerns. Did he see that they were not well, not happy?

* * *

Around this time my father suffered a disappointment with his job, as a promised promotion to become a traveling salesman did not materialize. He received the reassurances from his parents, in their letters, that I assume he yearned for.

My grandmother wrote that the news has "put me out very much, I am so endlessly sorry for you . . . you were treated terribly . . . but don't let this dampen your spirits. You will succeed sooner or later—and a young man must show what he can do." My grandfather echoed with "hold your head high, you will prevail."

But they must have worried. While they may not have known the full extent of it, the reality was that the United States was in the depths of a thirteen-month severe recession—the "Roosevelt Recession," from May 1937 until June 1938, with unemployment increasing from about 14 percent in 1937 to more nearly 20 percent in 1938. Recovery from the Great Depression was at a temporary standstill.[12] As my grandparents, albeit with ambivalence, finally began to consider emigration, perhaps they wondered about my father's financial ability to help them.

11

Germany, Early 1938

Frankfurt, 3. April 1938

My dear Rudolf,

After very beautiful spring days, the thermometer has dropped again very much. It is cold and unpleasant; there is even snow forecast for tomorrow. . . . Besides, it is not very tempting to go outside. I only go into town when I have to, otherwise I don't have much time or inclination to go for a walk. I enjoy the spring on our balcony with a view of the P.G. [Palmengarten], where everything is blooming now. . . . And now I am thinking very much of your birthday. I am sending you for your birthday all good wishes and all the best. I hope you continue to make such good progress, as you wish for yourself. And that your wishes come true, which is also our wish for you. Above all, stay well, cheerful and with good courage, so we can continue to have joy in you. . . . I will think of you very much on the 11th and do something special for myself. . . .

So, my dear, celebrate cheerfully and enjoy a very happy day. My thoughts are very much with you, I kiss you very cordially, Your Mutter

---

Frankfurt, 4. April 1938

My dear Rudolf,

I hope you received my letter from Leipzig. I have been back for a week. Business could have been better. . . . With us not much has changed, it only gets lonelier all the time. We stay home nicely and don't go out. On Monday and Wednesday evenings I go to the "Club," where I always meet a number of acquaintances. One doesn't know, for how long I still will be able to enjoy this, because the number of members is dwindling all the time. . . .

For your birthday, my dear Rudolf, the most cordial congratulations. I wish you everything beautiful and good and for the next year good progress! Celebrate the day very nicely. I hope to hear from you soon again. For today cordial greetings and kisses, Your Papa

For those trying to emigrate, the climate in the late 1930s and early 1940s in Europe—especially in Germany—was captured poignantly by the journalist Dorothy Thompson. In an article titled "Refugees: Anarchy or Organization" in the April 1938 issue of *Foreign Affairs*, she wrote: "It is a fantastic commentary on the inhumanity of our times that for thousands and thousands of people a piece of paper with a stamp on it is the difference between life and death."

Getting that stamped piece of paper—a visa—from various countries, including America, was proving to be more and more difficult.

As David S. Wyman writes in his authoritative history *Paper Walls*, "Three major factors in American life in the late 1930's tended to generate public resistance to immigration of refugees: unemployment, nativistic nationalism, and anti-Semitism. Debate, generally centering on the first two elements, often carried overtones of the third."[1]

If my father was going to help his parents escape Nazi Germany, the gates were slowly closing. It would never have been easy, but more made it to the United States in 1938 and 1939 than in the dark years to follow. After the *Anschluß* of Austria, FDR instituted what would be the first, and the most liberal, of four visa policies to be enforced over the next three years. That policy lasted eighteen months—from March 1938 to September 1939. Although the German-Austrian quota remained unchanged—at 27,370 persons per fiscal year from 1933 through 1945—it was not close to filled until the fiscal year 1939 (that is, July 1, 1938, through June 30, 1939), when the quota was not only met, but also surpassed, at 119.7 percent.[2] That means that 32,762 German-Austrian Jews were able to immigrate to America in that fiscal year. But that number was only a small percentage of those who wanted to come and sought visas: in 1938, three hundred thousand Germans, mostly Jews, applied for entry to the United States.[3]

In March, 1938, FDR pledged to take in refugees up to the quota limit.[4] He did this in part by relaxing the stricture of "likely to become a public charge," which had been interpreted highly conservatively to include any persons who did not have a guaranteed job upon entry to the States as well as a document of good conduct from the German police.[5] Previous to FY 1939, the quota fulfillment had gradually increased, from 5.3 percent in FY 1933 to 65.3 percent in FY 1938.[6]

At the same time, around the world, more and more countries decided not to permit entry of large numbers of Jews—decisions communicated at the July 5, 1938, Evian Conference, an international conference of thirty-two countries that FDR convened in the French resort town of Evian to address the Jewish refugee problem.[7] At the conference, FDR repeated his promise to accept refugees up to the quota limit.[8] Norman Bentwich, the British-appointed attorney general for the Mandate Palestine, who attended the conference as a representative of the German Jews, noted that the word *Evian* is *naïve* spelled backwards.[9]

In Germany, meanwhile, as of April 26, 1938, all Jews were required to register assets over 5,000 Reichsmarks—which then become available to Hermann Göring, the commissioner for the Four Year Plan, for use benefitting the German economy. And it became illegal for non-Jews to help conceal Jewish holdings.[10]

The Nazis were creating a Catch-22 for themselves regarding emigration. They continued to persecute the Jews in ways that caused many Jews to live in poverty; at the same time, they wanted as many Jews as possible to emigrate.[11] But the few countries that still had their doors ajar for immigration (such as the United States, Great Britain, and Cuba) were not interested in welcoming the poor. After the failure of the Evian Conference, a Nazi newspaper headline gloated, "Jews for Sale at a Bargain Price—Who Wants Them? No One." [12]

An immigrant to the United States needed approximately $450 ($8,313 in 2021 dollars or 1125 RM), based on the following charges in 1941 dollars:

Steamship Passage	$350.00
Embarkation Fee	$19.50
U.S Head Tax	$8.00
Maintenance at Lisbon (10 days average)	$10.00
Board money on ship	$10.00
Rail fare Spanish Border to Lisbon	$42.00
Cable Charge	$2.50
Balance to apply to possible additional cables	$8.00[13]

Until June of 1938, Jews leaving the country paid a 25 percent "flight tax" on their assets and were subject to arbitrary currency conversion rates—10 percent until June 1938—for their remaining assets, which were frozen in blocked accounts, whether they were emigrating or not. Each payment from a blocked account required special authorization. And, after June 1938, Jews were not allowed to bring any capital out of Germany.[14]

The Nazi policies were utterly schizophrenic—attempting to push German

Jews out of their country yet taking away the financial resources they would need in order to go.

These policies had a direct bearing on my grandparents. In 1938, my grandfather's assets, including his bank accounts and stocks, totaled 3,640 RM, or $1,462 in 1938 dollars—an amount that was unlikely to be sufficient for him and my grandmother to emigrate. They would have needed at least 3,813 RM, comprising: the minimum 25 percent tax–or 910 RM–for fleeing the Reich; the excise tax on Jewish assets, assessed at 653 RM for my grandfather; and then 2,250 RM for their travel and entrance to t,he United States. And that would have been *before* the Reich imposed its arbitrary currency conversion rates.

Did my grandparents make these calculations for what they would have needed to flee? It seems they were 173 RM short before being subjected to those conversion rates. Did that seem insurmountable to them and, if so, were they resigned to remaining in Germany?

12

Frankfurt and Dresden, April–June 1938

Frankfurt, 15. May 1938

Dear Rudolf,

I am very surprised, that you have been without news from us for two weeks; I cannot understand this. Now as ever I am sending a letter every week. During Easter week the mail was delayed a bit. But it goes without saying that I would not leave you without news for so long. As far as our health is concerned, we are well; Papa wrote to you from his trip, he has been back for eight days. Business was not good—also here it is quiet now. Everything is rather changed. I mentioned in my last letter that the Stolz family was here and had to tell me much about you. I also wrote that Frau Marx from our building arrived there on the 9th and that I hope very much that you will speak with her. You can get in touch with Erich Löwenstein, who will meet her at the boat and who knows the Beckhards. She will be in Boston for a few weeks. Erich L. has settled in well, by the way; he likes it very much and he earns good money, as far as he engages new customers for the bank. He now hopes very much that his mother will come over soon as well. . . .

Good night and many cordial greetings and kisses, Mutti.

The increased restrictions on Jewish life in Germany in the spring of 1938—while not explicitly addressed by Julie and Norbert in their letters to my father—were evident from their increasingly bleak tone.

On April 23, 1938, in Frankfurt, Jews were issued compulsory identification cards.[1] The context of such frightening new developments lends greater gravitas to my grandfather's words, in a handwritten addition to one of my grandmother's letters on April 4, 1938: "It only gets lonelier all the time. We stay home nicely and don't go out."

It seems that in 1938 my grandparents did not observe Passover with a Seder, which was traditionally held at the home of my grandmother's brother, Jacob, and his wife, Olga, as Jacob and Olga no longer had a housekeeper. And for all major occasions—the Passover Seder, their wedding anniversary, my father's birthday—my grandparents no longer expressed hopeful dreams of celebrating with my father soon again, as they had expressed in the previous year. In May and June their letters sounded increasingly desperate.

On May 1, 1938, my grandmother—for the first time—directly bemoaned the conditions in Frankfurt: "The last week and the last days were very upsetting for us—the situation has very much come to a head, none of us know any more what will happen in the coming weeks. You can imagine, how one worries, because we don't want to burden you yet today. But one still must think about it—what should be done in the extreme case of emergency."

Because of the censorship of the mail, presumably, my grandmother was not specific about what upset her. She mentioned other woes—her frustration in not finding a suitable boarder for their spare room, since the last boarder had left. And, she commented that she and the other two ladies in the apartment house were "always sharing" what was going on. Frau Löwenstein, in particular, had "many different plans," according to my grandmother. And in early May, Frau Marx sailed to America for a four-week stay to visit her son in Boston, beginning with a short stay in New York.

It seems strange in light of history, but Frau Marx was like many German Jews who continued to travel abroad, stay for a short time, and return to the horrific conditions in Germany. It is not clear how she and others did so, given that German Jews were allowed to travel only for business purposes or emigration. Those who traveled abroad for short stays must have believed that the oppressive conditions in Germany would cease sooner or later.

That they could ride it out, they could survive.

Assuming that my father met with Frau Marx, as my grandmother had requested, he must have not only received the parcel of cookies she had for him, but also heard a far more detailed account about the conditions in Germany than any of my grandparents' censored letters relayed. I am curious if it was around this time that my father began reaching out to his "contacts in New York," an allusion in his autobiography, to find support for his parents—if and when they would decide to emigrate.

Before closing her May 1 letter, my grandmother wrote, "I am today a bit distracted and nervous and therefore also not in the right mood for writing—there is a lot on my mind."

It was a troubling letter, perhaps, but not one that could have prepared my father for the letter my grandfather wrote, on his own from Luxembourg, where he was traveling for business and out of reach of the German censors. He wrote on May 5, 1938, a letter like none other my father had received to date:

> Luxembourg, Grand Hotel Staar, 5. May 1938
> *My dear Rudolf!*
> I hope you are well; with the exception that we are healthy I cannot write many nice things today. I am en route since Sunday and have arrived here yesterday; the past week I was in Frankfurt, a lot has happened there. All Jewish businesses were boycotted all week long. (For example, Saalberg, Josef, Blum, Leonh. Kahn, . . . and so forth.) Customers were standing in front of the shops; The police did not let anybody in; If someone summoned the courage to go in anyway, he was harassed. The shop windows were smeared with scurrilous slogans, signs saying "Jewish Business, Attention, Attention" stuck on; also on our store they had smeared "Jew"; the entire movement is directed at excluding all Jews from business. We don't know for how long we can keep going. Until now the customers here have not made difficulties for us, apart from a few exceptions; yet how long the customers are allowed to buy from us and for how long we will get deliveries of goods, is entirely uncertain. In addition, there is the new law about the registration of assets. You can imagine yourself, what that means. There is the view that the larger fortunes are to be invested in the *Hermann Göring Aktien or Schatz-Briefe* [Hermann Göring shares or treasury notes]. One cannot endure what this costs in nerves, the more so as we don't know what will become of us. Meanwhile I also have other worries—you know that I still have to pay back J.B. 160 Marks for the next six months. This time I could only manage half and had to ask for an extension for the remainder. This was a great problem for me. You know after all, that I can only take out a fixed amount for us. In addition to these 80M I have to pay again at least 160M by the end of October. I don't know yet today how I am going to manage this.
>
> As a consequence of the difficulties described above, business has also not been good. Also here I have not been able to work well due to the political circumstances. But I won't lose courage and it is lucky that Mutti's health is rather satisfactory again, because it is more than questionable, whether we can stay in Germany. What will become of us, I don't know, however!
>
> I am sorry that I cannot write to you anything more pleasant, but you

should be informed after all, one cannot write this from Frankfurt. You will yet see Frau Marx, she will tell you more of the details. Is there any opportunity for us in America?

Tomorrow night I'll come home again. Today I am sending you a small parcel of chocolate; enjoy it in spite of all this. Ella Weil also "steamed off" to America yesterday. Weils will follow within the year, because one does not feel safe in Germany anymore.

For today, my dear Rudolf, be greeted most cordially and kissed by your *Vater*.

[For a facsimile of the original letter, see Appendix, p. 260.]

And so my father knew my grandparents' harsh reality—not merely from conversations with newly arrived visitors or immigrants from Germany, not merely from extrapolating from my grandmother's intimations. For the first time, one of my grandparents directly asked my father about the possibility of coming to America.

Another aspect of that harsh reality, though unmentioned in that letter, was that my grandfather was required by the Nazis to register and identify his "Jewish industrial enterprise"—his wholesale tailor supply company. He also must have known that the Nazis were pressuring many Jews to sell their business holdings, as Friedländer notes, to "Aryan businessmen, entrepreneurs and the like . . . [who were] shamelessly attempting to grab up Jewish shops and factories, etc., as cheaply as possible and for a ridiculous price."[2] By April 1938, more than 60 percent of all Jewish-owned businesses that had existed prior to 1933 were no longer in existence.[3]

This startling letter from my grandfather from Luxembourg was followed by my grandmother's weekly letters throughout that May, including two with additional lines from my grandfather. These returned mostly to themes of day-to-day life, both in Frankfurt and America. She was curious how my father's sock-darning skills had progressed, what his new girlfriend was like, and whether he was going hiking in his free time. My grandparents were happy with my father's long-awaited promotion to becoming a driver for a traveling salesman, but worried when my father's boss, Mr. Heilbronn, advised my father to borrow money to buy a car to drive to Birmingham, Alabama. They were concerned about how Rudy would manage and advised him not to borrow.

My grandmother also continued to instruct my father about many obligations on which he should follow-through—that he should make a condolence call on the young photographer who had taken the pictures of my grandparents and had immigrated to New York City shortly before his father passed away; send sixtieth birthday greetings to Uncle Jacob; give regards to Leo Wohlfarth in the United States, a distant relative.

She also admonished him on several counts. From her perspective, my father often did not respond to her inquiries: How was it when he got together with the photographer? With their dear friend Arnold Kahn? What had been his correspondence with his cousin Hertha, who had a troubled life and was trying to immigrate to the States? Julie told Rudy which relatives he should try to help and which he should not. Consequently, on the next two letters that he received, my father wrote notes to himself, presumably as reminders about topics or people that he wanted to be sure to include in his response.

Through friends returning to Frankfurt, my father sent my grandmother a handbag and a small parcel, but nothing for my grandfather. My grandmother wrote about that on May 8, 1938, and she was less oblique than in the past about the situation in Germany:

> I thank you very cordially for it. Yet I was a bit disappointed, for I would have been even happier if you had sent something also for Papa. He could have used it very well. Don't you think that Papa would also have been happy if you had thought of him? You know full well that he still has lots of worries and that one also does not know now, how things will develop. I had written about this already months ago—you never took notice of it and never asked about how Papa is dealing with it. You know, dear Rudolf, how much we like to do everything for you and make use of every opportunity to send you even a small thing to give you joy. It is really the best thing for us, to keep thinking of you and Grete and to do everything we can—but now times are such that you also must think of us.

But she still continued occasionally to express some ambivalence about leaving, as in her May 21, 1938, letter:

> At the moment I cannot write to you anything new about the situation. . . . As you write yourself, there is no point in burdening you too much with the problem, because you are for now not in a position to do something positive. We cannot make a definite decision yet, but one cannot speak of burying one's head in the sand. . . . For now, Papa is earning our living and we don't

> have to make demands on you for this. It also would be very dire for us—but one does not know—Grete has also written to us a very worried letter, but also the problem "Palestine" is not simple and would have to be pondered very much. I have seen the country and know how hard it is over there and how hard Ruben has to work, so that I cannot imagine that we can expect him to take care of us. It is hard for all of us to solve the problem and how much I would like not to burden you children with it—but unfortunately we all are in the same boat.

What does "something positive" refer to? Money that they required to get visas but my father could not provide? Connections to still be contacted? Why was my father "not in a position to do something positive"? What had my father said to make his mother write that? Had he exhausted all possibilities to open new doors? Did he believe that he did not socialize in the "right circles" with those who could help? Was he too proud to ask others for money toward his parents' passage?

Just how extensive were his efforts to get his parents out of Germany?

In the next letter, on May 29, 1938, the day after a boycott of Jewish businesses in Frankfurt began,[4] Norbert wrote again, as he had on May 5, that he was required "to pay at least 160—by October 30th. As long as we are here now, we are all right; let me know if you come to an arrangement with J. B. because he demands this sum from me. How long the business can be kept up, one cannot know." Because my grandfather was now referring to my father's direct involvement with paying J. B., I suspect that these monies owed were about a loan that my grandfather incurred from J. B. to acquire the funds for my father's emigration. And was J. B. my grandfather's distant relative Josef Baum, with whom my grandparents occasionally socialized?

Julie continued to address her dilemma about emigrating, writing:

> We are already thinking with melancholy of the time when everything will change. Ya, Rudolf, it still remains to be deliberated very much, how our problem will be solved. Of course it might be easier for us to immigrate to Palestine, but Ruben does not have a secure income and has such a hard time. I have seen it after all and know that it would be a great burden for the children and I still don't know, if I can work there much. For Papa it will be quite impossible, it is a great worry for us, but one cannot come to a decision yet.

The difficulty of deciding to emigrate was expressed by others as, "Here we are somebody—abroad we might be beggars."[5]

We don't have my father's letter responding to his parents' suddenly explicit fears and worries, but he apparently did write back with some kind of plan or offer. My grandfather, in turn, responded to my father's letter, a "proper essay" as he described it, by minimizing some of my father's concerns: "Dear Rudolf, you write in your last letter that we should give up the business. As long as we can keep it, it is not necessary. I just can cope with my life. My worry is much more. What is going to happen later. We don't know what is going to happen to us and whether we old people can stay here."

But stay they did.

* * *

Two more letters followed, in June 1938, from my grandmother when she visited her sister Helene and brother-in-law Saemmi in Dresden.

Though not as explicit as my grandfather's letter from Luxembourg, these letters reveal more about the conditions in Germany and about Julie's fear and worry. "Dresden is still a beautiful city, but one does not have much

Saemmi and Helene (née Geiger) Stern, circa 1920s.

joy in it anymore, although there are still far more opportunities here," she wrote. My grandmother took strolls on "wonderful paths nearby," adding "one can relax a bit." She also went to the movies. Did she and Helene go to a traditional movie theater, or to the Dresden *Kulturbund*? In any event, they saw *Die Dreiklang* (The Triad), which was unlike other German movies of the time, as it did not promote German militarism. The female lead was Lil Dagover, who won the 1937 "Actress of the State Award" and was rumored to be friendly with Hitler.

The question of emigration was addressed in these two letters written from Dresden, though my grandmother's indecision and ambivalence clouded my grandparents' request—if there was one. "Both your letters from May 23rd and 24th have been forwarded to me here—there seem to be a few misunderstandings. You had heard from us already a few times directly and it struck me very odd that you never replied to any of it. This might lead to the impression that you perhaps don't want to reply to everything. We know exactly that you are not in a position today to do something positive [for us]—but one would be interested in some kind of response of yours."

As the letters themselves do not contain direct requests, what is meant by "you have heard from us already a few times directly"? Had messages been passed along through friends who had come to the States?

What was "any of it"? Did my father dissuade them from trying to immigrate to the States? Just what my father wanted to do, didn't want to do, tried to do, and didn't try to do remains a great mystery.

My grandmother continued:

> The proposal "Palestine" is possible, perhaps, but putting it into practice is very difficult. I cannot come to a decision, no matter how much I keep thinking about it. For Papa would not be able to work at all over there and for me it would also be difficult given this climate. It also is not possible to burden Grete and Ruben like this. It is not easy for them to take care of themselves, even if you provided some support. At any rate the thought of it weighs me down, unfortunately this is the fate of many elderly people. It is very hard for me that all of you out there are burdened by this. I don't really know what you mean to say by claiming that we should not fool each other—that was never my intent.

What is Julie trying to say in that infuriatingly opaque last sentence? Perhaps my father had implied that he and his parents should stop fooling themselves about the gravity of the situation; or perhaps he was referring to his ability to get them to America (thus leaving Palestine as the only tenable solution).

Is her writing so obtuse because she is trying to navigate censorship?

Julie also wrote that her physician, Dr. Billigheimer, was immigrating to England, and she felt "very sorry about this." In closing her first Dresden letter, my grandmother signed off not as *"Mutti,"* but as "Julie," which she had never done before.

Between his mother's letters from Dresden, my father received a short letter from his father. Norbert wished my father success as a traveling salesman and explained that his own business was "quiet at the moment." He spent Pentecost, the first Sunday in June, "very quietly. I was not even in the Taunus, because one cannot go to any restaurants anywhere. I don't know of any news, mother will have written to you." In all likelihood, Norbert did not know of any news he could write that would not be censored.

In her second letter from Dresden, Julie again wrote directly about the possibility of leaving Germany: "I hope we can continue living like this. I also have written to Grete about this problem in great detail. We cannot make up our minds—yet. I know what this would mean for you all and especially Grete and Ruben. These are thoughts one cannot shake at all. It is quite hard and one cannot imagine how an emigration would be possible." Yet, as was her norm, my grandmother shifted from the heaviness of the times to the lightness of fashion, from one sentence to the next. She again requested that my father try to speak to Frau Marx before her return to Frankfurt, and "If it still works out, you can give her a pair of shoes to take along for me, black with white or blue. That would be lovely."

She continued to express her maternal concerns—how would my father fare in his long-awaited position as a driver for a traveling salesman, particularly in the American South, with its oppressively hot weather? She cautioned him about driving, "Please, do be very careful and also think of me." She wondered about his wardrobe: "Of course you also use up more clothing and underwear, I understand that, how are your supplies in order?" She worried about how their weekly correspondence would proceed, given my father's travels.

And, in the closing paragraph of the second of her two letters from Dresden, on June 13, 1938, my grandmother wrote of the weather. "I had a few rather warm days, but now it has become very cool again, so that it does not look well for strawberries and cherries yet. I hope things will improve; one needs something to look forward to."

* * *

The June 13, 1938, letter is the last letter before a three-and-a-half-year gap in the trove of eighty-eight letters that I have. Where are the letters from July 1938 through September 1941?

They existed. In his autobiography, my father refers to the exchange of letters becoming sporadic, with months sometimes passing without correspondence after he had become a traveling salesman in the latter half of 1938. Then, with the outbreak of World War II on September 1, 1939, the sheer volume of mail exchanged was drastically reduced. Whatever letters arriving in the States were surely heavily censored. But my father received some letters. He wrote in his autobiography that, "by 1940, the letters from home started to sound alarming, as my parent's situation began to deteriorate."

Where are those letters? Did my father lose them? Unlikely. He was extremely organized, especially in safekeeping documents of personal importance.

Did my father throw away those alarming letters? Perhaps in the depth of one of his depressions?

After my grandmother's letter of June 13, 1938, there is a long silence. The three-and-a-half-year gap in the letters is beyond perplexing. It is deeply disturbing. An unknown haunting me forever.

13

Germany, Summer and Late 1938

The Director of the Exchange Control Office
Frankfurt am Main, 19. November 1938

Based on oral information by Mr. Jentges, Frankfurt/Main, Stegstr.67, the Jewish firm Norbert Harff, F[rankfurt]/M[ain], Gr. Kornmarkt 18, has about 8000–10.000 RM [Reichsmark] receivable in foreign accounts. These bills due are in danger, because it is suspected, that the owner of the firm or his wife, who has full power of attorney, is in the process of emigrating illegally and will cash in from his clients abroad, who are also Jewish.

Jentges makes a trustworthy impression. He says he was installed in this firm (wholesale of fabric lining men's clothing) as a trustee by the district economic counsel.

I am asking for immediate measures.

P. Devertin

To the Director of the Exchange Control Office "S"
Frankfurt am Main
Goethestr. 9

From the Hessian State Archives in Wiesbaden
in a file on Norbert's firm, the Norbert Harff Company

This late 1938 communication from the Exchange Control Office suggests that the Nazis planted an informer in my grandfather's tailor supply business. It is likely that this fellow Jentges is the "1st associate" whom my grandmother is referring to in her February 15, 1937, letter, when she wrote, "Papa, too, is doing much better, even though things still aren't easy for him—the 1st associate is the same after all, but we don't want to make things more difficult for ourselves. The business is going quite decently, but nothing can be said about that."

What led this Mr. Jentges to suspect that Julie and Norbert were in the process of emigrating? Did he see documents that indicated as such? Did he overhear explicit discussions of Norbert?

Around this time, in the summer of 1938, the elaborate trap the Germans had constructed for its Jewish citizens was slowly and steadily being put into place. That summer, new laws barred Jews from access to commercial services, such as real estate or credit information, and excluded Jews from stock and commodity exchanges.[1] They could not practice law, although two hundred lawyers were authorized as "consultants" for their fellow Jews.[2]

Already, Jews had been denied the right to hold public office or civil service positions, or—since 1933—to own land.[3] Jews had been banned from the cultural arena, could not be employed in radio or theater, and were not allowed to sell sculptures or paintings.[4] The summer of 1938 saw the destruction of the synagogues in Munich and Nuremberg.[5]

Also, in June 1938, Joseph Goebbels's "Asocial-Action" sent 1,500 German Jews, previously convicted of traffic violations, to concentration camps.[6]

In July 1938, it was decreed that, by the end of that year, all Jews were required to carry an identity card to be produced on demand at any time,[7] a ruling already being enforced in Frankfurt as early as April. In August, the Nazis issued a proclamation that, as of January 1, 1939, Jewish males must take *Israel* as their middle name and Jewish females must take *Sara* as their middle name.[8] Evidence of this decree appears in documents from that period relating to my grandparents.

On October 5, 1938, Jewish passports became invalid; Jews were forced to bring in their passports and have them stamped with a "J" to validate them. Thus no Jew could pretend to be a Christian.[9] It then became nearly impossible to emigrate anywhere, including to those countries that did not require a visa.[10] The narrow door out of Germany became narrower. Indeed, according to the US Holocaust Memorial Museum: "About 85,000 Jewish refugees (out of 120,000 Jewish emigrants) reached the United States between March 1938 and September 1939, but this level of immigration was far below the number seeking refuge. In late 1938, 125,000 applicants lined up outside US consulates hoping to obtain 27,000 visas under the existing immigration quota. By June 1939, the number of applicants had increased to more than 300,000. Most visa applicants were unsuccessful."

* * *

On November 7, 1938, Herschel Grynspan, a seventeen-year-old German-Polish Jewish refugee, out of revenge for the suffering of his fellow Jews in

18/4282 Baum
E Norbert
Futterstoffgroßhdl.
Wolfsgangstr.132
Frankfurt a/M.
jd/jd 8.12.71.

Einkommensteuer 1939

und Kriegszuschlag zur Einkommensteuer 1939

Finanzamt Frankfurt (Main)

Für endgültig erklärt am .... Bl. ....

Geändert am .... Bl. ....

From Norbert Baum's Income Tax File 1939.

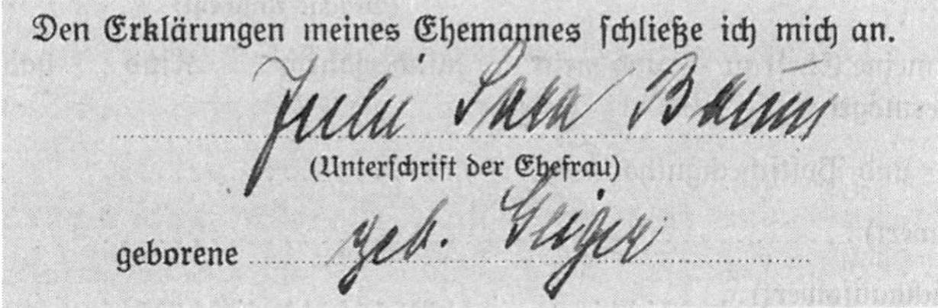

Den Erklärungen meines Ehemannes schließe ich mich an.

Julie Sara Baum

(Unterschrift der Ehefrau)

geborene ....

From a joint asset and expense statement submitted to the Exchange Control Office on December 1, 1939.

Germany, assassinated a low-level German diplomat, Ernst vom Rath, at the German Embassy in Paris. The Nazis manipulated the worldview of the event, casting it as the incendiary event (and opportunity) to launch their long-calculated campaign of terror against the Jews.

And so, the Nazis ordered a pogrom, which began on the evening of November 9 and lasted into the evening of November 10, 1938. It would come to be known as *Kristallnacht*, the Night of Broken Glass, although that name was supplied by the Nazis, and it actually took place in broad daylight, over two days. It is also referred to as the November Pogrom.[11]

Jewish businesses, including 7,500 stores, were looted and destroyed—among them, my grandfather's business—the wholesale textile supplier, Firma Norbert Harff, which my grandfather was subsequently forced to abandon.

Although most of the general population did not participate in the riots, many gathered to witness the destruction, arrests, and threats. As the historian Trude Maurer cites from Joseph Benjamin Levy's memoir: "The masses had already started gathering on the street, receiving us with shouting and mean insults, with chants . . . the most well-known of which was '*Juda verrecke!*' [Death to the Jews!] Upon the release of those over 65, the onlookers shouted:

'Hang them! Let them face a firing squad! Why should these criminals be released?'!"[12]

Was my grandfather among those released and taunted by those chants?

During the two days of anti-Jewish riots, almost all synagogues—267 in total—in Germany, Austria, and areas of Sudetenland, were desecrated or destroyed.[13] Frankfurt's Westend Synagogue, the Reform synagogue to which my father and his family belonged, was desecrated and severely damaged. Over time, it would become a storage space for Nazi armaments and supplies. The Unterlindau Synagogue, where my father became a *bar mitzvah*, was burned.

Years later, among the remains of synagogue files that were plundered, the state archives director in Frankfurt found a list of the approximately twenty-three thousand Jews living in Frankfurt.[14] My grandparents' names most certainly were on that list.

Thirty thousand Jewish males from throughout Germany were sent to concentration camps, such as Dachau, Buchenwald, and Sachsenhausen, as a result of the events the Nazis celebrated as *Kristallnacht*.

In a particularly perverse twist, victims of those two days of Nazi-inspired riots were made to pay for the very destruction wreaked upon them. The Nazis levied a one billion Reichsmark fine, referred to as the "*Kristallnacht* Atonement Fee," against the German Jewish community to pay for repairs necessitated by the damage inflicted by the SS. The fine was 20 percent tax on assets valued at more than 5,000 Reichsmarks that had been registered six months earlier, in April.[15]

In the coming weeks, because the riots did not impel as many Jews to leave as the Nazis had hoped, the regime concocted more regulations to penalize and restrict Jews, to segregate them to an even greater extent. Jews were no longer allowed to own stores or artisan businesses. Jewish children were expelled from German schools and only could attend Jewish schools.[16] The League of Jewish Women was dissolved.[17] Residential restrictions curtailed the freedom of movement and travel of Jews, with curfews enforced and more places declared off-limits. For example, my grandparents were no longer allowed in any public parks. They could no longer enjoy strolling through their beloved nearby Palmengarten, Frankfurt's botanical garden.[18] They were prohibited from attending movies, concerts, and other cultural performances outside of the *Kulturbund* events.[19]

My grandparents would have learned about the growing list of public orders and restrictions in the *Jüdisches Nachrichtenblatt* (Jewish News Sheet), a

Gestapo-controlled publication and the only Jewish paper that remained after the riots.[20] Although the newspaper also promoted emigration, that option had become more unlikely in the face of economic persecution. Many Jews simply did not have the required funds or a promise of employment, as required.[21]

By the end of 1938, approximately 200,000 of Germany's 500,000 German Jews remained in Germany, with approximately 150,000 having emigrated from 1933 to the beginning of 1938 and another 140,000 having emigrated in 1938.[22]

Of those Jews remaining in the Altreich, only 16 percent were under the age of twenty; almost 26 percent were between twenty and forty-five, and nearly 58 percent were over forty-five, according to Friedländer. He observes that "the Jewish population in Germany was rapidly becoming a community of elderly people. And it was also becoming hopelessly impoverished."[23] By the end of 1938, one in four Jews in Germany was on welfare—that is, welfare assistance from the Jewish communities, because Jews could no longer receive public welfare.[24]

The end of 1938—and the riots that the Nazis celebrated as *Kristallnacht,* in particular—was a turning point for many German Jews who, like my grandparents, formerly believed that the Nazi threats would soon subside and certainly would not seriously affect those who were older, especially those who had served in World War I.

My grandparents' shift from ambivalence to growing desperation must have been palpable in their letters to my father.

14

Birmingham, 1938

I took the train to Birmingham, Alabama. . . . I got a taste of what America was really like, especially life in the segregated South.

RUDY BAUM | "A Son of a Respectable Family"

On July 4, 1938, my father took a train to Birmingham. He had been promoted at last, and now he was going to be a driver for a traveling salesman, whose territory was Alabama, Mississippi, Louisiana, and Tennessee. I would not be surprised if before this promotion my father did not know exactly where Alabama was. His last long train ride had been one-and-a-half years earlier, when he said good-bye to his parents on the platform in Frankfurt.

This time my father probably took *The Pennsylvania Railroad's Congressional Limited* electric train. After passing through Wilmington and Baltimore, the *Congressional Limited* stopped in Washington, DC, where my father would have transferred to the renowned passenger locomotive the *Crescent*, which was ultimately destined for New Orleans after stops in Virginia, North Carolina, and Alabama. It would have taken another thirty-six hours to arrive in Birmingham. He would have arrived at the Birmingham train station, with its several hundred-foot-long Americana wrought-iron sign announcing "Birmingham, the Magic City."

Just days before he left New York City, my father had surely listened to accounts of a boxing match at Yankee Stadium that had reverberations around the world. The fight attracted the largest audience ever for a single radio broadcast, an estimated seventy million Americans—more than half of the population.[1] On June 22, Joe Louis, a black American, faced off in a rematch against Max Schmeling, the white German touted by the SS as the perfect specimen of Aryan superiority, for the heavyweight championship. Schmeling was not a member of the Nazi party and despite pressure had refused to part with his Jewish manager.

Nonetheless, a Nazi publicist traveled with him and issued statements, including one that said a black man couldn't win against Schmeling. Wrong. In the rematch, on June 22, 1938, the referee stopped the fight after two minutes and four seconds, during which Louis had landed a barrage of solid punches to Schmeling's two, and had knocked the German down three times, landing him in the hospital for ten days.[2]

I strongly suspect that my grandfather back in Frankfurt was among the many abroad who tuned in, as only some months before that date my grandmother wrote, "Papa sits next to it [the radio] with delight and listens besides the news also to beautiful music—but he still is crazy about sports. He would have liked best to hear about Schmeling until 3 in the morning in order to get the reports."

Barely two weeks later, when he took the train to Birmingham, my father surely spent time gazing out the window at the American South. He was giving up his cultivated comfort with the German Jewish community of Manhattan's Upper West Side, with his good friends and his Golo buddies, in exchange for moving up in his career. I doubt that he could fathom what the deep South would be like. The newspapers described Alabama's governor, Bibb Graves, as a Democrat, yet also as a supporter of the Ku Klux Klan, an organization all about white supremacy and not too fond of Jews, either.

His new boss, the traveling salesman, was a fat, cigar-smoking Jewish man named Bob Wiener. With a heavy southern accent, he was known as quite a personality and a successful salesman in Golo, although he was a bit of a Willy Loman character. My father was not only Mr. Wiener's driver, but also the packer of his shoe samples and a babysitter for his children.

For most of their customers, meeting a German refugee was a unique experience. And most were surprised that my father did not speak Yiddish, as was the case for German Jews, unlike Eastern European Jews, who almost universally spoke it.

At the same time, my father was surely trying to make sense of the customers' strong Southern accents. I suspect that it may have been then that Rudy decided to change the pronunciation of his last name, *Baum,* from *bowm* to *bomb*, believing that it was a better fit for the American ear.

One of the customers became my father's "benefactor," in the words of my father. He was a Jewish store owner who invited my father into his home many times and, in the fall of 1938, took him to High Holiday services at the Reform synagogue in Birmingham. (It must have been Temple Emanu-El, which had been founded in 1884.) Organ music filled the sanctuary, reminiscent of Frankfurt's Westend Synagogue. The rabbi was named Newfield,

Hungarian born, and it is possible that the topic of his sermon on the eve of Rosh Hashanah on September 25, 1938, was the deadly hurricane that had hit Long Island only four days earlier.

Eating in diners in the South must have been an entirely foreign experience for my father. It was not uncommon for a seven-foot partition to separate the front dining area from the back dining area, the front filled with white faces and the back with black ones. My father surely encountered new dishes such as biscuits and sausage in the form of a flattened patty, not the familiar cylindrical shape, smothered in a peppery mud-brown gravy. And pecan pie, which would become one of his favorites.

After only a few months of driving in the South, I imagine that he acquired a tan line on his left arm from his countless hours behind the wheel in short-sleeve dress shirts with the windows rolled down. On one trip, my father and Mr. Wiener were shocked by what they stumbled upon as they were driving down a highway. After noticing numerous cars parked on both sides of the highway, they saw the lifeless body of a young black man hanging from a tree, surrounded by a crowd of white locals, celebrating the event.

I am curious if my father recalled at that time his first encounter with a black man. It had been in 1920 in Frankfurt at the small grocer Schade & Füllgrabe, around the corner from Reuterweg 73. As he told the story, he and his sister Gretel, five and seven, respectively, at the time, were filled with fright when they saw a Senegalese soldier, one of the Allied French troops briefly occupying the Rhineland after World War I. But then the black soldier bought a hard-boiled egg and offered the egg, which was dwarfed by his peach-colored over-sized palm, to my father. My father's fear vanished.

* * *

As summer turned to fall in 1938, and after the events of early November in Germany, the American press was filled with editorials on the anti-Semitic riots that the Nazis called *Kristallnacht*. I am sure my father read about it. According to Friedländer, "Practically no American newspaper, irrespective of size, circulation, location, or political inclination failed to condemn Germany. Now even those that, prior to *Kristallnac*ht, had been reluctant to admit that violent persecution was a permanent fixture in Nazism, criticized Germany."[3] At that time, FDR extended the visitors' visas of some twelve thousand to fifteen thousand refugees already in the United States, most of whom were Jewish.[4] He withdrew the US ambassador in Berlin.

I wonder if my father, who was still in Birmingham during the riots, saw the November 11, 1938, *New York Times* headline "Nazis Smash, Loot, and Burn Jewish Shops and Temples Until Goebbels Calls Halt." How might such a headline have affected my father emotionally? Did he reach out to more people for help on his parents' behalf?

I wonder, too, the extent to which my father was in direct contact with the anti-Semitism spreading in the United States. Father Charles Coughlin, a Catholic priest and American radio broadcaster, aired many shows blaming Jews for Germany's problems and for Russian Communism. He established the American Christian Front, an organization of mostly working-class Irish and German Americans who promoted the idea of America as a Christian nation united against the Jews.

At the end of November 1938, Father Coughlin staged a rally in the streets of New York. Some twenty thousand people chanted "Send Jews back where they came from in leaky boats," and "Wait until Hitler comes over here." A few weeks after that rally, the New York *Daily News* reprinted, on two-and-a-half pages, a pamphlet of similar rhetoric written by the extremist William Dudley Pelley, founder of the Silver Shirts (à la Hitler's Brown Shirts). The next day, that same paper published an unusual editorial, vowing that the US Bill of Rights merely meant "that our government shall not officially discriminate against any religion. It does not mean that Americans are forbidden to dislike other Americans or religions or any other group. Plenty of people just now are exercising their right to dislike the Jews."[5]

By Thanksgiving 1938, in time for Father Coughlin's big rally, my father had finished his stint in Birmingham and was back in New York City.

15

Germany, 1939

NORBERT BAUM

to

TAX OFFICE FFM

Feb. 22, 1939

I ask for an extension for the prepayment due on March 10, 1939, for income tax for 1939 because I do not have an income any more for the year 1939.

Signed: Nathan, aka Norbert Baum, 132 Wolfsgangstr., Ffm

TAX OFFICE FFM

Frankfurt, Feb., 23, 1939

The company Norbert Harff has been transferred into other hands at the end of 1938.

In its January 2, 1939, issue, *Time* magazine named Adolf Hitler "Man of the Year" for 1938, a title "bestowed by the editors on the person or persons who most affected the news and our lives, for good or ill, and embodied what was important about the year."[1]

The magazine's cover was a black and white drawing of a pipe organ supporting a Ferris wheel of hanging naked bodies, virtual skeletons, with Hitler as the organist and Nazi officials as witnesses. The caption read: *"Man of 1938. From the unholy organist, a hymn of hate."* Excerpts from the cover story:

> Greatest single news event of 1938 took place on September 29, when four statesmen met at the Führerhaus, in Munich, to redraw the map of Europe. The three visiting statesmen at that historic conference were Prime Minister Neville Chamberlain of Great Britain, Premier Edouard Daladier of France, and Dictator Benito Mussolini of Italy. But by all odds the dominating figure at Munich was the German host, Adolf Hitler. . . .the greatest threatening force that the democratic, freedom-loving world faces today . . . had

> himself become the world's No. 1 International Revolutionist. . . . Germany's 700,000 Jews have been tortured physically, robbed of homes and properties, denied a chance to earn a living, chased off the streets. Now they are being held for "ransom," a gangster trick through the ages. . . . In five years under the Man of 1938, regimented Germany had made itself one of the great military powers of the world today.[2]

On January 30, 1939, the anniversary of his installment as chancellor, Hitler, for the first time, made his intentions about the annihilation of the Jews clear in a Reichstag speech: "Today I will once more be a prophet: If the international Jewish financiers in and outside Europe should succeed in plunging the nations once more into a world war, then the result will not be the Bolshevization of the earth, and thus the victory of Jewry, but the annihilation of the Jewish race in Europe!"[3]

The Nazi plan, outlined in an article in the SS newspaper *Das Schwarze Korps* (The Black Corps), was to allow 150,000 Jews to leave Germany over the next three years and keep two hundred thousand Jews—mainly the elderly—in Germany, thereby holding a significant number hostage so that international Jewry would behave positively toward the Reich. Yet, a few weeks later, another article appeared announcing the need for complete segregation of the Jews in Germany, and ultimately their total annihilation. So there was an ongoing dichotomy supporting emigration, on the one hand, and striving toward the extinction of the Jews in Germany, on the other.[4]

Even more restrictions on Jewish life were enforced. The Tenth Decree of the Reich Citizenship Law established the *Reichsvereinigung der Juden in Deutschland*—the Reich Association of the Jews in Germany—a compulsory organization of which all Jews, as defined by the Nuremberg Laws, were required to be members. The association was obligated to provide an independent Jewish welfare system and a Jewish school system such that henceforth Jews would no longer receive public welfare or attend schools outside of the provisions of the association.[5] Furthermore, the Ministry of Justice declared: "The exclusion of the Jews from the German economy must be completed according to plan. . . . Businesses and other properties in the possession of Jews . . . will become German property.[6]

Jews could no longer own export, distribution, or mail order businesses or retail stores. Owners were forced to sell those businesses to Aryans at a loss.[7] Jewish pharmacists, dentists, and veterinarians were barred from practicing their professions.[8] By the end of 1939, only 16 percent of Jews in Germany were employed.[9] Jews were ordered to surrender their gold, silver, diamonds, and other precious stones (except wedding rings) without compensation.[10] What gold and diamond jewelry did my grandmother surrender?

They were also ordered to turn in their radios to the police. As the order was decreed on the Jewish holiday of Yom Kippur, Jews who owned radios were forced to forgo attending the most important worship service of the year.[11] I assume that my grandparents, as others, instead of observing the holiday carried their prized radio, their cherished gift from their children, to a government office and waited in a long line to turn it in.

Jews also lost their right to rent protection, as non-Jewish landlords were forced by law to evict Jewish tenants. And Jewish landlords were allowed to lease only to Jewish tenants. So how did my grandparents' Aryan landlord, Philipp Schneider, rent to them? Furthermore, Jewish landlords and tenants were encouraged to register unused rooms to make them available for evicted Jews. I wonder if my grandparents ultimately had numerous boarders against their wishes. For any such boarder arrangements, the Reich drew up the necessary documents and then charged a fee to those involved.[12]

Additional restrictions dictated the freedom of movement of Jews. They had to abide by an evening curfew—8:00 p.m. in the winter and 9:00 p.m. in the summer.[13] That probably meant no more skat for my grandfather or late evening bridge games for both of my grandparents.

Their shopping access was also restricted severely, and then further constrained throughout 1939 and thereafter. They would have had a ration card stamped with the word *Jew*. Jews were restricted to a designated hour daily when all Jews were allowed to shop. Only designated stores could sell to Jews, and those stores were allowed to charge higher prices to Jews than Aryans, and to give them smaller portions, often of poor quality food. For example, Jews received less meat and butter than Aryans. As Marion Kaplan, in *Between Dignity and Despair,* quotes Erna Albersheim of Frankfurt, "the milk was of poor quality. . . . The bread was hardly edible. . . . Rolls were gray. . . . Onions [were] sold by the piece when the grocer had any. Butter was rationed."[14] Furthermore, Jews experienced decreasing food rations and an ever-increasing list of foods (such as rice and cocoa) that they were not allowed to purchase.[15]

Also, it was in 1939 that the exhibition of *Entartete Kunst* (Degenerate Art) opened in Frankfurt. A few months later, Frankfurt became home of the newly established Reich's Institute for the Study of the Jewish Question, led by

Alfred Rosenberg, a key ideologist of the Nazi Party. The institute was around the corner from one of my grandparents' favorite bakeries, Café Laumer, and only a few blocks from the Westend Synagogue, where my grandparents had attended services. The institute's library became the collecting point for books, documents, and manuscripts, and Rosenberg spearheaded the looting of more than twenty-thousand pieces of art across much of Europe.[16] Was my grandparents' Max Beckmann oil painting taken from them? I long to know which one of Beckmann's many works it was. What did it mean to them? Did they witness Nazis confiscating their painting?

* * *

On the other side of the Atlantic, in the United States, a fierce debate was underway about the nature of the Nazis, policies of immigration, and the fate of Germany's Jews. Along with another one of Father Coughlin's pro-Nazi rallies at Madison Square Garden in February 1939, the industrialist Henry Ford loudly voiced anti-Semitic views, blaming World War I on the Jews; attributing labor strikes, financial scandals, and agricultural depression to the Jews; and predicting that the United States could be embroiled in war again because of the Jews. He had a built-in forum in *The Dearborn Independent*, his hometown newspaper, which he owned. This small town newspaper had reach far and wide, as it was distributed to Ford's car dealerships across the country, sometimes placed on the front seat of the Model-T cars, and frequently quoted by local newspapers. In the face of anti-Semitic sentiments from someone as rich and powerful as Ford, many American Jews turned down the volume with which they were willing to express their fears.[17]

At the same time, a bill was drafted to allow twenty thousand children from Germany under the age of fourteen to enter the United States during 1939 and 1940, separate and apart from the quota system. The bill died in committee,[18] which was reflective of Gallup Poll results.[19] Other bills that proposed liberalizing immigration policy and expanding quotas were buried, usually by restrictionists, who contended that aliens caused unemployment.

The world was teetering on the brink of war in the spring and summer of 1939. President Roosevelt beseeched both Hitler and Mussolini to vow that they would not continue their aggression. He argued to both that war was unnecessary and that they should respect the independence of other nations, specifically, thirty-one countries in Europe and the Near East.

In June of 1939, meanwhile, FDR refused to admit the 930 Jews on board the *S.S. St. Louis,* which had set sail from Hamburg and was bound for Havana, but had been denied entry by the Cuban government. The Nazis spread propaganda, via their agents in Cuba, about the "criminal nature" of the Jewish passengers, in order to influence the Cubans to refuse the passengers entry.

As the ship's fate was being decided, the *New York Times* did not comment. Although a *Times* editorial described the *St. Louis* "as the saddest ship afloat" and stated that "no plague ship ever received a sorrier welcome," it was too little too late, appearing two days after the ship was on its way back to Europe. As pointed out by Laurel Leff in *Buried by The Times*, the editorial included no mention that the passengers were Jewish (although all but six were). It did not lay blame or express a plea for the United States to offer refuge, and only suggested that Cuba offer a temporary haven. And the editorial was placed inconspicuously, being the fourth of five.[20]

FDR was not being pushed very hard by senior members of the State Department. Of this response, my father offered the following during a panel discussion in 1997:

> When FDR was president, the Jews loved him and voted for him, but the truth was that he was indifferent to what happened to Jews. Cordell Hull had a clique in the State Department with Breckinridge Long, who made a point to keep out as many Jews as possible. He said there was a depression and it was not politically correct to let anyone in. The tragedy of the Holocaust is that the world closed its ears and eyes to what was happening. There was enough information and people knew what was happening.

Those days, too, carried strong messages of impending war. Winston Churchill delivered a fifteen-minute radio broadcast to America, warning of the increasingly serious threat of war in Europe and the likelihood of American involvement. "This is the time to fight—to speak—to attack!" FDR, upon the urging of Albert Einstein and in light of the rumor that Nazi Germany was building an atomic bomb, issued orders for a US effort to investigate building one as well.

Then, war.

Germany and the Soviet Union attacked Poland on September 1, 1939. Two days later, Britain, France, India, Australia, and New Zealand declared war on Germany.

The Nazi resolve became stronger, and they took even further steps against Germany's Jews. German authorities instructed that all Jews be transferred, via German railway freight cars, from the Reich to Poland.

But what was known in the United States of such steps? From the start of the war in Europe, and for the next six years, Leff writes:

> The *New York Times* and other mass media treated the persecution and ultimately the annihilation of the Jews of Europe as a secondary story. The story of the Holocaust . . . made the *Times* front page just 26 times, and only in six of those stories were Jews identified on the front as the primary victims. . . . Not once did the story lead the paper, meaning appear in the right-hand column reserved for the day's most important news . . . When the Holocaust made the *Times* front page, the stories obscured the fact that most of the victims were Jews, referring to them instead as refugees or persecuted minorities.[21]

* * *

The Nazis also raised the so-called *Kristallnacht* atonement fee at this time, and thus it is probably not coincidental that in November 1939, my grandfather requested of the *Devisenstelle* (Exchange Control Office) that his monthly government allowance of 300 Reichsmarks—$120 in 1939 dollars and $2,233 in 2021 dollars—be increased to 410 Reichsmarks, to match my grandparents' monthly expenses. This total comprised 130 RM for their rent, including utilities; 190 RM for general living expenses (for example, clothing); 25 RM for household help; and 65 RM for miscellaneous. After much back-and-forth, including conversations mentioned in official correspondence, the *Devisenstelle* granted my grandfather's request for the increase to 410 Reichmarks monthly. To make ends meet, they probably spent down their assets, comprising 2,350 RM in the bank and 1,290 RM in stocks. If they had been considering emigration, they were nonetheless being forced to spend down any resources toward that possibility.

Another letter written by my grandfather on November 29, 1939, provides further context of the financial restrictions being imposed. It was addressed to the postal service regarding his postal bank account and an identical version addressed to another bank. The purpose of the letters seems to be that my grandfather was notifying both banks that he could only receive payments to a special account (presumably an account for the deposit of the monthly allowance from the government), that cash payments to him or to "persons in his favor" were no longer allowed, and that he understood that any action to the contrary would be punished with not only a steep monetary fine, but also deprivation of liberty.

Meanwhile, in addition to financial hurdles, emigration became ever more difficult. Until the war began, emigrants had been able to travel on passenger liners, largely through German ports and other European harbors.[22] By the spring of 1939, so many people from Germany as well as Czechoslovakia had applied for US visas that, had they all been accepted, they would have filled the quotas for those countries for four to six years.[23] But then, from September 1939 through May 1940, foreign passenger lines refused German currency, so only people with foreign currency, usually from relatives, were able to leave Germany. Of those who became eligible for emigration based on their visa numbers, most were prevented from emigrating because they could not get the foreign currency.[24] Yet so high was the demand that the US quota was still 95 percent filled in FY 1940.

Slowly, the noose tightened. A second US visa policy was enforced for most of FY 1940, from the onset of the war in September until July 1940: the American consuls required proof of payment for the ship voyage. Furthermore, the affidavit sponsor had to be a relative. Although exceptions were made in rare instances involving a wealthy non-relative sponsor, those sponsors were required to make cash deposits into American banks. Only 10 percent of those whose visa numbers came up could emigrate under this new policy, though many from the waiting list had success.

Some of those who still had money could buy expertly forged passports and other necessary documents. The Latin American consuls were known to sell visas for several hundred dollars; for example, a Cuban transit permit cost $300.[25] Simultaneously, Palestine became a less viable option when the British government deemed that only ten thousand immigrants would be allowed in annually, from 1939 to 1944.[26]

Meanwhile, although the United States declared its neutrality, it began rearming for war.

16

Texas, 1939–1941

After leaving New York City to travel to Texas, my first stop was in Pennsylvania. When I started out the following morning, I was so excited that I headed in the wrong direction and did not realize it for over an hour. Nevertheless, I eventually arrived in Texas, and Dallas became my headquarters for the next two-and-one-half years. There was a small group of refugees there and it did not take long before I met almost everyone. A few of us were traveling salesmen and we all struggled together trying to make a living.

RUDY BAUM | "A Son of a Respectable Family"

After a few short months in New York City, once again, my father finally received the promotion he had long desired—to be a traveling salesman. Golo had fired their salesman in Texas and repossessed his car. In early 1939, my father drove from New York to Dallas.

Among my father's first connections were Edith and Walter Florsheim. They had been in the States since 1933, and Walter was a distant cousin. Walter's grandmother and my father's great-grandfather (i.e., father of Rosalie Fuld, August Geiger's wife) were brother and sister. Edith was a terrific cook and made many of my father's favorite traditional German dishes, such as *rouladen* and *spätzle*.

My father quickly became immersed in the Dallas community of German Jewish refugees, a small, tightly knit group of about fifty that was part of a larger Jewish community of some eight thousand.[1] He became particularly close to the other eight to ten German Jewish traveling salesmen, including Manny Marx, who had worked with my father at Ada-Ada.

How much did members of that German Jewish community discuss what they were reading in the papers and magazines and hearing on the radio? What did they think of FDR's Fireside Chat on September 3, 1939, just after the war began in Europe?

> My fellow Americans and my friends:
>
> . . . This nation will remain a neutral nation, but I cannot ask that every American remain neutral in thought as well. Even a neutral has a right to take account of facts. Even a neutral cannot be asked to close his mind or his conscience.
>
> I have said not once, but many times, that I have seen war and that I hate war. I say that again and again.
>
> I hope the United States will keep out of this war. I believe that it will.[2]

What was it like for my father to hear such "chats" about the neutrality of the United States, and simultaneously to know of the growing threat to his parents in Germany?

* * *

Compounding the complexity and confusion of it all for my father was that his regular correspondence with his parents became less frequent and unpredictable, perhaps because life as a traveling salesman meant that he was often out of town for five consecutive days, sometimes for as much as a few weeks. On the other end, of course, was increased censorship and a war, which reduced the flow of mail from Germany. In any event, the correspondence became sporadic, and often a few months could pass between letters.

But some did get through, and their tone had changed. The letters my grandparents did send during this period were once in my father's possession, but have gone missing. Perhaps my father could not bear to look at them anymore.

But at some point, it is clear that Julie, the devoted mother, and Norbert, the proud father and the former German soldier, finally entreated their son for help in escaping their country. At some point, they saw their peril as impossible to survive unless they fled Germany and "burdened" either Gretel in Palestine or my father in the United States. The words in those letters must have burdened my father for a lifetime.

My father was apparently trying to save enough money to try to rescue his parents, penny-pinching in the process, according to a second cousin. Rudy filed a transmigration voucher with the American Jewish Joint Distribution Committee (JDC), naming himself as the depositor with his address as the Hotel Adolphus in Dallas and the beneficiaries as Norbert Baum and wife, both of Frankfurt. A transmigration voucher was an account of the monetary deposits made by friends and family in America to pay the full or partial travel costs for Jews emigrating from Europe, since those Jews usually could not purchase steamship tickets in local currency. Most of these Jews were emigrating to the United States on steamships departing from Yokohama or Lisbon, the site of the central office of the JDC. While the transmigration voucher that my father filed is undated, it is likely that he filed it shortly after the JDC established the Transmigration Bureau on June 21, 1940.[3] No deposit amount is listed on my father's voucher, which was not unusual.

Was he saving money prior to 1940 for his parents' possible emigration, albeit not saving into a specific account? If not, 1940 was late to begin to cobble together funds. Had he wished he had started earlier? Did that haunt him?

As the cost to immigrate to the United States was approximately $450 per person, my father would have needed $900—$16,745 in 2021 dollars—for both his parents, requiring steep savings. In 1937 and early 1938, he was earning $18 a week (or approximately $335 in 2021 dollars), up from the $15 a week he earned when he first arrived in the United States in 1936.

And, again, by this point the number of people trying to get out of Germany was much, much larger than the number who were successful.

17

Germany and America, 1940 and 1941

TAX OFFICE

(Large J written in blue pencil)

RE: Baum, Nathan Israel

PROFESSION: old age pensioner

Wolfsgangstr. 132

Vol. 1, assembled 1940

NAME: Baum, Nathan Israel

DECLARATION OF ASSETS 1940

Nathan Baum

Now without profession, before, wholesale merchant in lining fabric

Fm, Wolfsgangstr. 132

Were you married by 1. Jan. 1940? *Yes.*

If yes, to whom? Julie Sara, née Geiger

Do you live in separation from your spouse? *No*

Which persons mentioned [here] are Jews? *Nathan Baum, Julie Sara Baum, née Geiger*

PROPERTY AS OF JAN. 1 1940

(All crossed out)—basic property, business property, other property, esp. capital

BANK ACCOUNTS

Savings account Frankfurter Bank nr. 3980 Nathan Baum: 1755 RM

Checking account Deutsche Effekten und Wechselbank b. 30, Nathan Baum: 257 RM

(Added in red pencil) total: 2012

Minus 1000

Result:1012

STOCKS

[Illegible]: value: 995.-

I.G. Farben Stocks, value: 313.-

Total: 1308.-

1308 plus 1012 equals 2320. (added in red pencil)

My grandparents' struggle to get by day by day only became worse.

The list of restrictions on their daily lives continued to grow. German Jews could no longer buy meat, nor most fruits and legumes. They were no longer eligible to purchase new shoes, clothing, or even material to make clothing. Their shoes could be repaired only by Jewish shoemakers. They no longer had access to public laundries, nor were they allowed to have telephones.[1] More distribution shops were set up to give out used clothing and shoes.[2]

So my grandparents must have been deeply appreciative when their dear friend Hedwig Kahn arranged to give them 200 Reichsmarks monthly as a direct deposit from her bank to their official government account. Yet I wonder whether my grandparents actually received—and had access to—that money, or did that account become a "blocked account," because the assets of Jews were in blocked accounts after June 1938? And, according to my grandfather's 1940 property tax file, he held stock in I.G. Farben, the company that ultimately produced the Zyklon B pesticide that was repurposed for the gas chambers at the concentration camps.

Their opportunities to continue to enjoy the concerts and plays that they so loved became more and more restricted. German composers and playwrights, unless they were Jewish, were banned from the *Kulturbund* programs. Already in 1934, Schiller and works of the Romantic period were banned; in 1936, Goethe's works were banned; and after the annexation of Austria, Mozart was banned.[3] The *Kulturbund* became a venue only for works *by* Jews to be performed *for* Jews, and Jews could not attend cultural performances offered anywhere other than the *Kulturbund*.

At the same time, the Reich reached the German film-viewing public with anti-Semitic films to stoke disdain and hatred. The film *Jud Süß* won awards and received many favorable reviews for its depiction of Jews as extortionists, seducers, and demons. In the documentary-style film *Der Ewige Jude*, the movement of Jews from Palestine to other countries was depicted as analogous to rats running underground. The text read "Where rats turn up, they spread diseases and carry extermination into the land. They are cunning, cowardly, and cruel; they mostly move in large packs, exactly as the Jews among the people."[4]

Then came the real-life fate with deportations, ghettos, and camps. With one thousand German Jews deported from eastern German towns such as Stettin to the Lublin area in February 1940, the expulsions began. Auschwitz was established that year, and its forced labor began producing synthetic rubber and gasoline. And, on April 30, 1940, the first major ghetto for Jews was created in Lodz, Poland's second largest city and a major industrial center.[5]

The Lodz Ghetto held 160,000 Jews in an area that was approximately two-and-half square miles, with extremely poor living conditions. Seven people might be forced to live in one room. One outhouse for many was the norm.

The Germans changed the name of Lodz to Litzmannstadt, in remembrance of a German general. German became the official language of Lodz, and the names of the streets and squares were changed from Polish to German names.[6]

The ghetto was sealed on May 1, 1940.[7] The rationale was that pure Germans coming in from the Baltic were moving into the former homes of the Jews, and the Germans wanted to keep those residents away from their old neighborhoods. Other ghettos were sealed because the Germans were afraid that the sanitary conditions could lead to the spread of epidemics beyond ghetto walls.[8]

In November, the forced labor of Jews built what would become the largest ghetto in Europe, the Warsaw Ghetto, by erecting a wall over ten feet high and topped with barbed wire, around a 1.3 square-mile area for over four hundred thousand Jews.[9]

On May 10, 1940, Germany invaded France. And on June 10, Italy entered the war as Germany's ally. Later that day, FDR delivered prepared remarks at the commencement exercises of the University of Virginia, where his son was graduating from law school. At one point, FDR went off script to declare, "On this tenth day of June, 1940, the hand that held the dagger has struck it into the back of its neighbor." This line, in what became known as the "Stab in the Back" speech, referred to the duplicity of Mussolini, who had promised to keep the war out of the Mediterranean but then proceeded to attack France. The president continued: "Some indeed still hold to the now somewhat obvious delusion that we of the United States can safely permit the United States to become a lone island, a lone island in a world dominated by the philosophy of force. Such an island may be the dream of those who still talk and vote as isolationists. Such an island represents to me and to the overwhelming majority of Americans today a helpless nightmare." He was no longer expressing neutrality or vacillation about *if* the United States should help Hitler's victims; it was now a question of when and how.[10]

One of the first steps was to aid Great Britain, one of the few Western

European countries not controlled by Germany. Within a few weeks of the "Stab in the Back" speech, FDR supplied Britain with artillery and arms by "selling" the goods to a steel company that then "resold" the goods to the British government, thus bypassing US neutrality laws.

Yet the internal debate in the United States continued. In the summer of 1940, the United States's third visa policy was put into effect. That policy essentially constructed a "paper wall" around Central Europe, making it virtually impossible to emigrate from Germany; thus the number of German immigrants to the United States steeply declined.

In September, meanwhile, the United States instituted its first peacetime draft, requiring seventeen million men to register. Only a few weeks later, the film *The Great Dictator*, Charlie Chaplin's first talking movie, was released, mocking Hitler, Mussolini, and the Nazis as "machine men with machine minds and machine hearts."[11]

In November, FDR was re-elected for a third term as president of the United States. Although he was an "interventionist," Congress and the American people, for the most part, were more isolationist. Just a few months earlier, the America First Committee (AFC) had formed, a group that was opposed to the United States entering the war. The AFC was one of the largest anti-war groups in the history of the United States, with Charles Lindbergh as its renowned spokesman. Lindbergh had lived in Europe from 1935 to 1939 to seek privacy for his family after the fatal kidnapping of his infant son; he visited Germany and toured the *Luftwaffe*, the German Air Force, and was impressed with Germany's "organized vitality."[12] He was awarded the honorary Order of the German Eagle medal by Göring, as commanded by Hitler, for his aviation accomplishments, just as Henry Ford had been honored, ostensibly for his assembly line accomplishments.[13] A few months after the war had started in 1939, Lindbergh elucidated his white supremacist beliefs in the widely circulated *Reader's Digest*, writing: "We, the heirs of European cultures, are on the verge of a disastrous war, a war within our own family of nations, as war which will reduce the strength and destroy the treasures of the White race, a war which may even lead to the end of our civilization. . . . We can have peace and security only so long as we band together to preserve that most priceless possession, our inheritance of European blood."[14]

Among the AFC's eight hundred thousand members were Brigadier General Robert E. Wood (CEO of Sears, Roebuck and Co.), Gerald Ford,

Sargent Shriver, e.e. cummings, Sinclair Lewis, Gore Vidal, and Walt Disney. The young JFK even sent a $100 contribution, stating, "What you all are doing is vital."[15] The influence of this thinking spread to Chile and Brazil, which also closed their doors to German Jews in 1940.[16]

In FY 1940, more than twenty-one thousand people emigrated from Germany to the United States.[17] By the end of calendar year 1940, approximately 315,000 Jews remained in the Greater Reich (Germany, Austria, and the Greater Protectorate).[18]

My father's parents, Norbert and Julie, were among them.

* * *

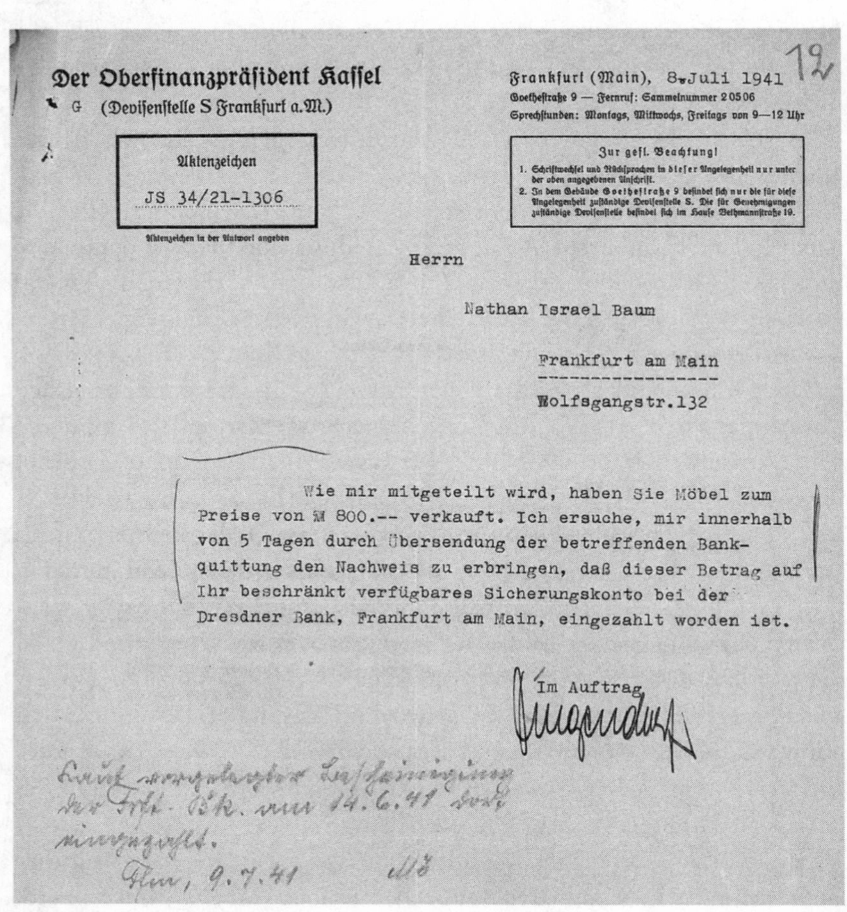

Der Oberfinanzpräsident Kassel
G (Devisenstelle S Frankfurt a.M.)

Frankfurt (Main), 8. Juli 1941
Goethestraße 9 — Fernruf: Sammelnummer 20506
Sprechstunden: Montags, Mittwochs, Freitags von 9—12 Uhr

Aktenzeichen
JS 34/21-1306
Aktenzeichen in der Antwort angeben

Zur gefl. Beachtung!
1. Schriftwechsel und Rücksprachen in dieser Angelegenheit nur unter der oben angegebenen Anschrift.
2. In dem Gebäude Goethestraße 9 befindet sich nur die für diese Angelegenheit zuständige Devisenstelle S. Die für Genehmigungen zuständige Devisenstelle befindet sich im Hause Bethmannstraße 19.

Herrn

Nathan Israel Baum

Frankfurt am Main

Wolfsgangstr.132

Wie mir mitgeteilt wird, haben Sie Möbel zum Preise von RM 800.-- verkauft. Ich ersuche, mir innerhalb von 5 Tagen durch Übersendung der betreffenden Bankquittung den Nachweis zu erbringen, daß dieser Betrag auf Ihr beschränkt verfügbares Sicherungskonto bei der Dresdner Bank, Frankfurt am Main, eingezahlt worden ist.

Im Auftrag

Laut vorgelegter Bescheinigung der Frkf. Bk. vom 14.6.41 dort eingezahlt.
Ffm, 9.7.41

Documentation from Regional Tax Office, July 8, 1941. (Translation on opposite page.)

Meanwhile, in October 1940, my father was eager to join the army. He registered for the draft, in a room above the post office in Palestine, Texas.

His lottery number was low, so he received "greetings from the President," ordering him to report for duty to the US Army on June 16, 1941. My father would later write that his company, Golo, wanted to get him a deferment, "but I felt not only an obligation, but also a moral responsibility to do my share."

In an interview at home in late 1999 or early 2000, he would ask: "Who had a better reason to fight against Hitler than I did?"

* * *

Norbert and Julie scrambled to subsidize the insufficient monthly allowance that the Reich had determined they could have. To that end, they sold furniture, in June of 1941, for 800 Reichsmarks, and again in late September 1941, for 350 Reichsmarks. As it was not a move to another apartment that precipitated these sales, my grandparents must have desperately needed money far more than they needed furnishings. And perhaps they were forced to share their apartment with more people, Jews, of course—and getting rid of furniture created space.

July 8, 1941
File nr. JS 34/21-1306
Mr. Nathan Israel Baum
Frankfurt/Main
Wolfsgangstrasse 132

As I am informed, you sold furniture for the price of RM 800. I request that you furnish proof within 5 days, by submitting the relevant receipt, that this amount was deposited into your security account with limited availability at the Dresdner Bank, Frankfurt/Main.

On behalf of

Signed: 'Augendorf'

handwritten note on bottom of page: According to the receipt of the Frankfurter Bank, which was presented, the sum was paid in on June 14, 1941.

Signed, dated: Frankfurt/Main, July 9, 1941 "Mö"

34-1306- 13

Frankfurt a.M., 14.10.41

Vermerk.

Mit Genehmigung vom 23/9. der NSDAP. Kreisleitung, Kreiswirtschaftsberater, hat der Jude:
Nathan Baum, Ffm, Wolfsgangstr. 132
Möbel im Werte von RM 350.-
an Herta Pass, Ffm, Stiftstr. 39
verkauft. Der Verkäufer wurde seitens des Kreiswirtschaftsberaters auf die devisenwirtschaftlichen Bestimmungen aufmerksam gemacht.

Mö

Documentation from Regional Tax Office, October 14, 1941. (Translation below.)

October 14, 1941
Frankfurt/Main
MEMORANDUM:

With the permission granted on Sept. 23 by the NSDAP Kreisleitung (County Government), Kreiswirtschaftsberater (The Business Counsel of the County), the Jew Nathan Baum, Frankfurt/Main, Wolfsgangstr. 132, has sold furniture valued at RM 350 to Herta Pass, Frankfurt/Main, Stiftstr. 39. The seller was informed about exchange control regulations by the business counsel of the county.

"Mö"

By 1941, two-thirds of the Jews in Germany were beyond middle age.[19] In March, Jews up to age sixty-five—including those down to the age of fifteen and some older than sixty-five—were forced to work a minimum of ten hours each day, often in difficult jobs, such as construction, road work, trash removal, or cleaning public toilets. My grandmother was fifty-seven and my grandfather sixty-nine, at that time. What was my grandmother's job? Was my grandfather forced to work as well?

Meanwhile, it was getting harder to eat. More foods became forbidden for Jews: fish, poultry, coffee, canned foods, apples, tomatoes. Milk was only available to Jewish families with young children. Any shortage of permissible foods caused shop owners to display signs stating "Foods in Short Supply Are Not Sold to Jews." If my grandparents did acquire forbidden goods on the black market, they were taking a risk, as their home could be among those randomly searched by the Gestapo.[20]

On the anniversary of his chancellorship, on January 30, Hitler reiterated that Jews would no longer have a role in Europe in the coming months and years: "Finally this year will help to assure the basis for understanding between the peoples, and thereby, for their reconciliation. I do not want to miss pointing out what I pointed out on 3rd September [1940] in the German Reichstag, that if Jewry were to plunge the world into war, the role of Jewry would be finished in Europe. They may laugh about it today, as they laughed before about my prophecies. The coming months and years will prove that I prophesied rightly in this case too."[21] The Nazis were working to fulfill those prophecies, too. The April 5, 1941, edition of the newspaper *Cologne Zeitung*, reported, "Although the Lodz Ghetto was intended as a mere trial, a mere prelude to the solution of the Jewish question, it has turned out to be the best and most perfect temporary solution of the Jewish problem."[22] This first ghetto, conceived to be a holding place before extermination, became a place of humiliation, psychological torture, starvation, and widespread epidemics.[23] As of April 14, 1941, any Jew attempting to escape the ghetto was shot immediately.[24]

In March, at a pinnacle meeting at the Reich Institute for the Study of the Jewish Question, the head of the Nazi Party's Office of Racial Policy, Dr. Walter Gross, who before the war had favored sterilization and even euthanasia of Jews, said: "The definitive solution must comprise the removal of Jews from Europe." To that end, he assisted in creating the system of mass murder in the killing centers.[25]

In October 1941, Hitler stated that the reason to export Jews to the East was to exterminate them for their crimes.[26]

In November 1941, the German authorities opened the largest concentration camp to date, Theresienstadt, in the town of Terezin in former Czechoslovakia as well as centers for mass murder by gas in the eastern territories. They also enlarged Auschwitz, the concentration camp complex constructed in May 1940, increasing the capacity from a few thousand to thirty-thousand inmates. And then the first killing centers, otherwise known as extermination or death camps, were established in late 1941 and throughout 1942. No one can say that death was not rampant in the concentration camps, which were technically labor or detention camps. But at the killing centers, such as Chelmno, Treblinka, and Auschwitz-Birkenau, the Nazis were able to murder thousands with swift and brutal efficiency by shooting or gassing.[27] The first mass gassing experiments using Zyklon B took place at Auschwitz, in the summer and autumn of 1941.[28]

Meanwhile, extensive bombing occurred throughout Europe, including a British air raid of Frankfurt. Fifty to sixty bombers attacked Frankfurt over five-and-a-half hours during the night of September 12 into September 13, 1941, with some of the greatest destruction only 1.5 miles from my grandparents' Wolfsgangstraße apartment. More than two hundred people lost their homes; seventeen people were injured, and eight died.[29]

America, meanwhile, was at a crossroads. Before it would enter the war at the end of the year, it took on the role of providing aid to other countries through what was called the Lend-Lease Program. As FDR put it: "If a neighbor's house is on fire, the man who owns a hose does not say: 'My garden hose cost fifteen dollars and you must pay this sum before you can have it.'"[30] Shortly thereafter, in New York City, Mayor Fiorello LaGuardia announced that in the previous six months, 238 people had been arrested for inflammatory and anti-Semitic speeches and actions.[31] Mayor LaGuardia was a staunch opponent of Hitler, perhaps, in part, because his own mother had been raised as an observant Jew in Trieste.[32]

Yet in June, a Gallup Poll indicated that 79 percent of Americans were opposed to entering the war.[33] And in October 1941, polling data revealed that 48 percent of Americans believed that Jews had too much power in the United States, a number that would climb to 58 percent by June 1945.[34]

In July 1941, the fourth visa policy of the United States had been established, essentially strangling visas in process and destroying the hopes of those wanting to apply and gain refuge in the United States. The policy was predicated on the fear—as stoked by the State Department—that foreign agents would enter the United States and endanger the country's security. Some believed that Nazi agents in the United States pressured refugees from Germany, Poland, and Russia to become spies by threatening harm to those refugees' family members left behind.

Secretary of State Breckinridge Long centralized immigration control in Washington and successfully advocated for a complex bureaucratic process to slow the rate of immigration nearly to a halt.[35] Protesting this turn of events, Albert Einstein wrote to Eleanor Roosevelt that the United States had basically closed its doors to refugees "by erecting a wall of bureaucratic measures alleged to be necessary to protect America against subversive, dangerous elements." Upon receipt, Eleanor Roosevelt sent a handwritten note to her secretary at the bottom of the letter: "Tell Dr. Einstein I will bring this to the attention of the President."[36]

In August, FDR and Churchill met and drew up the Atlantic Charter, a joint declaration of eight principles affirming their shared view "of certain common principles in the national policies of their respective countries on which they based their hopes for a better future for the world." The sixth principle read: "After the final destruction of Nazi tyranny, they hope to see established a peace which will afford to all nations the means of dwelling in safety within their own boundaries, and which will afford assurance that all the men in all the lands may live out their lives in freedom from fear and want."[37]

Yet America still seemed divided. Shortly thereafter, Charles Lindbergh addressed an audience of approximately eight thousand people in Iowa. His speech, "Who Are the War Agitators?" aggressively blamed the British, the US administration—and the Jews. He exclaimed: "No person with a sense of the dignity of mankind can condone the persecution of the Jewish race in Germany. But no person of honesty and vision can look on their pro-war policy here today without seeing the dangers involved in such a policy both for us and for them. Instead of agitating for war, the Jewish groups in this country should be opposing it in every possible way for they will be among the first to feel its consequences."[38] Did my father read or hear about this speech? If so, what was his reaction?

By then, in my grandparents' Germany, Jews were required to have police authorization to leave their area or residence. To make it easier for authorities to track the movements of Jews, as of September 1, all Jews over the age of six were required to wear a yellow cloth Star of David, inscribed with the word *Jude* in faux Hebrew letters, not only separating the Jews, but also stigmatizing and humiliating them.[39] How and when did my father acquire a yellow cloth Star of David, the one that I have pressed among my father's many documents?

Also in September 1941, the Gestapo dissolved the *Kulturbund*.[40] It was the end of Jewish cultural events. The musicians' instruments were confiscated, their albums recycled.[41]

But, of course, there was much worse. Deportations had begun in 1940—and then massive deportations of Jews from Germany, Austria, and Czechoslovakia to ghettos and killing sites began in October 1941.

Among German Jews, initially there were only whisperings of incomprehension and disbelief about what was happening. What will people do when they arrive at wherever they were being taken to? Would they work? Why take the elderly? Gradually such questions were muted by rumors of gas wagons and mass shootings.[42]

Meanwhile, in October 1941, Jewish emigration from Germany was stopped, with approximately 164,000 Jews remaining.[43]

The door was shut.

18

Frankfurt, October 1941

With the outbreak of World War II, the mail situation worsened, and by 1940 the letters from home started to sound alarming, as my parents' situation began to deteriorate. My contacts in New York were unresponsive to my request for help for my parents and there was no one in Dallas I could turn to. The last letter I received, dated October 15, 1941, was a desperate cry for help, and it was clear that they felt doomed and that I would be unable to rescue them.

RUDY BAUM | "A Son of a Respectable Family"

In previous (now, missing) letters, my father must have discussed a plan to get Julie and Norbert out via Cuba, because the letter dated October 15, 1941—the last he would receive—begins by mentioning that plan. In the letter, my grandmother suggests two people whom my father should solicit for help—one man named Warburg, and another named Steigerwald. Warburg may have been one of the relatives of the renowned banker Felix Warburg, whom my father's sponsor and grandmother's second cousin Martin Beckhard, knew. And Steigerwald may have been related to Minna Steigerwald, who lived at Reuterweg 73, according to historical records.

This last letter was typed, except for my grandfather's lines at the end. Here is the letter in its entirety:

> My dear Rudolf, we receive your letter, No. 8 from 9/18, only today; this time the mail took somewhat longer again. We last wrote to you on 9/29. We now await further news from you concerning Cuba, because the matter is very urgent and becomes more urgent every day. Were you able to contact Warburg? You can imagine that one longs for news at a time such as this, and this time your letter once again took very long. We still live in the hope that you will succeed in accomplishing something for us, because that's the only hope we have left.
>
> In the meanwhile we hear that orders were issued via Washington to issue visas for the USA in Berlin or Lisbon. We know of such a case in exact detail. This appears to be another possibility. We had asked you on a number of occasions, how your naturalization is going? We hear everywhere that you should

Abs.Norbert Baum
an Rudolf Baum

No 12

Frankfurt,15,10.41.
Wolfsgangstr.132.

Mein lieber Rudolf,wir erhalten erst heute Deinen Brief,Nr.8
vom 18,9. u.hat dieses Mal die Post wieder etwas länger gedauert.
Wir schrieben Dir zuletzt am 29,9.Wir erwartennun weiter Deine Nach
richt betr.Cuba,da die Sache sehr dringend ist u.jeden Tag dringli-
cher wird.Hast Du mit Warburg in Verbindung kommen können?Du kannst
Dir denken,dass man in solcher Zeit sehnlichst auf Nachricht wartet
u.diese Mal war Dein Brief wieder sehr lange unterwegs.Wir leben
immer noch in der Hoffnung,dass es Dir gelingt etwas für uns zu er-
reichen,denn das ist die einzige Hoffnung,die wir haben.
Wir hören inzw.dass durch Washington,die Anweisung gegeben wurdee
im Berlin resp.Lissabon ,Visen für U.S.A. zu erteilen.Ein solcher
Fall ist uns auf das Genauste bekannt.Es scheint,in dieser Beziehung
wieder eine Möglichkeit zu geben.Wir hatten Dich doch schon verschie
dentlich angefragt,wie es mit Deiner Einbürgerung steht ?Wir hören
übrigens allgemein,dass Du durch Deine Stellung,darin bevorzugt wür-
dest,wie verhält sich dieses? Es wäre für uns u.für Dich die beste
Lösung u.für Dich die billigere.Vielleicht kann Dir Herr Steigerw.
bei einer Information behilflich sein,da er in Washington lebt.
Ich gebe Dir die Adr.unten an.Wir überlegen uns dauernd,jede Möglich
keit zu erfassen u.nichts unversucht zu lassen,da keine Zeit zu verlieren ist.Wir hoffen doch unbedingt,dass Du es fertig bringst uns
zu helfen,dass wir von den furchtbaren Sorgen endlich befreit werden
Es ist weder schön,solche Briefe zu schreiben,noch ist es schön,dies
zu erhalten,doch bleibt uns keine andre Wahl.Es ist erstaunlich,dass
trotz aller Schwierigkeiten u.Kosten,soviele Leute,visen nach Cuba
erhalten.Von unsren Bekannten gehen eine ganze Anzahl dahin u.der
Kreis wird immer enger.Du kannst Dir denken wie traurig das für uns
ist,dass uns nicht gelingen will,was sovielen gelingt,von denen wir
es nie für möglich gehalten hätten.Wir glaubten,nachdem Du nun so-
lange drüben
bist,es Dir nicht so schwer fallen würde u.es Dir nicht
solche Sorgen verursachen würde.Du musst aber sehen,der Schwierigkeiten Herr zu werden,denn es muss sein.Ich kann Dir vn uns sonst
wenig berichten,wir sind mit unsren Nerven sehr strapaziert,das ist
bei den Aufregungen nicht zu verwundern.Ich kann auch augenblicklich
keine Briefe an Freunde schreiben,da ich zu deprimiert bin u.nichts
Erfeuliches zu berichten habe.Ich weiss nicht,ob Du meine Stimmung
verstehen kannst,aber sei versichert lieber Rudolf so ernste Feiertage haben wir noch nie verlebt.Gestern waren wir bei Rolfs Ettlinger,
die jetzt ein Zimmer in einer Pension haben,in der gleichen Pension wohnen
auch Unas mit Carmen.Es ist dies natürlich eine grosse Umstellung,u.
billig ist es auch nicht.Von Hirschs habe ich direkt noch nichts gehört,sie können von Glück sagen,dass sie ihr Ziel erreicht haben.
Wären wir nur schon auch schon soweit,ich bitte Dich innigst u.herzl.
alles zu tun um uns zu helfen,wir hoffen auf Dich.xxxxxxx
Es tut mir leid,dass meine Freundin Toni,solche Schwierigkeiten
hatte,ich hoffe dass sie bald Beschäftigung findet,sie ist ja auch
nicht mehr die Jüngste.Hoffentlich konntest Du etwas helfen.
Ich weiss nicht ob ich Dir schon geschrieben habe,dassElse Nathan
vor einigen Wochen ausgewandert ist,nach N.Y.Ihr Bruder,der selbst
erst ein Jahr drüben war,hat ihr die Ausreise ermöglicht.Sie hat
immer noch gute Freundschaft gehalten u.kam öfter zu uns.Da sie viel
Schwierigkeiten hatte,hat sie sich oft mit Papa beraten.Sie hat sich
dafür recht freundschaftlich benommen,indem sie uns,eine Zuwendung
machte,die uns monatlich ausbezahlt werden soll.6Monate lang,das ist
uns sehr viel wert.Sie hatte eine furchtbare traurige Ankunft in
N.Y.,da ihr Bruder während sie auf der Reise war,an einem Hirnschlag
gestorben ist.Wir haben natürlich Grüsse für Dich mitgegeben,wahr-
scheinlich hast Du inzw.von ihr gehört.
Hoffentlich hast Du angenehme Feiertage gehabt u.es geht Dir gut.
Bleibe gesund u.lasse baldigst wieder von Dir hören,hoffentl.Gutes

[illegible]

Last letter from Julie to Rudy, October 15, 1941.

be favored on account of your position/job, is that true? It would be the best solution for us and you, and the cheaper one for you. Perhaps Herr Steigerw.[ald] can assist you with any information, as he lives in Washington. I add his address below. We are constantly thinking about how to grasp every opportunity and to leave nothing untried, because there is no time to lose. We hope at all cost that you will succeed in helping us, so that we shall finally be relieved of these awful worries. It is neither nice to write such letters, nor is it nice to receive them, but we have no other choice. It is astonishing that, despite all the difficulties and costs, so many people are receiving visas for Cuba. Quite a number of our acquaintances are going, and our circle continues to shrink. You can imagine how sad it is for us that we shouldn't succeed where so many others are succeeding, of whom we never would have expected it. We believed, now that you have been over there for so long, that it wouldn't be so hard for you and that it wouldn't create such trouble/worry for you. But you will have to figure out, how to master the difficulties, because it must happen. Other than that there's only little to report about us, our nerves are very stressed, which is no wonder given the causes for alarm. At the moment I can't write letters to friends, because I am too depressed and have nothing pleasant to report. I don't know whether you understand my mood, but be assured, dear Rudolf, we have never lived through such solemn holy days. Yesterday we visited the Rolf Ettlingers, who now have a room in a boarding house, the same one where the Unas are living with Carmen. It is a big adjustment, of course, and it's not cheap either. I have not heard anything directly yet from the Hirschs; they can thank their lucky stars that they reached their destination. If only we were that far along, too, I ask you fervently and sincerely to do everything to help us, we place our hopes in you.

I am sorry my girlfriend Toni encountered such difficulties. I hope that she soon finds a job, she's not a spring chicken anymore. I hope you could be of some help. I don't know, whether I already wrote you that Else Nathan immigrated to N.Y. a few weeks ago. Her brother, who himself had been over there for only a year, made it possible for her to emigrate. She remained good friends with us and visited us frequently. Because she had lots of difficulties, she often consulted with Papa. In return she proved her friendship by generating a stipend, which is to be paid to us monthly. For 6 months, that means a great deal to us. She had an awfully sad arrival in N.Y., because her brother died of a stroke while she was still en route. Of course we passed along greetings for you, you probably have heard from her by now.

3145 Mt Pleasant St. N. W.
Washington D.C.

Last letter from Norbert to Rudy, October 15, 1941.

I hope you had pleasant holy days and you are well. Stay healthy and let us hear from you as soon as possible, hopefully with good news.

(Handwritten) With fervent regards and kisses, M[utti]

My dear Rudolf:

Yesterday we received your letter. I hope that you spent the holy days well and are healthy. Here we noticed little of the holy days. We go out very little, only if I have to buy something. Mutti already wrote to you in greater detail. I have the urgent wish that we can get away. I am still hopeful that you can accomplish something. From Aunt Helene we received another very sad letter. She hasn't heard from Hertha for 7 weeks and is very worried. The fact that her pension is almost gone creates problems; I would help her if I could. Other than our nerves our health is o.k. I hope we soon have news from you again.

With heartfelt regards and kisses, Papa.

Steigerwalds' address:
Jak. Steigerwald
3145 Mt. Pleasant St. N.W.
Washington, D.C.

* * *

Four days after that letter was written, on October 19, 1941, the deportations began in Frankfurt. Unannounced.

Jews were simply taken from their homes and marched through the streets to the *Großmarkthalle*, the big wholesale produce market hall. There, they were processed. Among the first to go were my grandparents, Norbert and Julie Baum.

When they were deported, their property and assets were confiscated by the Reich, in accordance with the Eleventh Decree of the Reich Citizenship Law, as documented in a court order (based on the Gestapo list of evacuated Jews) to the Frankfurter Bank on November 6, 1941:

> Re: Assets of Jews evacuated to the East
> I call attention to the fact, that the assets of the persons [Nathan Baum and Julie Sara Baum] named below have been confiscated to the benefit of the Deutsche Reich.

Although twenty-six thousand Jews lived in Frankfurt in 1933, fewer than six hundred survived in Frankfurt.[1]

Weeks later, on December 7, 1941, Japan launched a surprise attack on Pearl Harbor. On December 8, the United States declared war on Japan, thus entering the war. On December 11, Germany and Italy declared war on the United States. The news traveled via radio broadcasts, more than eleven thousand newspapers, and the newsreels shown prior to movie screenings in American cinemas.[2]

* * *

It would be some time before my father would learn of his parents' fate.

As the historian Marion Kaplan explains: "Exact figures of those who left Germany as a result of racial persecution cannot be established, but a good estimate is between 270,000 and 300,000 Jews. That is, close to three-fifths of German Jews managed to flee Germany. Yet approximately 30,000 of those who got out were later caught by the Nazis in other European countries. Ultimately, about half of those Jews who had lived in Germany in 1933 could save themselves through emigration to safe countries. Their friends and relatives who remained behind were murdered."[3] By September 1942, my father would know that his parents were dead. An obituary in German was placed in the *Aufbau*, a newspaper, published in New York City that served German Jewish immigrants:

Wir erhielten die tieferschütternde Nachricht, dass unsere geliebten Eltern, Gross-Eltern, Schwester, Schwägerin und Schwager

Norbert Baum und
Julie Baum geb. Geiger

(früher Frankfurt a. Main)
in kurzer Folge in Polen verschieden sind.

In tiefer Trauer:
Rudolf Baum, Reception Center Fort Logan, Colo.
Reuben Bloch und Frau Grete geb. Baum, nebst Sohn Mischa, Palästina
Helene Stern-Geiger, Dresden
Jacob Geiger und Frau Olga geb. Liebmann, 54 Mentelle Park, Lexington, Ky.

Obituary in the *Aufbau*, September 4, 1942.

> We received the deeply shattering news that our beloved parents, great grandparents, sister, sister-in-law, and brother-in-law
> Norbert Baum and Julie Baum (born Geiger)
> (Formerly of Frankfurt am Main)
> Died in short order in Poland.
> In deep mourning:

Then it lists the survivors—my father's sister Gretel and her husband and son, in Palestine; Helene Stern-Geiger, my grandmother's sister in Dresden (deported on August 25, 1942 to Theresienstadt and perished there on November 1, 1942)[4]; and Jacob and Olga Geiger, my grandmother's brother- and sister-in-law, in Lexington, Kentucky, who had successfully emigrated.

And, at the top: Rudolf Baum, my father, whose residence was listed as the reception center of Fort Logan, Colorado, where he was training for army duty.

* * *

More than seventy years later, in the Hessian State Archives housed in Wiesbaden, I would find this handwritten memo bearing the stamp of the Frankfurt Tax Office and dated January 16, 1942:

1. The Jew Norbert Israel Baum was deported to Poland in the month of December 1941.
2. The entire property is considered to be impounded.
3. Therefore the property tax is to be revoked as of April 1, 1942.

It was initialed by two signatories and stamped again, on January 17, 1942.

Part Four

THE WAR AND THE PEACE

Now we have become part of history.

RUDY BAUM

19

Fort Sill, Fort Logan, St. Louis, Camp Lee, Camp Ritchie, and Camp Sharpe, 1941–1944

My late parents borrowed considerable amounts of money,
that I am obligated to pay back over here.

RUDY BAUM | letter to his future wife, Hannelore Schoenfarber

Between 1942 and 1944, German authorities developed an even stronger resolve, including their determination to rid Europe of its Jews.

In June 1942, Germany attacked the Soviet Union, beginning the months-long battle that would eventually result in Germany's retreat. Just six months before that attack began, Hitler and his associates officially declared "the Final Solution" for the Jewish problem—the decision to exterminate the Jewish people. What ensued was three years of increasing torture, systematic deportations, and killings of millions of Jews throughout Europe. The first gassings occurred at Auschwitz. Many more concentration camps and killing centers were established.[1]

My father, meanwhile, had begun his US Army service—in June 1941—and was stationed in Fort Sill, Oklahoma, before being transferred to Fort Logan, Colorado, near Denver. At Fort Logan, his military orders were often confused with those of another Rudolf Baum, who was stationed nearby. This other Rudolf Baum, it turned out, was also from Frankfurt, attended the Westend Synagogue, and was only a few years older than my father. There was no family relationship, but Rudie—as he was known—was a welcome Frankfurt connection with whom my father stayed in touch for the rest of his life.

With the attack on Pearl Harbor in December 1941, which officially brought the United States into WWII, the likes of my father—German Jewish refugees serving in the US Army—became "enemy aliens" overnight. At the same time, his term of military service expanded—from one year to "the duration of the war." Then, in 1942, amendments to the Soldier and Sailor Relief Act enabled these "enemy aliens" to become naturalized citizens—with the recommendation of their commanding officers and without the usual requirements of a declaration of intention, a waiting period, and examinations in knowledge of the US government.

On June 12, 1942, upon the recommendation of his commanding officer, my father and four other "enemy aliens" were in the Denver Courthouse chambers of Colorado's US District Judge J. Foster Symes, who believed that the naturalization process had been hurried and lacked sufficient interrogation. Judge Symes addressed the Chief Naturalization Examiner, F. C. Emmerich, with these words: "It would be the easiest thing in the world for a German spy to use this method of getting citizenship—all he has to do is enter the Army. The officers who have known these men for three or four months, and on that acquaintanceship swear the men are attached to the principles of the Constitution, don't know what they are talking about. I'll naturalize them, if you and the army officers recommend it, but I'll not take the responsibility." These words of welcome were followed by the oath of citizenship declared by my father and four fellow immigrant US soldiers—Englebrecht, Oberlander, Unger, and Zadera. These men repeated after Emmerich in unison, phrase by phrase: "I hereby declare, on oath, that I absolutely and entirely renounce and abjure all allegiance and fidelity to any foreign prince, potentate, State, or sovereignty, and particularly to Germany of which I have heretofore been a citizen; that I will support and defend the Constitution and laws of the United States of America against all enemies, foreign and domestic." The combination of their heavy accents and the "fill-in-the-blank" format to renounce their homelands must have made for a garbled "in unison" chorus. My father, at the age of twenty-seven, and two other soldiers renounced Germany; a fourth renounced Poland; and a fifth, Canada.

When Judge Symes finally declared "I hereby grant you citizenship," I wonder: Did my father consider himself an American Jew or a Jew who was American? Until that moment, my father had been a *German* Jew.

As newly anointed American citizens, my father and his fellow soldiers raised their right hands and recited: "I pledge allegiance to the flag of the United States of America, and to the Republic for which it stands . . . " One by one, they received their certificates of citizenship. Then they returned to their posts—my father to Fort Logan. Corporal Rudolf Baum was an American citizen.

Still, when Corporal Baum applied for Officer Candidate School, or OCS, the FBI conducted lengthy background checks. He easily furnished the

Denver Post,
June 13,1942.

FIVE SOLDIERS GET CITIZENSHIP THRU NEW LAW

Symes Disapproves Act But Admits Denver Aliens.

Altho he emphasized that he was not taking the responsibility for the action, United States District Judge J. Foster Symes admitted to United States citizenship five Denver soldiers of alien birth Friday, in the first local application of a new federal law.

The war powers act, recently enacted, set forth that an alien serving in the military or naval forces could be naturalized providing his commanding officer will testify he is a man of good character and attached to the principles of the constitution. The usual declaration of intention, waiting period and examinations in knowledge of government are not required.

SAYS SPY COULD GET CITIZENSHIP EASILY.

Expressing himself as feeling that the matter had been rushed thru too quickly and without sufficient interrogation, Judge Symes declared:

"It would be the easiest thing in the world for a German spy to use this method of getting citizenship—all he has to do is enter the army. The officers who have known these men for three or four months, and on that acquaintanceship swear the men are attached to the principles of the constitution, don't know what they're talking about.

"I'll naturalize them if you and the army officers recommend it, but I'll not take the responsibility."

The remarks were addressed to F. C. Emmerich, chief naturalization examiner, who emphasized that the procedure was being followed in accordance with the letter of the law and the urging of government officials.

"An examiner is even being sent to India to naturalize aliens in American service there," he said.

Judge Symes deferred conferring citizenship on two other soldier-petitioners, pending further study to learn whether they should have registered as enemy aliens. Several of those admitted also were citizens of enemy nations.

ALL BUT ONE ARE "NONCOM" OFFICERS.

The men who received citizenship were:

Rudolf Baum, 27, of Dallas, Tex., a corporal at Fort Logan; Samuel Tobias Unger, 27, of New York city, a sergeant at Lowry field; Curt M. Engelbrecht, 25, of Burlingame, Calif., a corporal at Fitzsimons General hospital; Alexander Zadera, 28, of Detroit, a private at Fitzsimons, and Siegfried David Oberlander, 25, of Chicago, a corporal at Lowry.

All the men came to the United States within the last five years, except Zadera, a Canadian, who entered in 1923.

required letters of recommendation from friends he had made in Denver. But weeks went by before he heard about the status of his application, causing him to question if he could become an officer in spite of his German background.

Finally, in April of 1943, Rudy was accepted to OCS in Camp Lee, Virginia. My father referred to himself as a "ninety-day wonder" because he then became a second lieutenant in only three months.

* * *

On his first furlough from Denver, in April 1942, my father took a train to St. Louis to visit friends, Walter and Evelyn Mainzer, a German Jewish couple who had emigrated from Frankfurt. They were in their late thirties with a five-year-old daughter. Walter's parents had been friendly with my father's parents in Frankfurt. The Mainzers fixed up my father with a date, a young woman named Hannelore Schoenfarber.

Hannelore (also known as Hanne) was from Nuremberg, and had emigrated in 1934 with her parents and younger sister, Inge, when she was fourteen and Inge was six. They first settled in Des Moines, where they had relatives, and later moved to St. Louis.

Hanne was almost twenty-two when she met Rudy, who was five years older. She was attractive, with great legs, coal black hair, and a warm smile.

Hanne had dropped out of high school because of a conflict with a teacher. My mother's telling of the story was that she and the teacher strongly disliked one another. When my parents met, my mother held two jobs. She worked at the St. Louis Transportation Corps for a captain who was in charge of the freight cars coming through St. Louis to pick up hospital supplies. She also was a saleswoman at the big Stix, Baer & Fuller department store.

They likely met shortly before my father learned of the death of his parents in Poland.

My father returned to St. Louis a few times, including the following September of 1942, just before the Jewish holidays. Upon his return to Denver, he wrote to my mother that he had barely slept on the sleeper train due to the "icy cold" weather, and so spent most of the next morning sleeping before spending the rest of the day in synagogue for the holidays. He wrote about what a pleasant memory his trip was, and how he found my mother to be "a real swell girl" with "a lot of sense." He returned to St. Louis again in January 1943.

Hannelore Schoenfarber, circa 1942.

But their visits were few. So their romance blossomed through letters.

At one point, my mother was writing to my father every day. And ten months after meeting Hanne, Rudy proposed to her—in a letter dated February 15, 1943. The letter was most practical and decidedly unromantic:

> Hello Darling:
>
> I myself have been giving the idea of our getting married a lot of thought, and I feel for sure, that it is going to happen. . . . As I am writing this letter, I get to realize, that I am proposing to you. . . . Now then the thing that I have been thinking was to get married after I get through with OCS, provided I get through, or rather, get to go, before I get shipped. The question is would that be fair to you for several reasons. One is, that I might be shipped let's say, about 6 months later, and then you'd be home, and I some place else. . . . Another thing is, I wouldn't know ahead of time, where I would be stationed, and whether or not I could have you with me, and that would be worse. . . . Another angle that's important is the financial side, which is rather a sore spot. Actually, and to put it very bluntly, I don't have anything, except what I am making. And that must sound very strange to you, but here is the reason. My late parents borrowed considerable amounts of money, that I am obligated to pay back over here, and that has been taking just about all I've ever been able to save, I am still paying on it. We could make a living on my

pay, after school (about $220 net), but that might not be the kind of living you like and not the kind I'd want you to have. So here it is off my chest and in your lap. . . . I know, Sweetheart, if we can come to a solution of all those problems, the rest will take care of itself. I know we love each other as much as any two people can, so the mental and physical adjustment as part of the marriage should be easy enough and no problem at all. . . .

Now if I can still concentrate on something else, I'll try to write another letter or two. So, for today, Darling,

With all my love and loads of kisses,

Rudy

My father refers to the "problem" of paying back the debt that his parents had incurred. I suspect that he was referring to a continuation of the loan payments to Josef B., a debt that his parents had requested that he take over as of 1938.

Against her parents' initial objections, presumably about a young unmarried girl spending time away with a single young man, my mom—along with a close girlfriend, as a chaperone—visited my dad in Denver, to become officially engaged.

And I have to wonder: To what extent would getting married serve as a balm for the hole in his heart, for his deceased parents? My father sent a mother's day card in 1943 to his future mother-in-law, who replied immediately, signing her letter "all my Love, your Mom."

After sorting out their wedding date through the mail, Rudy and Hannelore married on July 18, 1943, the Sunday after my father graduated as a second lieutenant, and just ten days before my father was to report to Quartermaster School, for officer candidate training.

It was a wartime wedding: the rabbi in St. Louis who was to officiate was called into military service, so another rabbi was recruited at the last minute. The ceremony was performed in the rabbi's study. In attendance were my mother's parents, the Mainzers, and three of my mother's close girlfriends. The wedding reception was small—only the closest friends who lived nearby were invited, as difficulties with civilian traffic precluded out-of-town guests. The reception was a luncheon in The Blue Room of Forest Park Hotel, known for its Circus Snack Bar nightclub, where the likes of Liberace, Louis Armstrong, and Sarah Vaughn performed.

My parents spent their honeymoon in Cincinnati. While strolling through

Rudy's and Hanne's wedding, July 18, 1943.

Rudy and Hanne, 1943.

the Cincinnati Zoo, they happened upon my father's uncle Jacob, his mother Julie's brother, who was living an hour and a half away, in Lexington, and had immigrated to the States either in late 1938 or during 1939. I assume that, upon meeting Jacob, my father experienced a rush of memories with a wave of sadness, as I believe that this was the first relative my father had seen since he left Germany—and a close relative at that. Prior to this chance encounter, Jacob and Rudy must have been in touch by mail or telephone about the death of Julie and Norbert, as it must have been one of them who placed the obituary in the *Aufbau* almost a year earlier. How did they acknowledge their loss now in-person?

After their honeymoon, my parents took separate trains—my mother returning to St. Louis and my father, probably on board the *Fast Flying Virginian*, returned to Camp Lee near Petersburg, Virginia, to which he had transferred in April. They reunited six weeks later, when my mother joined my father, first for a brief stint in Camp Lee and then later in Camp Ritchie, Maryland, where he was sent next.

* * *

When my father returned from his honeymoon, he reported to the Quartermaster School as an officer candidate. A telegram awaited him: the Office of Strategic Services in Washington, DC, requested his presence. The Office of Strategic Services was recruiting volunteers to parachute behind enemy lines. My father asked to be excused, citing two reasons: he did not feel physically fit for such a challenge, and he had recently married.

Instead, he taught at Officer Candidate School for three or four months and then asked to be transferred to military intelligence. That is when he was sent to Camp Ritchie, the US Army Military Intelligence Center, where he became a member of the Interrogation of Prisoners of War Unit and underwent further commanding officer training for ninety days during the cold winter of 1943–1944.

Camp Ritchie was the first centralized intelligence training facility in the US, and some say the birthplace of modern psychological warfare. Not far from Washington, it was a few miles south of the Pennsylvania-Maryland border, at a remote location in the northern tip of the Blue Ridge Mountains, about ten miles north of FDR's presidential retreat, which came to be known as Camp David.

My father likened his arrival at Camp Ritchie to a homecoming, because the camp was filled with soldiers who were German Jewish refugees, likely sporting a dog tag with "H" for Hebrew, as opposed to "C" for Catholic or "P" for Protestant. Dog tags issued between 1941–1952 denoted a soldier's religious affiliation, so that the appropriate religious rituals could be rendered in the event of serious injury or death. Because the letter "H" could cause increased risk for Jewish soldiers in the face of the enemy, how many of these Camp Ritchie soldiers eventually got rid of their dog tags, blurred the legibility of the "H," cited no religious preference on their tag, or chose instead a "P" or "C" affiliation?[2] Most of the Camp Ritchie soldiers spoke English with an accent—if not German, then Italian or French. Hence the Camp Ritchie slogan: "I spick six langwitches, English da best."

The German Jewish soldiers referred to themselves as *The Ritchie Boys*. Because they spoke German and understood German culture and behavior, they were ideally suited to be trained in interrogation, investigation, psychological warfare, intelligence, and counterintelligence techniques. Their goal was to psychologically reach the captured enemy soldiers; to get them to talk and continue talking so they would divulge as much information as possible. The work demanded brains and not brawn, the typewriter—not a gun—as its weapon, which I am sure made my father happy. Many of the men did not consider themselves front line fighters either psychologically or physically. My father, in particular, had a small frame, minimal muscle tone, and little physical prowess.

The courses were rigorous and covered a range of subjects, including Morse code, aerial photography, scouting skills, marksmanship, weapons maintenance, German military maps, German insignia, and the German Order of Battle. One of the tests was on identification of enemy artillery and armor, captured examples of which lined the roadway leading to the camp's headquarters.

Classroom instruction was augmented with extensive roleplaying and reenactment in order to train these soldiers if and when they went behind the lines. Soldiers honed their interrogation skills by interviewing German POWs brought from North Africa. It was often a surreal scene: There was a reenactment of a Nazi rally, with Nazi banners hanging from the balconies. Swastikas decorated the walls. And from time to time, someone impersonated Hitler, with the aid of a glued-on mustache. The *Sieg Heil!* (Hail victory!) salute resounding loudly. There was even a reenacted German ambush in the countryside, complete with plywood scenery to depict a small German town. One of the scouting assignments required each soldier to find his way back in the dark to camp from a remote location, relying only on a compass and night sounds—no flashlight, map, walkie talkie, or radio.

Alongside the rigor was humor. The Military Intelligence Training Corps—MITC—was nicknamed Military Intelligence Total Confusion. As a practical joke, a few Ritchie Boys made up a story about capturing Hitler's latrine orderly, who divulged details about Hitler's genitalia. This story took on a life of its own—to such an extent that senior military brass showed up to hear the story firsthand. Some of their tactics in the field were equally original: in a "good cop, bad cop" routine, two Ritchie Boys teamed up to play on German soldiers' fear of Russian captivity—the good cop threatened the prisoner with Russian captivity if he did not cooperate, escorting the prisoner into a tent decked out with Russian paraphernalia, to be interrogated by a "Russian Commissar"—the other Ritchie Boy disguised in Russian uniform and feigning a Russian accent.[3]

Overall, it was a friendly, almost familial atmosphere. The officers' mess had excellent food and service, meeting the expectations of the senior military officers from DC who visited frequently. The chef was from New York City's Mayflower Hotel, and the cooks were mainly of Italian and German descent.

Table service, one of the perks at Camp Ritchie, was provided by Italian POWs. And it was either at Camp Ritchie or back at Fort Logan that my father, though right-handed, began to drink his coffee "left-handed," because he believed he would be more likely to be sipping from the less used, and thereby cleaner, side of the cup.

My father was surrounded by many Ritchie Boys who were, or would become, famous. Klaus Mann was the author of almost a dozen books and the son of Thomas Mann, the famous novelist and Nobel Laureate. Richard Schifter would become the Assistant Secretary of State for Human Rights and Humanitarian Affairs, from 1985 to 1992, and would serve on numerous UNESCO and UN committees.[4] Ernst Cramer became the chief editor, managing director, and publisher at the publishing house Axel Springer Verlag AG as well as the closest confidant of Axel Springer himself. And Cramer became a lifelong friend of my father.

My father never referred to himself as a "Ritchie Boy." He seemed to shy away from the topic. I wonder if there was some aspect that caused him to be conflicted about his identity as a "Ritchie Boy." Or for some reason did he feel inadequate to describe the Ritchie Camp experience?

* * *

After three months at Camp Ritchie, my father was assigned to a Mobile Radio Broadcasting Company as a foreign language propaganda officer. He was transferred to Camp Sharpe, an adjunct of Camp Ritchie, located on the Battlefield of Gettysburg. While stationed at that seminal site, my father took the opportunity to learn about the American Civil War. Rudy and Hannelore lived in a furnished room outside of Gettysburg, socializing on weekends with other young military couples.

Under the instruction of Hans Habe, a Hungarian Austrian newspaper editor and correspondent, my father, along with his Camp Ritchie buddy Ernst Cramer, learned how to write radio broadcasts and airborne leaflets. Hans Habe was eccentric, highly extroverted, and a flashy dresser. He would become an acclaimed author, with more than two-dozen books. Ernst later wrote that he remembered my father "as a dapper young lieutenant . . . who of course obeyed his superior's (Hans Habe's) orders, but who made it known that he not always agreed with the captain's antics and especially grinned about Habe's tailor-made uniforms."

The goal of Habe's classes was to create non-threatening leaflets encouraging the enemy to surrender. The class analyzed leaflets that had been used thus far, such as one with only a picture of an expansive open field dotted with thousands of graves of German soldiers. My father helped design a two-sided leaflet with a two-word lead, *ONE MINUTE*, followed by six short points informing the enemy of the Allied soldiers' intention to spare lives and, on the back page, explaining how to surrender.

Due to his training and subsequent wartime experience with this Mobile Radio Broadcasting Company, my father briefly toyed with the idea of becoming a radio broadcaster after the war. He was a talker, had a deep voice, and truly enjoyed the radio. He never pursued the notion, perhaps because of his practicality—could he make a living in a new field?

With the opening of the second front, most of the Ritchie Boys were sent to Europe in the spring or summer of 1944. On June 6, 1944, D-Day, the Allies began to shift the balance of power in the war. Before the actual invasion on the beaches of Normandy, the Germans had been deceived into believing that they would be attacked much farther north, in the Pas de Calais region.

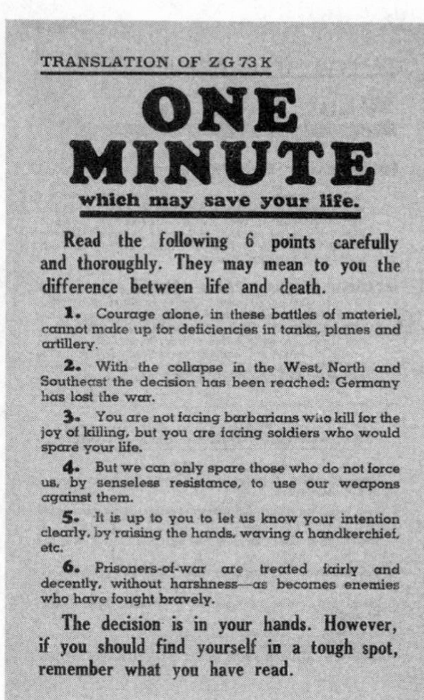

TRANSLATION OF ZG 73 K

ONE MINUTE

which may save your life.

Read the following 6 points carefully and thoroughly. They may mean to you the difference between life and death.

1. Courage alone, in these battles of materiel, cannot make up for deficiencies in tanks, planes and artillery.

2. With the collapse in the West, North and Southeast the decision has been reached: Germany has lost the war.

3. You are not facing barbarians who kill for the joy of killing, but you are facing soldiers who would spare your life.

4. But we can only spare those who do not force us, by senseless resistance, to use our weapons against them.

5. It is up to you to let us know your intention clearly, by raising the hands, waving a handkerchief, etc.

6. Prisoners-of-war are treated fairly and decently, without harshness—as becomes enemies who have fought bravely.

The decision is in your hands. However, if you should find yourself in a tough spot, remember what you have read.

TRANSLATION OF ZG 73 K

What is to be done?

Individual Surrender : Small groups of not more than 5 men surrender by putting away weapons, helmet and belt, raising their hands and waving either a handkerchief or a leaflet. If Allied soldiers are in the immediate vicinity, they are to be called. Safe conducts, although helpful, are not absolutely essential. Collection points for prisoners-of-war are located along the main highways and thoroughfares.

Group Surrender : As long as units surrender in small groups, the same applies as above. For larger units it is provided under the Hague Convention that officers surrender their men under the sign of the white flag, to the nearest Allied officer (if possible, of equal rank). If parlays are required, accredited parlamentaires may take up personal contact with the nearest Allied command post.

Treatment of prisoners-of-war

1. Decent treatment. According to the Geneva Convention, you are treated like soldiers.
2. Good food. You receive the same nourishment as we, the best-fed army in the world.
3. Hospital care. Your wounded and sick are treated just like our own.
4. Mail connection. You can write 4 post cards and 4 letters home per man per month.
5. Return home. After the war you are returned home as soon as possible.

WHEN TAKEN PRISONER, SHOW THIS LEAFLET TO YOUR CAPTORS.

Z G 73 K

Leaflet distributed by Allied soldiers.

Rudy and Hanne, Gettysburg, 1944.

Although the Germans held back the Allied troops for about six weeks, the Allied forces finally were able to begin the liberation of Paris and northern France and destroy much of the German Army stationed near Normandy.[5] Meanwhile on the Eastern Front, Hitler suffered his greatest setback when Stalin's military operation in Belorussia destroyed three times as many troops as the Allies had destroyed in Normandy.[6]

My father received orders at the end of April 1944 to go to Paris. It was a difficult good-bye for Rudy and Hannelore, who had only been married nine months.

My mother returned to St. Louis to live with her parents. They never spoke about the obvious possibility that my father might not survive. I suspect that they also never talked about the psychological trauma he might experience—facing the enemy, witnessing towns and cities destroyed, seeing the Jewish victims of the "Final Solution."

General Patton and Major General Walker, November 1944.

20

London, Normandy, Paris, and Trier, 1944–1945

It did not take long to come face to face with my first German prisoner. I don't remember whether he or I was more nervous during my first interrogation. I felt a sense of revenge, as now I was in charge and it was the German who had to be afraid.

RUDY BAUM | "A Son of a Respectable Family"

My father set foot on European soil again in Southampton, England, the same port from which he had left for America seven and a half years earlier. He was now part of General Patton's Third Army and, more specifically, Major General Walker's Twentieth Corps.

His tour of duty began in London, where he received additional training, conducted primarily by journalists. During this period, the Germans regularly bombarded London with their V1 missiles. Whenever the sirens sounded, my father and others sought protection by crawling under their beds and hoping for the best.

On July 4, 1944, my father and his fellow soldiers, most of whom were refugees like him, crossed the Channel to Normandy, where they stayed for thirty days. As this was nearly a month after D-Day, the attacking Allied soldiers were in a stronger position than the defending Germans. My father, as a Propaganda and Psychological Warfare Officer, helped lead the efforts to drop leaflets and broadcast across enemy lines to get the German troops to surrender. He interrogated German prisoners to secure information on the order of battle, the positions of German units, and the morale at the front and in Germany. That information was then used to write the Safe Passage Leaflets, either sent by shell or dropped by planes, that assured the German troops safe passage if they held up the leaflet.

The Allied troops had the opportunity to mingle with the local residents in France, who welcomed them with open arms. Many of the soldiers were busy writing home to recount the events. Although my father, as an officer, had the responsibility of censoring the mail of the troops under his command; about

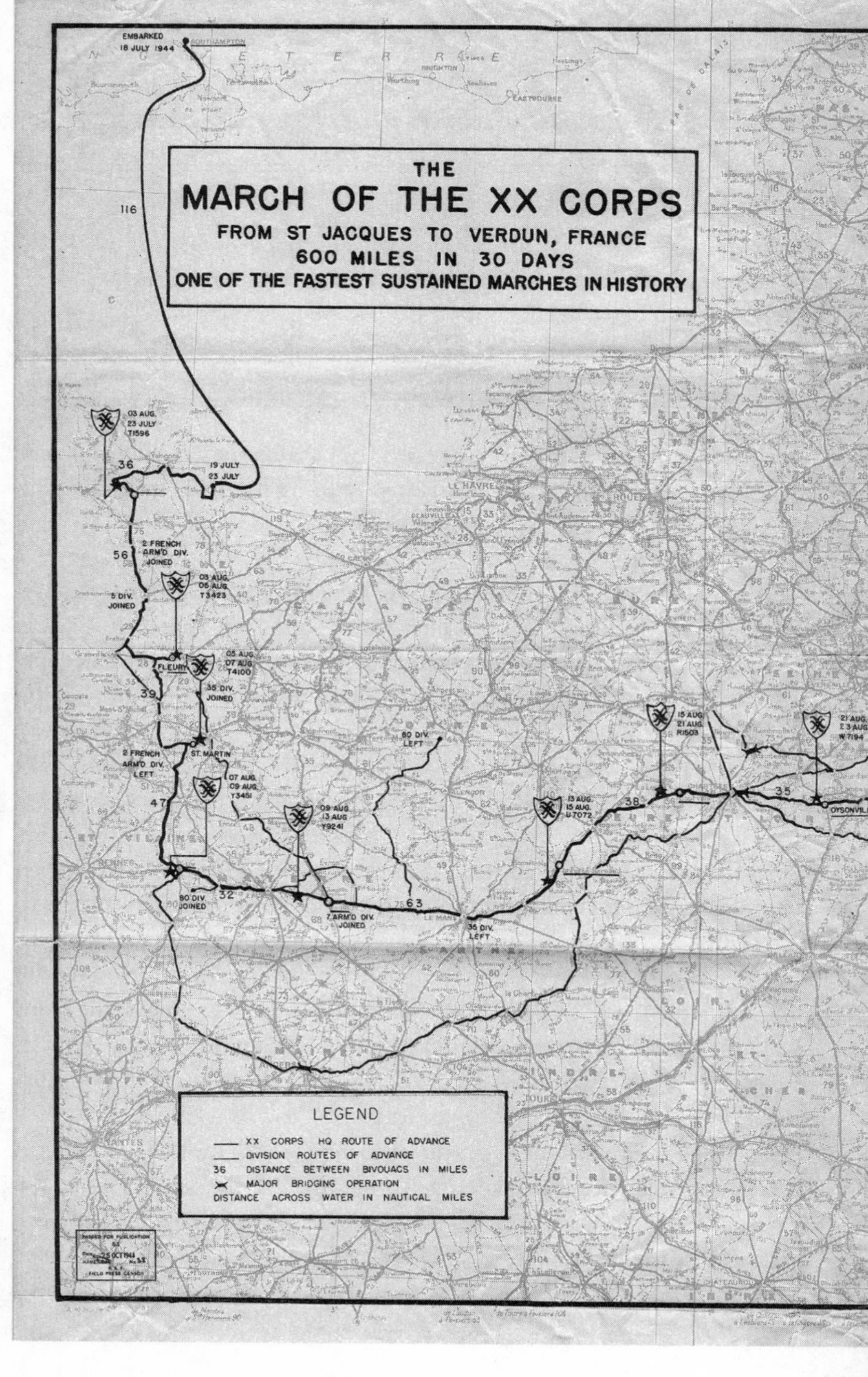
THE
MARCH OF THE XX CORPS
FROM ST JACQUES TO VERDUN, FRANCE
600 MILES IN 30 DAYS
ONE OF THE FASTEST SUSTAINED MARCHES IN HISTORY
EMBARKED
18 JULY 1944
SOUTHAMPTON
116
03 AUG.
23 JULY
T1596
19 JULY
23 JULY
36
56
2 FRENCH
ARM'D DIV.
JOINED
03 AUG.
05 AUG.
T3423
5 DIV.
JOINED
FLEURY
05 AUG.
07 AUG.
T4100
35 DIV.
JOINED
39
ST. MARTIN
2 FRENCH
ARM'D DIV.
LEFT
07 AUG.
09 AUG.
Y3451
47
09 AUG.
13 AUG.
Y9241
80 DIV.
LEFT
80 DIV.
JOINED
32
7 ARM'D DIV.
JOINED
63
35 DIV.
LEFT
13 AUG.
15 AUG.
U7072
15 AUG.
21 AUG.
R1503
38
35
21 AUG.
23 AUG.
W7194
OYSONVILLE
LE HAVRE
ROUEN
LE MANS
RENNES
TOURS
NANTES
LEGEND
XX CORPS HQ ROUTE OF ADVANCE
DIVISION ROUTES OF ADVANCE
36 DISTANCE BETWEEN BIVOUACS IN MILES
MAJOR BRIDGING OPERATION
DISTANCE ACROSS WATER IN NAUTICAL MILES
PASSED FOR PUBLICATION
FIELD PRESS CENSOR

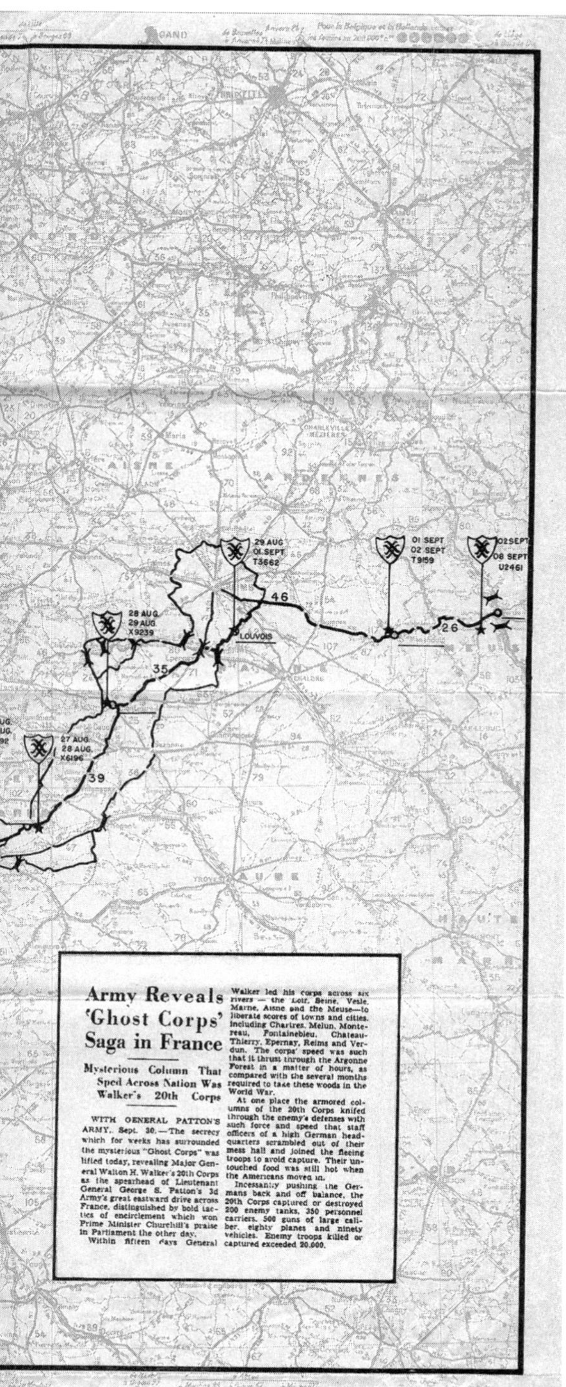

Army Reveals 'Ghost Corps' Saga in France

Mysterious Column That Sped Across Nation Was Walker's 20th Corps

WITH GENERAL PATTON'S ARMY, Sept. 30.—The secrecy which for weeks has surrounded the mysterious "Ghost Corps" was lifted today, revealing Major General Walton H. Walker's 20th Corps as the spearhead of Lieutenant General George S. Patton's 3d Army's great eastward drive across France, distinguished by bold tactics of encirclement which won Prime Minister Churchill's praise in Parliament the other day.

Within fifteen days General Walker led his corps across six rivers — the Loir, Seine, Vesle, Marne, Aisne and the Meuse—to liberate scores of towns and cities, including Chartres, Melun, Montereau, Fontainebleu, Chateau-Thierry, Epernay, Reims and Verdun. The corps' speed was such that it thrust through the Argonne Forest in a matter of hours, as compared with the several months required to take these woods in the World War.

At one place the armored columns of the 20th Corps knifed through the enemy's defenses with such force and speed that staff officers of a high German headquarters scrambled out of their mess hall and joined the fleeing troops to avoid capture. Their untouched food was still hot when the Americans moved in.

Incessantly pushing the Germans back and off balance, the 20th Corps captured or destroyed 200 enemy tanks, 350 personnel carriers, 500 guns of large caliber, eighty planes and ninety vehicles. Enemy troops killed or captured exceeded 20,000.

The March of the Twentieth Corps, July 18, 1944.

this duty, he wrote that he "never became comfortable about snooping in the private lives of people I lived with on a day-to-day basis."

To my father, the liberation of Paris was "the most exciting and uplifting event of the war." For days, jubilant crowds of soldiers, civilians, and journalists joined in a celebration of victory and freedom. Celebration replaced sleep. The French could not do enough for the soldiers, with plentiful food and drink. "The French," my father said, "could make good meals out of nothing."[1]

My father and his driver delayed their departure, ostensibly to continue to enjoy Paris. Might their delay also have been due to my father's mixed feelings about their next stop: Germany? On the one hand, as my father would write, "There was the satisfaction of returning as an American officer and seeing the German civilians, who were looking starved, scared, and poorly clothed. As far as I was concerned, every German was a Nazi and a war criminal." On the other hand, there would be a return to a homeland that was no longer his home, to where Jews had suffered and died.

Due to the nearby Battle of the Bulge—the final German offensive, fought from mid-December 1944 through the end of January 1945—my father and his troops were stationed for a few months in a small town in Alsace-Lorraine, staying in private homes with French families. They advanced through the Moselle/Saar area toward Trier, the first major city they occupied.

Then they crossed the Rhine and headed toward Frankfurt. My father described this experience in an interview:

> In January 1945 I entered Germany for the first time since I left. To land back on the continent that I didn't think I'd see again and then being close to the Germans was a traumatic experience. I didn't know what to expect—how much danger we'd be exposed to, I had the feeling of exuberation and uncertainty. One fear was that if I was captured and taken prisoner, what would happen? It was a mixed feeling to get so close, because it was all bottled up.
>
> When I was first back in Germany, everyone was a war criminal. I had a deep-seated hatred of the Germans. As miserable as the conditions were, I couldn't feel compassion —only hatred and contempt. I couldn't feel any other way—they're still alive and what happened to all the Jews?[2]

21

Frankfurt, 1945

"Give me ten years and I shall change the face of Germany."
This Hitler prophecy has found its full realization in the City of Frankfurt.

Annex No. 2 to G-2 Periodic Report NO 236
HQ Twentieth Corps
2 April 1945
[written by Rudolf Baum, Second Lieutenant]

On March 29, 1945, my father, dressed in his US Army uniform, had his hand on the doorknob that once provided entrée to the oak stairway that led to his family's fourth-floor apartment at Reuterweg 73, his home for the first nineteen years of his life. But the third and fourth floors, the top floors, had been destroyed by bombs. And the names next to the doorbells were unfamiliar. He pulled his hand away.

It had been nine years since he left Frankfurt. Everything had changed. Destruction was everywhere. The streets were deserted.

Still, as part of Patton's Third Army capturing Frankfurt, my father could take the opportunity to visit places of his youth. He went to the Philantropin, his elementary Jewish day school, only to discover the site of red crosses painted on the school's rooftop, indicating that the SS had confiscated this Jewish property to serve as a German Army hospital.

As he describes in his autobiography, he next proceeded a few blocks away to the Musterschule, the boys' *Gymnasium*, or secondary school, that he had attended. While the front of the building was still standing, most of it had been reduced to rubble. As he looked at the playground, he wondered what had happened to his classmates, how many had been killed.

He went to the Rat-Beil-Straße Cemetery, the Jewish cemetery where his grandparents and other family members were buried. But he was unable to locate any of their gravesites. Instead, he found broken and overturned headstones, headstones defiled with graffiti, headstones strategically stacked to build a useless anti-tank wall. Weeds overgrew it all.

Reuterweg 73, March 1945.

He went to Kaiserstraße, only a few blocks from the central train station, in search of his father's office. The entire block was razed. Nothing remained.

Before leaving Frankfurt, my father's final quest was to see the shoe factory Ada-Ada in Höchst, where he had worked for five years. He was surprised to find it still standing. However, as he walked through gates and doors that had been left wide open, he saw frenzied looting. Shoes, like most goods, had been rationed during the war, and people were fighting over them, mixing up pairs, trampling shoes that had fallen on the floor.

Forcing his way through the chaos, my father went upstairs to the offices, where a ghostly silence greeted him. He stood alone among the overturned filing cabinets and chairs of this once thriving business. Empty desks with familiar nameplates caused him to wonder—what happened to those people?

My father and his fellow soldiers had arrived in Frankfurt the night before, to sights that foreshadowed the destruction he would find. They had approached the River Main, bringing back my father's memories: "I thought back to the time when I had my canoe and spent summer weekends on the river."[1] He and his fellow soldiers initially were unable to cross because the retreating troops had blown up the river's seven bridges. They were delayed thirty-six hours while engineers erected pontoon bridges.

They then came upon bombed out streetcars with electric wires dangling overhead. That tangled mess marred the formerly inviting entrance to the *Stadion*, the sports complex where he swam and watched many a soccer game as a boy.

At the request of his commanding intelligence officer of the Twentieth Corps, my father, as a mere second lieutenant, wrote an annex about Frankfurt to the daily intelligence report under his commanding officer's name.

> The City of Frankfurt
>
> "Give me ten years and I shall change the face of Germany." This Hitler prophecy has found its full realization in the City of Frankfurt. Even for one who lived in the city for twenty years it is hard to find the way around since most of the prominent landmarks have been razed. Those still left standing are burned out shells. The parks, once the pride of the city, and today parking lots for U.S. Army vehicles, look neglected. Not a single house in the business district is left standing, and the store that once occupied the buildings have signs pinned to the ruins of their former stores, indicating that they either left the city or moved to the suburbs. . . .

Rudy, Frankfurt, March 30, 1945.

The civilian population appears to be about 2–300,000 which is roughly half of the original population. . . . The population of today is dispirited and demoralized. The people loot anything they can find, preferably food and alcohol. . . .

If given another ten years the face of Frankfurt will probably have changed some more. Entire city blocks will have been cleared away by bulldozers and grass will have grown over many famous sights of this once proud city.

Annex No. 2 to G-2 Periodic Report NO 236
HQ XX Corps
2 April 1945

My father made his way to the outskirts of town to reunite with his unit as it prepared to advance northeast.

In later years, he acknowledged that his prediction that "entire city blocks will have been cleared away . . . and grass will have grown over many famous sights" was far from what became reality. Frankfurt was rebuilt. He observed that, "Where there is grass, it is where they [the Germans] want it to grow. And where there is grass, there are signs that say 'Stay Off the Grass.'"

22

Buchenwald, 1945

I felt an enormous rage against the perpetrators of this evil, and a desperate feeling of helplessness in the face of all this suffering.

RUDY BAUM | "A Son of a Respectable Family"

It was the morning of my father's thirtieth birthday, April 11, 1945. It was the beginning of spring, so the weather was mild. As a member of a division of General George S. Patton's US Third Army, my father marched into Weimar, home to Goethe, Schiller, and Bach, and, later, the birthplace of the German Democratic Republic.

On their route of advance, my father and his fellow soldiers encountered something shocking: the smell of burning flesh.

And then, the site of one of the largest concentration camps in Germany: Buchenwald.

At the entry was a massive red brick structure with a third tier that served as a guard tower. The tower was surrounded by an oversized widow's walk and topped with a prominent clock and the SS flag. A barbed wire fence ran along the perimeter of the camp. The German guards were gone.

The troops passed through entry gates inscribed with *Jedem das Seine* ("to each his due"). Black smoke billowed from an imposing chimney. The acrid stench of death hung in the air.

And then there were the survivors. Walking skeletons drifted about, barely able to put one foot in front of the other. Flesh tautly wrapped around their bones, like drum skin stretched over a shell. A collage of skeletons covered the ground, too. Some were alive; many were not. The ghostly silence was occasionally stirred by a movement or shallow breath.

In some areas, only the dead remained—naked corpses lying face-up on wagons, many with their mouths wide open. As my father described it, they formed massive mounds of human flesh—shriveled bodies entwined with one another, blurring any distinction between one lifeless form and another. Layers of bodies had an apparent order—one with heads at the far end alternated with another that placed heads at the near end. They had been neatly stacked six feet high, like cordwood. [1]

Wagon after wagon of these ashen gray stacks awaited its turn in front of the still-burning crematorium. An eight-foot-tall brick wall housed the burning ovens, each of which had artfully carved arches framing a two-foot-by-three-foot door. Each oven held three trays. Each tray held three bodies. With almost ten ovens, nearly one hundred bodies could be burned simultaneously.[2]

I remember my father recalling that "the ovens were still burning" when the American troops entered the camp. He and the other soldiers referred to the survivors as "the walking dead" or the "living dead," as inscribed on the back of one of his photos.

In a speech my father would deliver years later, on February 12, 1995, he recalled: "The sights of the camp were shocking to non-Jewish American servicemen—how much more so for me, a Jew. But for the fortuitous circumstances of my life, I was standing there, not as a forlorn German/Jewish survivor, but as a determined American/Jewish officer." He saw emaciated survivors barely cloaked in the remnants of vertically striped dark blue and dirty gray fabric, like wire hangers dangling filthy rags. They were mostly men and some children, but the gender and age of many of them was indiscernible. Some sat propped up against a wood-shingled building. Some lay scattered among the dead in the wooden bunks.

My father and other soldiers walked through the quarters that had belonged to the camp's commandant, Hermann Pister. Scattered about were branding irons, cat-o'-nine-tails, sharp metal pointers wrapped with barbed wire, cudgels that sat like baseball bats waiting to be used.

There was also the notorious handiwork of Ilse Koch, the previous commandant's wife, more aptly known as the "Beast of Buchenwald." She was obsessed with skin and shrunken heads: tanned human skin, often with tattoos, made into book covers and lampshades of all sizes and types; a small ship with sails made of tanned human skin adorned with pictures of the Virgin and Child; multiple crosses made of human skin. A cross-section of a diseased human lung preserved in glass. A shrunken human head with a thick mop of brown hair and a brown closely shaven beard. Glass jars contained shrunken and shaved human heads that seem to stand at attention. And a huge jar held a human head of normal size, like bounty from a victorious hunting expedition.

Years later, my father would write: "I felt an enormous rage against the perpetrators of this evil, and a desperate feeling of helplessness in the face of all this

WS 10475

"Living Dead"

Buchenwald

April 1945

128

RUDY BAUM
6231 DEL[illegible]E LANE
DALLAS, TEXAS 75225
(214) 361-1483

Buchenwald, 1945.

suffering." After General Patton inspected the camp, he ordered the military police to round up Germans living in Weimar and force them to witness the horrors of Buchenwald before any of the dead were buried. He ordered the German-speaking American officers to prepare an exhibit of instruments of torture and of Ilse Koch's creations.

Patton's soldiers ushered the German citizens through the exhibit and the camp. Rounded up at bayonet point from the neighboring villages were three thousand well-dressed German citizens who reluctantly marched eight kilometers uphill to the camp.[3]

Greeting them upon their entry was a guard hung in effigy on gallows crudely constructed by camp survivors. The horrified townspeople seemed fearful of what awaited them. My father and his fellow soldiers formed a row on either side of the civilians to keep them in line. The civilians, in their finery, walked by the nearly lifeless skeletons leaning against the barracks and passed the mounds of bodies stacked on the wagons in front of the ovens.

The responsibility of the German-speaking American soldiers was to keep the line moving and ensure that each person saw the spectacle in its entirety. They showed no mercy, forcing the citizens to walk through with their eyes open wide, despite protests of denial and attempts to break away. Medics revived those who fainted.

After the seeing the camp, the mayor of Weimar died by suicide.

Years later, my father would write, "All denied knowing anything about the murders and the brutal conditions at the camp that had been going on a scant few miles from their homes for over seven years. These denials fueled the hatred I felt for all Germans. I had come to the conclusion that they were all guilty. Nothing I have experienced in my entire life can compare with the impact Buchenwald had on me. When I talk or think about the Holocaust it brings back to my mind pictures of the emaciated, dying victims in the camp." Pictures my father took of the Ilse Koch collection were kept in albums among our traditional family scrapbooks. I remember, as a child, sitting on the floor of our den, combing through stacks of bulging photo albums and scrapbooks—the old albums, with their black heavy pages, displaying photos held in place with black photo corners. The two pages of photos of the Ilse Koch exhibit and the German citizens marching through Buchenwald are burned in my memory.

Today, on those two pages, only the photo corners remain. My father donated several of the photos to the US Holocaust Memorial Museum in DC.

Rudy Baum, first American soldier on left (with his right hand on his pocket), along with other American soldiers, showing Weimar citizens the atrocities at Buchenwald, April 16, 1945. Photo taken by Walter Chichersky, US Signal Corps photographer. National Archives.

Yet those empty pages have tremendous impact on me, almost as much as the photos themselves.

Did my father reach a point of not being able to bear having those photos in his possession? He had said, "Man's inhumanity to man doesn't even describe it. It's almost unbelievable that something like that could have happened. . . . It was absolutely horrifying, and it was difficult to deal with. I lost quite a few in my family, and of course that affects you because you know when you see this, you have an idea what they went through . . . the image stays with you, and it stays with you forever."[4]

My father was unaware of photojournalists or cameramen at Buchenwald during the liberation. So, years later, in the 1970s, as he was reading *Time* magazine before going to sleep, he was amazed to stumble upon a picture of himself escorting the residents of Weimar through Buchenwald. I can't imagine he fell asleep too quickly after that.

Later, in the early 1990s, when he and my mother visited the US Holocaust Memorial Museum, he unexpectedly viewed a US Army newsreel documenting the liberation of Buchenwald. And there he was again, ushering the citizens of Weimar through the Ilse Koch exhibit and the camp. He subsequently requested a copy of the footage, which ultimately became a focal point of his talks with schoolchildren about his wartime experiences.

I once observed my father talking with eighth-graders visiting the Dallas Holocaust and Human Rights Museum. While most of the students were attentive, it was painful for me to hear some giggling and some making fun of my father's struggle to understand their questions or to hear them. But I have to assume that the video footage stayed with them.

After one such session, a student wrote:

> Dear Mr. Baum,
>
> I enjoyed your presentation very much. The facts that you presented during your speech were very informative. I hope that this horror will not happen again in the history of the earth. So for the rest of my life I will pass the word of the Holocaust to my family and to my children when I go to have children and I will hope my family passes it on from generation to generation.
>
> Thankful listener, Kaleb

At one of the many venues where my father spoke in the 1990s, he met a man—an elderly man, though younger than my father was at that point—who had been one of the young boys at Buchenwald who was barely alive, staring out from the bunks. The man was one of the one thousand young boys among the twenty-one thousand survivors liberated at the camp. He was Elie Wiesel, the Romanian-born Jewish American professor, author, and activist who dedicated his life to ensuring that the Holocaust would not be forgotten. My father thanked Wiesel for being "a wonderful example." Elie Wiesel thanked my father.

Almost sixty years after my father's experience at Buchenwald, my sister and I came across my father's footlocker from his army days. We were helping my parents to move out of their house of fifty-two years. We lifted the trunk from a high shelf in the garage and carried it to the driveway to unlock its treasures. After jostling the creaky locks, we opened the lid.

The interior was lined with yellowed paper printed with tiny flowers. When we saw that the removable top tray was filled with coloring books, children's books, and drawings that once belonged to our older brother, we anticipated that the main trunk, beneath the tray, would contain *our* childhood mementos, a treasure trove that would bring smiles to our faces.

But no.

Instead, we discovered two cat-o'-nine-tails, a wooden nightstick, a French bayonet, a Nazi officer's knife, an SS dagger in its scabbard, and two SS helmets.

We wanted to load it all into a giant trash bag and throw it out as quickly as possible. But once we got past the initial shock, we spoke with our father, who suggested that he might sell it to a collector. With a brief conversation, we convinced him to donate the items to the Dallas Holocaust and Human Rights Museum. That afternoon, the museum sent someone to pick up the trunk and its contents. I was glad to see it go.

23

Marburg and Palestine, 1945

We lived like kings.

RUDY BAUM | on his experiences in Marburg, Germany

In June 1945, Rudy's tour of duty was extended. As a first lieutenant, he was appointed media control officer, a member of the Western Military District's field office, District Information Services Control Commands (DISCC) 6871, in Marburg, Germany.

His mission on behalf of the US Army? To try to reestablish Marburg's cultural life, to restore the German culture and freethinking that the Nazis had destroyed.

A picturesque university town, Marburg has medieval architecture and an atmosphere reminiscent of a Grimm's fairy tale, which in fact were collected and published by the Brothers Grimm in Marburg. The town was spared significant damage during the war because it had been designated a hospital city from 1942 to 1945, with some of its schools and government buildings converted to hospital wards to house wounded German soldiers.

My father and three enlisted men, all former members of the US Army Intelligence Service and fluent in German, took up residence at Georg Voigt Straße 33, a rambling, fully furnished, three-story house with a tiled roof, which became known as the Marburg Billet. Tucked in the hillside, it offered a magnificent view of the landscape from its balcony. The house also served as their office, their typewriters lined up side by side like soldiers ready to take orders.

One of the first people my father hired was his "right hand" to manage the house. Ewald Cordes was a displaced East German. He hired most of the house staff, including cleaners and local *Hausfraus* as cooks, who prepared spectacular German fare. My father and his enlisted men hosted all sorts of dignitaries, including fellow military men from abroad, and threw parties for the locals. As reported in the pamphlet "A Personal History of the Marburg

Rudy, 1945.

Newspaper Conference," by Tim Aronson, a British sergeant, "The Marburg billet was famed throughout the land for its food, view, and hospitality."

My father also hired a driver, Samson Knoll. He and his enlisted men lived like the royalty that had once inhabited the nearby castle, the Marburger Schloss.

How did my father reconcile his deep anger about what he witnessed in Buchenwald with his efforts to gain favor from the locals and help Germany revive itself?

My father's highest priority was to launch the *Marburger Presse*, similar to other postwar free presses such as the *Aachener Nachrichten* and the *Frankfurter Rundschau*—licensed and supported freethinking newspapers in the US Zone. His challenge was to hire a publisher and an editor who not only had the right blend of journalistic and technical skills but also held democratic political views and had never been sympathetic to the Nazis. For candidates for all positions, my father and his fellow soldiers ran extensive background checks and administered questionnaires about the candidate's political activities during the period of 1933 to 1945. They verified the information through an extensive network they had developed.

After a two-month search, my father hired Hermann Bauer, a native of Marburg, and Karl Bremer, as the publisher and editor, respectively. They had little time to lay the groundwork for the newspaper. Six weeks later, on September 14, the *Marburger Presse* would be launched.

During the week before the launch, my father traveled to Frankfurt, only sixty miles away, to attend Rosh Hashanah services at the Westend Synagogue, the synagogue of his youth. Parts of the synagogue had been sufficiently restored to host the services. Years later, my father recounted, "I spent Rosh Hashanah in Frankfurt, in the synagogue that had been partially rehabilitated, with a couple of friends who were also in the service. In fact, I have a total namesake [Rudolf Baum], who lives in St. Louis, who also comes from Frankfurt. And we met, and another fellow met, and we spent the holiday together. And, of course, that's something that you'll never forget. You'll always remember. And, of course, that was in a way, a traumatic experience to go back to."[1]

The *Marburger Presse* would be launched to extensive fanfare, including a cocktail party that my father and his troop hosted for a small group of military government officials and local German dignitaries. The newspaper born that day still exists. After merging with the *Oberhessische Zeitung*, it is known today as the *Oberhessische Presse*, comprising a regional daily newspaper with a circulation of approximately 28,000, three weeklies with a circulation of approximately 118,000, a Saturday magazine with a circulation of approximately 85,000 as well as an online presence.

The next major responsibility for my father was to be the man on the ground for the *Presse Konferenz*, a major newspaper conference to be hosted by the *Marburger Presse.* It was the first of its kind, and the idea was to encourage licensed publishers and editors of the German press in the American occupation zone to discuss how to manage a newspaper without political censorship. It brought together newspaper people from the American, British, and French zones. Among the attendees were concentration camp survivors, communists, and liberals, including Dr. Theodor Heuss, who would become the first president of the Federal Republic of Germany only a few years later. The conference was the brainchild of Cedric Belfrage, a member of the British Security Coordination, or BSC, a covert organization that had been set up in May 1940 in New York City's Rockefeller Center by the British Secret Intelligence Service (MI6) to promote British interests in the US, counter Nazi propaganda, and protect the Atlantic convoys from enemy sabotage.

My father was responsible for ensuring housing for the conference (without knowing how many would attend), planning meals (in the face of food shortages), scheduling meetings, and booking meeting rooms. Essential in the planning was Eugen Siebecke, the *Oberbürgermeister* (mayor) of the City of Marburg. He was a large man, who, like Bauer and Bremer and many Germans, did not quite fill out his clothes because he had not consumed his accustomed bounty of food during the war.

As described in "A Personal History of the Marburg Newspaper Conference," the *Oberbürgermeister* tripped over himself trying to please the American and British hosts of the conference. He insisted that Marburg would cover the entire cost of the conference. He placed ads in the *Presse*, asking the townspeople to open their homes to the visitors. He arranged for anti-curfew permits. He booked the required rooms, including the large conference room and the smaller rooms at the university. As Tim Aronson observed, "The conference took place in the *Kinderklinik* (children's clinic), which was full of newborn babies and kids with bandaged heads. A strange setting, but symbolically appropriate for the new press."

Siebecke arranged for the Europaischer Hof, a local hotel, as the venue for the elaborate meals, which included tongue, goose with baked apple, and several varieties of cake. The *Oberbürgermeister* requested that the American officers attend the formal Saturday night banquet, to offer the Americans everything that the Germans in attendance would have.

Upon entering the conference, participants encountered the equivalent of an extensive Christmas celebration, creatively assembled by Cordes. Fir trees lined the room and a dazzling electric sign, *Welcome, DISCC 6871, Marburg,* decorated the entrance. A brightly lit Great Seal of the United States was braided with evergreen and had an "eternal flame" continually roaring, with the help of a hair dryer. My father served as the master of ceremonies and acted as the chairman until the election of a conference chairman.

For my father, holding a microphone was as natural as holding a pen. Was that venue where he showed the first signs of a talent for public speaking? He provided the opening remarks, publicly crediting Cedric Belfrage and introducing the *Oberbürgermeister* and Lieutenant Colonel John B. Stanley, commanding officer of the 6871 DISCC Western Military District. The agenda unfolded, with publishers and editors reporting on the history and current problems of their respective newspapers. Some of the dignitaries went to the Georg Voigt billet for lunch. Dessert was a big cake decorated as an American flag in red, white, and blue, complete with its thirteen stripes and forty-eight stars.

My father was so exhausted by the end of the day that he went to bed early and skipped the Saturday banquet. The next day, after a debate about the pros and cons of journalism schools and a discussion about forming a Free German Publishers' Association, he delivered the closing remarks. My father later reflected that watching that conference unfold and come to a successful conclusion was the highlight of his stay in Marburg. Because it gave him a chance to shine in a new context? Or did he feel that such pro-democracy action was stomping on any seeds of a future Nazi-like movement?

* * *

In the fall of 1945, my father applied for a leave from Marburg to visit his sister Gretel in Palestine. After navigating much bureaucracy, my father agreed to serve an additional sixty days of overseas duty with the understanding he would be granted the two-week leave, plus travel time, and would be promoted to captain. For that period he was attached to a leave center that was part of the Middle East Service Command.

The trip, too, was somewhat arduous. Rudy hitched a ride on a bomber, probably from nearby Frankfurt, to Nice, France. He then took a train to Marseille, where he was able to get military transport to Rome. But due to unrest in Palestine, he learned, it was off-limits to all personnel that did not have priority clearance. By chance, he ran into an army friend whose orders authorized unrestricted travel. Rudy and his friend went to the officers' club, made a copy of the friend's orders, and typed in my father's name on the copy.

My father was then off to Cairo. After sightseeing for a few days, he took a commercial flight to Lydda Airport, near Tel Aviv. Upon arrival, he gave the taxi driver his Gretel's name and address. By chance, the driver was a German refugee who already knew her.

Gretel and her handsome, blond ten-year-old son, Micha, were living in Petah Tikvah, a town about six and a half miles east of Tel Aviv. Her husband, Reuben, who before the war had struggled financially, was serving in the British Royal Air Force, bringing home monthly pay. Gretel worked as a clerk at a nearby British Army base. For the first time, she and her husband could count on a steady income as long as the war continued.

Rudy arrived unannounced, and no one was home. My father slipped a

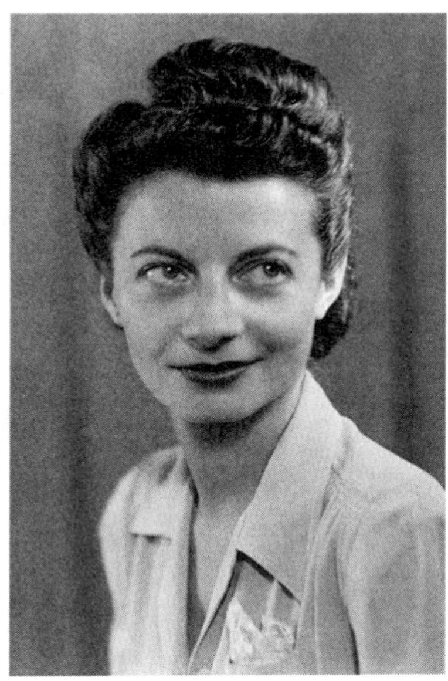

Gretel, Palestine, 1947.

handwritten note under her door. His walk through town confirmed the unrest, with British tanks and soldiers visibly in force.

When Gretel finally did come home, she accidentally pushed the slip of paper aside with her foot, not seeing it at first, only to later discover the reunion that awaited her. She immediately went shopping for something special for dinner—liver and onions, among my father's favorites.

Rudy and Gretel had not seen each other for eleven years, and had had little communication over the last two of them. Since they had last seen each another, Gretel had attended an agricultural school, worked in orange groves, and lived in a tent in sand dunes as part of a process toward the founding of the Ein Gev Kibbutz, where she had lived for a number of years.

In that time period, my father had made a life for himself in America. Gretel was proud to walk the streets—past curfew—with her little brother, an American Army officer now and much taller than she was. The two walked and talked for hours, wondering together about the fate of many family members and friends, sharing what they each knew. Their reunion had to be bittersweet, with the realization that they had survived their parents, and that they did not know the circumstances of their parents' deaths.

* * *

When my father returned to Marburg in November 1945, he received word that he had been promoted to captain, as promised, and that he must close the military intelligence unit on Georg Voigt Street by the end of the year and return home in the next eight weeks. Knoll, my father's driver, sent a Western Union telegram to my mother, announcing "Captain Baum due home about first of year." My father sent her two more telegrams—one a few days before he left and another upon his arrival in New York City.

By way of a formal goodbye, my father and his Marburg crew hosted an American-style open house on Christmas Day, inviting a vast number of their military and civilian friends. The "by invitation only" party became the most sought after event in town.

The guests filled the house, wall to wall. The community hailed my father with many toasts, including poetry. One of the townspeople recited this verse, among others:

For many long, long months has he
Been staying now in Germany,
And more than 4 years even passed
Since "Mister" Baum wore mufty [*sic*] last.

This work was often pretty tough
And caused him grief and pains enough.
Not only Chief but Soul was he
Of Marburg DISCC.

And now the day has come when he
Returns to Texas actually.
We by this fact are rendered sad
Yet we enjoy that *he* is glad. . . . etc.

And not to be outdone, another recited:

If any one here in this town ~
Be he of small or great renown,
Be he artiste or licensee,
Professor of a faculty,

Sportsman, reporter for the press
has trouble with his business,
Straight to "kind Mister Anthony"
(i.e., Lieutenant Baum) goes he,
Who not a single time denies
A cigarette and his advice.

Such patience and such helpfulness
You don't find anywhere, I guess;
And many clients heard I say,
"I wish he would for *ever* stay!" . . . etc.

In all likelihood, my father prepared remarks and took the microphone, if there was one, given his ease and pleasure in addressing a crowd. His words would likely have been those of an American Army captain who felt connected to many of the locals. He often later recounted how the people of Marburg had treated him and his men well and made them feel welcome—and been indispensable in helping his group accomplish its goals. In the end, Rudy's record would earn him the Bronze Star Medal for meritorious service in connection with military operations against an enemy of the United States.

Shortly after the Marburg celebration, my father wrote one of his last wartime letters to my mother. Based on the numbering on the handful of their letters that remain, they may have written as frequently as every other day, especially during the first six to eighteen months. In addition to airmail, they occasionally used the slightly faster victory mail, also known as V-mail, which censored, photographed, and then sent letters abroad via microfilm to be printed upon arrival at the destination post office.

On January 21, 1946, my father wrote to my mother:

Hello Darling:

Well, this is the letter I've been long hoping to write. The last one from Marburg. In about 1½ hours I'll be leaving here to go down to Headquarters. Knoll is going to drive me down. This morning I mailed you two boxes and one package. The latter contains some dirty laundry and a couple of pairs of shoes in need of repairs. The small box has the typewriter in it and the large one has all the things I didn't want to carry or throw away. Wonder who'll arrive first, the boxes or I.

Made about 10 farewell visits which I finished yesterday afternoon. . . .

So this is good-bye Marburg after eight months. It felt quite a bit like home here and the leaving is accordingly. But the things I have to look forward so much outweigh the little I leave behind. . . .

All my love and loads of kisses. I love you! Rudy

One of the items in the large box that my father shipped home was a Turkish sword from the early 1800s known as a *yatagan*. With its gold and brown tapestry-covered scabbard and coral hilt, the *yatagan* subsequently hung in our home in Dallas. In 2002, my father gave it to my oldest son, Matthew, for becoming a *bar mitzvah*. That sword is our tangible connection to Marburg.

Our intangible connection to Marburg is my father's enlightened view about collective guilt. Prior to his experience in Marburg, my father felt rage at "the Germans," as a collective entity, viewing every German as a war criminal and perpetrator of evil. After his eight months in Marburg—interviewing, interacting with, and working side by side with scores of non-Jewish Germans—he gradually came to view "the Germans" as individuals.

He would later write, "In screening so many different people I got to meet individuals who proved to be decent human beings who had been active in the anti-Nazi movement. Yet I still had problems dealing with the Germans. I did a lot of soul searching . . . and reluctantly concluded that not every German could be held responsible for the heinous crimes committed during the Nazi years."[2]

And, as my father put it years later, "I came to the conclusion that the concept of collective guilt that everyone is a criminal is not the right approach. The generations of Germans today can't be held responsible for the actions of their parents and grandparents."[3]

When my father left Marburg, he took the train to Le Havre to board the *Smith Victory*, one of the fleet of Victory ships transporting troops home. As he wrote later, it was "the beginning of the end of a long journey."

24

Dallas, 1959

Ultimately, the petitioners are not to blame for their lack of evidence.
MAX CAHN | attorney for Rudy and Gretel, defending restitution claim

It would be just over twelve years after he left Marburg, in the late 1950s, that my father and his sister, Gretel, hired a Frankfurt lawyer, Max Cahn, to file their restitution claims in pursuit of the property my grandparents had left behind when they were taken out of Frankfurt and, one way or another, sent to their deaths. At that time, many victims of Nazi persecution from Germany, Austria, and elsewhere as well as descendants of those who had perished in the Holocaust filed such claims.

Mr. Cahn's office was at Kaiserstraße 18–20, just a few doors down from where my grandfather had moved his office in the late 1930s. What was it like for my father to engage in a claim against his country of birth, a "restitution claim by Rudolf Baum against the Deutsches Reich," requiring ongoing correspondence with the financial authorities of Germany?

Whatever the emotional ramifications, it was far from an easy legal process. The initial documentation, sent to the State Office of Asset Control and Restitution in Frankfurt am Main, comprised a notarized copy of the certificates of inheritance, confirming through German consulate forms completed by Rudy and Gretel that they were the rightful heirs of both Julie's estate and Norbert's estate. The certificate for Julie's estate said that she "last lived in Frankfurt/Main and died on May 3, 1942 in Litzmannstadt," and then stated that she had left three-eighths of her estate to each of her children, and one quarter to her husband, Norbert, "who has been declared dead effective Dec. 31, 1945, as of the judgment of the Court in Frankfurt on Jan. 24, 1956."

My father and Gretel also provided the State Office with a notarized copy of a certificate by the Jewish Community Frankfurt/Main dated August 28, 1955, stating that "the married spouses Baum were deported to Litzmannstadt on October 19, 1941. As a result their personal property must have been confiscated at this time."

How did these words . . . *died on. . .who has been declared dead effective . . . Litzmannstadt. . . their personal property must have been confiscated* . . . echo in my father's consciousness?

Max Cahn forwarded a notarized record from the Frankfurter Bank, stating the amount of Reichsmarks in Norbert's savings account on April 15, 1942, all of which had been transferred to the Treasury Office (*Finanzkasse*) on that date as property forfeited to the Reich, and certifying that no special Jewish surcharges (*Jüdische Sonderabgaben*) had been paid from this account and no added deposits had been made into this account.

The Regional Tax Office of Frankfurt wrote to the State Office of Asset Control and Restitution, in a letter dated March 17, 1959, "objection concerning the restitution matter," without specifying why. A few weeks later, the Regional Tax Office sent a follow-up statement, saying that "it cannot make a decision at present due to insufficient substantiation of the claim," and encouraged "further proof of the dispossession, such as a receipt for the objects of precious metal, or files for foreign currency."

My father sent a sworn statement about his parents' household inventory, as "further proof of the dispossession," for the restitution claim:

> I, the undersigned Rudolf Baum, 6231 Del Norte Lane, Dallas 25, Texas, herewith swear to the following, having been told about the significance and instructed that a false oath would be punishable by law.
>
> For my person, I emigrated from Frankfurt/Main in Oct./Nov. 1936. My parents, the spouses Norbert Nathan Baum and Julie Baum, née Geiger stayed back in Frankfurt/Main, Eysseneckstr. 20. I last saw the apartment and its contents in October 1936.

He listed the contents of the living room/study, the dining room, and kitchen, and bedroom. In addition, he claimed "the inventory of a complete household, including bed and table and household linen, a radio, clothing etc., curtains, chandeliers" as well as specific sets of china and crystal. Also, his father's gold pocket watch with its gold chain; the items of his mother's jewelry; and the silver, including cutlery, vases, and bowls.

He then stated: "As the co-owner of the firm Norbert Harff oHG, Frankfurt/Main, Grosser Kornmarkt 18, wholesale in lining fabric and notions for tailors, my father had such an income that he had no need to sell off household items or items of jewelry and precious metal during the following years [after 1936]. Therefore I am certain that my parents surrendered the items of jewelry and precious metals mentioned above in the spring of 1939, when all Jews had to give up their possessions of jewelry and precious metals." My father had forced himself to remember and recount the contents of the home in which he grew up. But the response from the Regional Tax Office was dismissive: "R. Baum's sworn statement can only be regarded as supporting evidence, (not as proof), because the petitioner already emigrated in 1936 and therefore was not witness to the confiscation process. The confiscation of these objects would have to be proven by providing requisite papers or statements by witnesses."

Supporting evidence. Insufficient proof.

So Max Cahn provided the authorities notarized sworn statements from two more people. In a notarized and sworn testimony, Emil Hirsch, a close friend of Julie and Norbert, stated: "My wife and I used to live in Frankfurt/Main. We had known Mr. Norbert Nathan Baum and his wife Julie, née Geiger, for many years. Based on many visits to their apartment we can confirm that they owned a complete inventory comprising furniture and other furnishings such as porcelain, crystal, silver etc. Concerning jewelry we knew that Mrs. Baum had quite a few pieces, but we cannot remember the exact number and type."

The second testimony was from my father's first cousin, Albert C. Baum, to whom Julie often referred in her letters. Albert stated:

> Mr. Norbert Nathan Baum, who used to live in Frankfurt/M, Wolfsgangsstr. 132, was my uncle. I myself lived in Frankfurt until 1937 and visited my uncle regularly over many years. I last saw my uncle's apartment in the fall of 1937, when I traveled from Holland to Leipzig to attend a trade fair and also stopped in Frankfurt. I have been presented with the sworn statement of Rudolf Baum dated April 2, 1959. Most of the items enumerated in this statement are known to me. I remember the gentleman's study with the bookcase, desk, easy chair, and paintings; also the dining room comprising the sideboard, dresser, dining chairs upholstered with leather, the piano and pictures, as well as the bedroom and the kitchen. I also recall the radio and the precious china, as well as the silver, which I always admired there. Of course today I cannot make a detailed statement any more about the number of items, but I know that the named items were present there in those numbers.

At the same time, Max Cahn was told by the Frankfurter Bank about another savings account that existed already in January 1, 1940, with a smaller amount of money. The Regional Tax Office of Frankfurt was willing to recognize those two accounts, but was not "able to acknowledge" the rest of the claim "based on the sworn statements presented. Such statements only have the status of additional evidence, as long as other sources of evidence have not been exhausted." It continued: "As the persecuted ones had a bank account with the Frankfurter Bank, we ask to inquire there, if there was a payment recorded in 1939 by the municipal loan institution due to forced confiscated precious metals. There is also no proof regarding the confiscation of the inventory of the apartment and other household items. Besides, the inventory remaining at the time of the deportation would have to be detailed more precisely. Perhaps the claimant is still able to name persons (acquaintances, neighbors, co-tenants) who knew their circumstances. We cannot do without an additional proof."

My father and Gretel had no choice but to continue to fight to evidence the material possessions that their parents were forced to abandon when they were deported.

The next witness they found was someone who had not left Frankfurt: Lucie Bermann. In an interview conducted by both a representative of the Regional Tax Office and a partner in Max Cahn's firm, Lucie Bermann stated:

> My name is Lucie Bermann. I am 71 years old, housewife, and live in Frankfurt/M, Gagernstr. 36. I am neither related nor related by marriage to the claimant. As far as I remember I have visited the apartment of the persecuted in Reuterweg only once on the occasion of the confirmation of their son Rudolf. My daughter and the co-petitioner Grete Ramati were of the same age, they attended the same school and the same dancing lessons. These dancing lessons were so-called "roving dance lessons" which took place in the apartments of the participants. From this fact it can be concluded that also the persecuted had enough space and inventory to host the dancing lessons also occasionally in their apartment.
>
> For me it was obvious, that the persecuted couple Mr. and Mrs. Baum were living in well-situated /i.e. comfortable/ circumstances. As I only visited the apartment once, I cannot provide detailed information about the inventory of objects made of precious metals.

After hearing my father's sworn statement regarding the inventory of his parents' home, she commented: "I think it definitely possible, even very probable, that the statement of the applicant Rudolf Baum is true. I believe that Mrs. Julie Baum also wore jewelry, but I cannot make a statement about the appearance or the quality of that jewelry. I can only confirm once again that the statement of the claimant appears to be thoroughly credible."

And then, two more sworn statements, from friends who had emigrated from Frankfurt to Palestine. A dear friend of Gretel's, Liesel Bernstein, stated:

> I, Liesel Bernstein, née Bermann, was born in Frankfurt/Main on May 12, 1912, and lived there first on Gaertnerweg 44 and subsequently until my emigration in Beethovenstraße 38. Mrs. Grete Ramati, née Baum, was my classmate and friend, first in the Elisabethenschule, and later in the Viktoriaschule. We often visited each other at home. I remember that her parents had a spacious four-room apartment on Reuterweg 73. As a child I was invited there frequently for larger children's parties and later on as a teenager I was there quite often for dance events in a larger format. The Baum Family had a haute-bourgeois inventory, among other things a piano, carpets, crystal, china, silver, table linen, a gramophone and a library. I remember that Mrs. Baum wore jewelry, but I cannot recall individual pieces and therefore cannot describe them. I wish to emphasize that the household and the lifestyle of the Baum Family was equal to a well-situated family.

And then a sworn statement by Karoline Oppenheimer:

> I am Karoline Oppenheimer and was born in Mannheim on Oct. 9, 1892. I emigrated from Frankfurt in June 1938. In Frankfurt I was well acquainted with the couple Norbert Nathan Baum and Julie Baum, née Geiger. I often came to their home in order to play music with Mrs. Baum, while my husband played cards with Mr. Baum. Therefore I got to know the household of the family quite well. The Baum Family lived in a very spacious, well appointed four-room apartment in the best neighborhood. They had a gentleman's study with a large library, the floors were covered with Persian carpets. The dining room was very elegant. The buffet and the sideboard were laden with china, crystal and silver. I especially recall a large silver tea service, because I frequently remarked that I would not want to clean it. There also was a richly equipped box of silverware. Although I never entered their bedroom, I am sure that they had one. The kitchen was upper middle class and appointed generously with all sorts of implements. From my own observations I know that the Baum Family was amply supplied with linens, they owned especially damask table linens with hemstitching. I often was

able to admire that elegant linen. I also know that Mrs. Baum owned lots of jewelry, but I cannot recall individual pieces.

In response, the Regional Tax Office on July 11, 1960, stated that it regrets being unable "to acknowledge the expropriation of the precious metal objects and household items due to the lack of appropriate documentation, because the statements of Lucie Bernstein and Karoline Oppenheimer do not clarify what happened to the precious metal objects and how much of the inventory was still present at the time of deportation."

Do not clarify . . . how much was still present at the time of deportation. Even now, insufficient proof.

The Regional Tax Office also stated that "the scrutiny of the foreign currency file led to the result that the persecuted ones had to secure their living by selling their household items and were supported by Mrs. Hedwig Kahn during 1941. According to the foreign currency file, the [Norbert Harff] company was liquidated at the beginning of 1939. Therefore it is questionable, if the inventory of the apartment as claimed by the petitioner was still complete at the time of deportation. Is the petitioner able to provide further proof for this, especially suitable witnesses? Considering the values in question we unfortunately cannot do without supplemental proof."

Thus, if the Nazis forced them to sell items off before they were confiscated, no restitution would be awarded. They would receive compensation only for what they had when the Gestapo came to the door. My father and Gretel had no more witnesses to provide. No more proof. Their parents dead. Their parents' possessions likely taken by the Nazis, though Germany was demanding a dizzyingly high bar of proof.

As a final plea, Max Cahn wrote to the State Office of Asset Control and Restitution:

> The petitioners are unable to provide further proof concerning their claims for restitution. Regarding the household goods, it is impossible to understand the connection between the liquidation of the company and the household inventory. All Jewish companies were forced to be dissolved at the end of 1938. This does not mean at all that this also caused the household inventory to be dissolved. This objection could be made by the Regional Tax Office in practically every restitution claim. As can be seen from the foreign currency files, the persecuted one still owned bank accounts totaling 3.640 RM on Dec. 1, 1939. Therefore there was no reason for the persecuted ones

> to sell household goods due to financial need. The same is also true for the objects of precious metal and jewelry in their possession. The expropriation of items of jewelry and precious metals is known to have taken place already in the spring of 1939, that is, at a time, when the persecuted ones still had enough money to live on.
>
> If some part of the household items had to be sold in 1941, as can be gathered from the foreign currency files, then this part of the inventory may be deducted from the claims for restitution. One cannot, however, completely deny any claim for restitution for this reason. Since every sale was reported to the Exchange Control Office, it follows that no other sales have taken place other than the ones reported. Besides, the Regional Tax Office cannot ask the impossible concerning the proofs. Ultimately, the petitioners are not to blame for their lack of evidence. Further objections of the Regional Tax Office only serve to delay and are not helping to resolve the issue.

The response of the Regional Tax Office, on October 25, 1960, was: "In the present restitution claim the proof for expropriation of the items mentioned in the list of inventory is still missing. The petitioner may declare which sum he thinks adequate for a settlement. Thereby it needs to be considered that the proof of expropriation is still missing and that the insufficiently clarified matter cannot remain without influence for the amount of the settlement. If these circumstances are taken into consideration, there is a prospect for an amicable settlement."

On January 9, 1961, Max Cahn engaged in oral negotiations with the Regional Tax Office in Frankfurt and negotiated a settlement for a sum that took into account the bank records and "the expropriation of objects of precious metal and jewelry, a radio, and household items." Although the settlement was far less than what my father or Gretel believed they were entitled to, they had no other avenues to pursue. Their settlement was but a tiny drop of the $70 billion negotiated in the 1950s to be paid by Germany. These types of claims continue today.[1]

On January 23, 1961, came another letter from the State Office of Asset Control and Restitution, one that declared, "The case is resolved."

Baum family, 1956.

Rudy, circa 1956.

25

Dallas, 1961–1963

"How do these young girls please you?"
JULIE BAUM | words written on the back of a 1938 photograph

In 1949, my parents moved to Dallas and became immersed in the Dallas German Jewish community. By 1956, they had three children: Richard ("Dick"), then Diane, and, lastly, me.

My father was a seasoned traveling shoe salesman, most recently representing the women's footwear brand Buskens.

Sometime around 1961, my parents were poring over photo albums with Ruth and Albert Heydemann, their newest friends in the German Jewish community in Dallas. Ruth (née Simon) Heydemann and my father were both from Frankfurt, but had not known each other there, in part because Ruth was five years younger than my father.

Ruth and Albert had moved to Dallas from Baltimore in 1961. When Albert first came to scout out Dallas, Ruth suggested that he look up this fellow Rudy Baum who had been mentioned in the *Aufbau* as the president of Dallas Selfhelp, an organization to help German Jewish refugees assimilate into American culture.

When Albert called, my father invited him over for dinner. Albert, a stocky jovial man with curly brown hair, entered our house and, upon meeting me, immediately said, "I have a little girl just your age. Lynnie is her name."

Albert placed a present in my five-year-old hands—a coloring book with a red cover. Ecstatic to have a present, I was also thinking, "Yuck. I don't like the kids of my parents' friends." But when Lynnie Heydemann and I met a few short months later, we became fast friends.

As Ruth and Albert and my parents looked through the photo albums, one image, in particular, grabbed Ruth's eye. It was among the sepia photos sent to my father by his parents in the late 1930s, from their Wolfsgangstraße apartment. It showed my grandparents seated next to one another, with two young women in their late teens leaning on the back of another chair. And in that chair sat a woman in her fifties, a contemporary of my grandmother.

Standing from left: Ruth Simon and Trudy Rohm. *Seated from left:* Frau Löwenstein, Julie, and Norbert. January 1938.

Pointing to one of the two young women leaning on the back of the chair, Ruth asked my father if he knew who that young woman was. At that moment, my father realized that Ruth was that very woman.

I imagine a mix of smiles with nods and comments such as "*ja*" and "*natürlich*" [naturally] followed. My father must have then removed the picture from the safekeeping of its four photo corners, perhaps to verify a date on the back, only to see, once again after these many years, my grandmother's handwritten words: "An evening by Frau Löwenstein with Trudy Rohm and Ruth Simon, the young girls who remember Eric [Löwenstein]. How do these young girls please you? January, 1938." I find myself wondering: how did the rereading of my grandmother's words, more than two decades later, jar my father at that moment?

The connection of Ruth to my grandparents? Frau Löwenstein, the woman seated in the picture, was the neighbor whom my grandmother frequently mentioned in her letters. She was not only a dear friend of my grandmother, but also the mother of Ruth's boyfriend at the time, Eric Löwenstein.

So Ruth knew my grandmother. She knew her at a time when my father knew her life only through correspondence. Ruth had been in their Wolfsgangstraße apartment. She knew many of the people mentioned in the letters. That Frankfurt connection was the foundation of what came to be a lifelong friendship.

* * *

In 1963, my father—at the age of forty-eight, with three children—was fired from his job as a traveling salesman for the Viva! Americana division of US Shoe Corporation, after one too many clashes with his boss. That meant he was home almost all the time. I wasn't running to greet him on Fridays, after his week of travel, which had always seemed like an eternity to me.

When he lost his job, I remember wondering, as a seven-year-old would—Will I still get to have my birthday party when I turn eight on April 3? Will I still get a new bathing suit just like all my friends?

I heard hushed conversations between my parents. One night, my mother was giving me a bath, a night I remember because I did not want my bath to end, as the bath was the last part of our evening routine before sleep and dreams. And it was dreams I feared that night. Every night we had dinner at 5:30, then washed and dried the dishes, then bath and bedtime. On Sunday evenings, we would watch *The Ed Sullivan Show*. But this time, during the previous night, I had had a vivid nightmare after watching *The Wizard of Oz*. The Wicked Witch of the West had chased me, yelling "my pretty" in her bloodcurdling voice, and, for some reason, tried to cut off my thumb.

As my mother bathed me, I could not stop thinking about that dream. I knew that I was far from the Wicked Witch, that I was in my house on Del Norte Lane in Dallas, where I felt comfortable and safe, and nowhere near Oz. But still . . .

I remember my mother got up from kneeling beside the tub and went outside the bathroom to talk with my father. I could barely hear their voices. My father was voicing his worries—about paying for my brother's upcoming college tuition, making the mortgage payments and the car payments, putting food on the table. I heard my mother attempting to comfort my father, to reassure him that they would somehow manage. If they had known I overheard, then they would have stopped mid-sentence.

I remember that my father was shaky during this period, and hardly ever smiled. He did not have that spicy smell from his aftershave. He wore his loose-fitting one-piece zippered jumpsuits, not work clothes, and he lost weight. His blue eyes had a faraway look.

* * *

The depression that seemed to begin with my father's firing appeared to lift later that year. He took a job with Desco Debs for less than a year, and then subsequently with the Dunn & McCarthy Shoe Company based in Auburn, New York, representing the women's footwear brand Enna Jetticks.

My parents, German Jews living in the Baptist Bible Belt town of Dallas, were well assimilated into Texas and into America. My father became a Dallas Cowboys fan, and later a fan of the basketball team, the Dallas Mavericks. He became a grill master, known far and wide for his mesquite-grilled burgers and smoked chickens. My parents knew the Mexican restaurants in town. My father ate in all-American hole-in-the-wall restaurants in the countless small towns he stopped in as a traveling salesman. My mother adopted a bit of a southern drawl. They continued to pronounce *Baum* as the Americanized *bomb*, not the German *bowm*.

Our synagogue, Temple Emanu-El, was a contemporary structure whose sanctuary was surrounded in modern stained glass and had an arena-like high-domed ceiling. The congregation included descendants of many Texas Jewish pioneers. The paid choir, made up of mostly non-Jews, was conducted by the renowned Simon Sargon, and accompanied by an organist. All were tucked away in the choir loft—a setting more common in churches than in synagogues. Men did not wear the traditional *tallit* or *yarmulkes*. Our synagogue was a late adopter in the broader Reform Jewish movement to offer becoming a *bat mitzvahs*, the ceremony when girls are called to read Torah and lead services—a rite of passage for Jewish females, usually at the age of thirteen, the equivalent to becoming a *bar mitzvah* for Jewish boys. Because my dad felt strongly that his daughters should learn Hebrew, regardless of becoming a *bat mitzvah*, my older sister and I were the only girls in the Hebrew school, that we both attended from age nine to thirteen. Then, in middle school and high school, I became an assistant Hebrew school teacher. By the time becoming a *bat mitzvah* was offered at Temple Emanu-El, I was seventeen and a senior in high school. I wanted to become a *bat mitzvah*, but my father responded with, "For what, the party? You already know Hebrew."

I think that his negative response had to do with money for a celebration. I was disappointed. It lingered as unfinished business for me.

In our house, spending money on seemingly frivolous pursuits was never allowed. When my sister and I took ballet lessons, for example, we were not allowed to be in the recitals because the tutus cost money. And money for what? For a one-off performance for a few hours. Feeling denied and deprived, we served as understudies for those absent during rehearsals. We didn't attend the recital, but instead pined away, wishing to be there.

Having a "maid," meaning Mexican or African American household help, was part of the norm of middle- and upper-class Texas life. Blanche worked for us once every two weeks during my growing up years. I believe that my parents always felt that hiring her was a bit of a luxury, but also incredibly helpful to my mother, who was raising three kids while my father was traveling. Blanche did the heavy-duty cleaning and ironing. She made the most amazing southern fried chicken in my mother's cast iron pans. My parents did not allow her to operate the washing machine or dishwasher. And she was not allowed to eat off of *our* dishes or with *our* silverware or to drink from *our* glassware. She had her own dish, silverware, and glass, because who knew what kind of germs we could get from "those people"? I knew of no other household—Jewish or otherwise—that had such a practice. I still cannot reconcile my parents' attitude and actions with their background of fleeing Germany, where Jews were thought to be germ-carrying scum.

Also difficult for me to reconcile was my parents' unwillingness to provide assistance—material or otherwise—directly to the Russian Jewish immigrants who came to the US in the 1970s, although my parents continually contributed to the Jewish Federation benefitting many agencies. Many of my parents' German Jewish friends offered money, goods, or services such as English lessons or transportation. My parents' attitude was that they themselves had survived and thrived in the US without such help, therefore these immigrants could do so, too. No one helped my parents, so they weren't going to help anyone else. I was embarrassed by this point of view.

Like most in the Jewish community, my parents clearly stated, and telegraphed often, their expectation that their children must marry someone Jewish. They made clear that life would be easier if we did so. That it would be a slap in the face to them—and our ancestral history—if we did not. News of a Jewish kid in a serious relationship with a non-Jew or, worse, an engagement or marriage, would warrant clicking of the tongue, shaking of the head, or even a mournful facial expression.

Dick, Karen, and Diane at Karen's Harvard graduation, June 1978.

26

Frankfurt, 1972, and Dallas, 1990

If anything should happen. . . .

RUDY BAUM | prior to major surgery, 1990

My parents managed to have all three of their children marry Jews, after sending them all off to college.

Having more financial freedom and seeing their children settled, my parents began to travel more.

And, twice, they traveled to Frankfurt.

The first trip was in 1972. I went with them on this trip, and we spent a few days together there before I went on to Israel and my parents continued through Europe. I was sixteen. I remember going with my parents to visit the Musterschule, the secondary school that my father had attended, and seeing the exterior of Reuterweg 73, my father's home until he was nineteen. We stood outside of the Westend Synagogue. He said that he never dreamed he would go back and visit such places with his own child.

In the late 1970s and the mid-1980s came three Jewish weddings. Although my husband is Jewish, he is, in part, of Russian descent. My parents' attitude that the German Jews were higher brow than Russian or Eastern Jews—that same attitude my grandparents had in the Lodz Ghetto—was palpable. Subtle, but not so subtle. It became obvious when my father was explaining the expectations of who would pay for which aspects of our wedding weekend, how the rehearsal dinner would be handled.

And then, after the marriages, my parents had the joy of one by one, their six grandsons arriving on the scene. Life seemed full and joyous.

* * *

In February 1990, I made a routine call home from my business travels. I was in Charlotte, North Carolina, for a few days. I called my husband, Bob, from a restaurant pay phone to check in and find out how our son, Matthew, who was all of nine months old at the time, was doing. Bob said I should call my father. Something about Dad having a stress test and needing surgery.

I immediately called my parents. My dad reported that his stress test had shown severe blockage in one of his arteries and that the doctor wanted it addressed immediately. He was scheduled for triple bypass heart surgery the next day. Standing in that phone booth, I began to tremble. After some conversation about the blockage—where it was, how much there was—I asked when exactly the surgery was scheduled. My father reported that it would be at 7:00 a.m. the next morning, and "how lucky" he was to get the first slot.

With none of his children there? After much back and forth, he agreed to a new plan: the surgery was delayed to late the next morning, and my brother Dick and I flew down to Dallas.

The next day, we walked into the hospital room where my father was waiting for his surgery. He talked about "if anything should happen" to him—then, about his will and where important papers were. Tears welled up in my eyes. I could not take in that conversation.

He came through the surgery just fine, but I was unprepared to see him in the ICU afterwards—his bloated face, the maze of tubes running in and out of him, the continually beeping machines.

A month or two later, my mother told us that my father seemed out of sorts, maybe depressed. He was not much interested in socializing. He said he didn't want to buy a new pair of inexpensive pants, for fear he couldn't afford them. That's not him.

Dick and I returned to Dallas, only to find that it was worse than we feared: my father was severely depressed—low-spirited, disinterested in the world around him. We have since learned that depression after triple bypass surgery can be the result of any of a number of factors: patients may not know what to expect; they may be unable to do simple tasks without becoming extremely tired; and going under anesthesia for four or five hours, or on a heart-lung machine, can change a brain's chemistry. And of course, such an operation makes a person face his mortality.

We found a psychiatrist whom we thought would be a good fit. Although he was twenty years younger than my father, the psychiatrist's parents were also Jews who had emigrated from Germany. We had been told he had helped many geriatric Jewish patients, and, presumably, people whose lives had been touched by the Holocaust. He prescribed an antidepressant for my dad and began to see him weekly.

After three or four months, my father was his old self. To what extent was that depression the result of the surgery and to what extent did my father have a proclivity to depression? To what extent had his memories, his conscience, his pain, come back to overwhelm him?

He certainly seemed to recover. And it was shortly thereafter that my father would begin to speak and write more freely about his childhood and wartime experiences.

27

Dallas, 1991

And now, I know.

RUDY BAUM

It was one of our weekly check-in calls. I was letting my parents know that I was still alive and well in New York City, despite their concerns that I rode the subway, lived in an old building, and didn't have parking. Then my parents would update me about who they had dinner with, which movies they'd seen, who died, whose kids had babies, what new restaurants had opened.

As I cradled the cordless phone to my neck, I continued emptying the dishwasher. But on this particular call in 1991, my dad, with a slightly serious tone and a tremble in his voice, interjected that "something interesting had happened" that week. My curiosity was piqued, as my dad was not one to readily label anything as "interesting."

He proceeded to tell me that he had been at the Dallas Holocaust and Human Rights Museum (where he was a docent), waiting to give our neighbor's twelve-year-old daughter, Dede Cole, a private tour. It was there that he found the book *The Chronicle of the Lodz Ghetto,* a day-by-day account written by a group of ghetto inhabitants and based on first-hand information and documents. In a subdued voice, he explained that he had looked up his parents' names in the index and found his mother's name there.

"And now," he said, "I know."

Know what? I stopped with the dishwasher.

"My mother committed suicide," he said.

My left hand held my head. I closed my eyes for what seemed like a long pause. All I could think to say was how sorry I was. How hard this must be.

I was imagining my stoic father, then seventy-six, in that library, which was adjacent to the museum's cattle car, one of those used to transport Jews to the ghettos and camps. I imagined the silence and the loneliness of that moment of discovery for my dad.

Suicide.

My dad continued, "Now at least I know. So I think my father must have died before then." I could hear the relief of knowing the fate of his mother and the ongoing pain of the unknown fate of his father.

Perhaps this new knowledge provided him some closure when he would observe their *yahrzeits* in the future. Every year, he would light two *yahrzeit* candles before the Yom Kippur *Yizkor* service as well as on the first Friday night in May. The flickering lights reminded him of his parents and reminded my brother, sister, and me of the grandparents we never knew. All of us would attend Shabbat services on an appointed Friday night in May, anticipating the end of the service when the rabbi's booming voice would read the names "Julie Baum . . . Norbert Baum," among others on the lengthy list of those remembered.

Sometime later, after I read the entry myself, I imagined my father's trembling hands turning the pages in *The Chronicle of the Lodz Ghetto,* from the index to the page with the entry: "May 4, 1942: This morning, in the collective house at 70 Zgierska Street, 60-year-old Julia Baum from Frankfurt am Main hanged herself." And I imagine the echo that my father must have heard then, of the desperation of my grandparents' last letter to him.

28

Frankfurt, 1991

One of the biggest lies is that time could help. Time does not help. It only deepens the feeling that something is missing.

EVA FAHIDI | survivor of Auschwitz

In 1991, the same year after finding out the fate of his mother; and six years after my father retired, he and my mother returned to Frankfurt, this time as guests of the city.

Over the years—and to this day—many cities in Germany have a visiting program for Jews who lived there before or during World War II. Frankfurt's program, which began in 1980, is for "former Jewish Frankfurt citizens and the ones who were politically or religiously persecuted." These days, the program has expanded the offer to include the children and grandchildren of that generation.

My parents were members of a group of 133 people—Jews formerly of Frankfurt, each with a spouse or other companion. In recounting the trip, my father wrote: "While everyone had a different story, it was the same in many respects. We all had to leave. We survived. We made it and lived to come back."

They received "the red carpet treatment," beginning with accommodations at the Frankfurter Hof, one of the most plush hotels in the city at the time. Their rooms welcomed them with lavish flower arrangements and an overflowing bowl of strawberries. Throughout the two weeks, my father had the opportunity to eat the near-perfect preparation of many of his favorite foods—white asparagus, *grüne Soße* (green sauce), *rote Grütze*, and *Handkäse mit Musik,* literally "hand cheese with music," a translucent pungent cheese marinated in vinegar and oil with onions and caraway seeds.

My father noted many positive developments in the city since his last trip, in the 1970s. "The rubble is gone and the streets are clean. It is now a vital, bustling, growing city with construction cranes everywhere." Pedestrian malls. Shoppers with money. A fast and efficient public transportation system.

My parents again visited the Musterschule and Reuterweg 73. They toured the Jewish cemetery with its administrator, Klaus Meier-Ude, who had restored the cemetery to its original dignity and with whom they developed a friendship. They traveled to Höchst, where my father had worked for the shoe manufacturer Ada-Ada. And to Königstein, the home of the castle, and of wonderful pastries, where the Baum family had gone on weekends.

Reflecting on this trip, my father's sentiment was that we "can't hold younger Germans responsible for the misdeeds of their parents and grandparents. It's unreasonable to blame them." He felt "more tolerant," he said, "except when I see someone my age with a beer belly—I can see them in a black SS or brown SA uniform—and I can't help but think this guy looks like a real Nazi."[1] Perhaps because the food shortage in the war years had an impact on all except the Nazis.

Frankfurt had become a melting pot of ethnicities, thanks to the *Fremdarbeiter*, or foreign workers, from places such as the Balkans, Turkey, and elsewhere in the Middle East. My parents went to a flea market where most of the vendors and customers were foreigners. My father's observation: "So much for the master race."

The Jewish Museum Frankfurt brought back many memories for my father, with its exhibit of memorabilia, much of it attached to familiar names. He updated the museum library's copy of the Geiger family tree to include Gretel and himself and their respective families. "Now we have become part of history," he later wrote.

On Friday night, my parents attended services at the Westend Synagogue, which had only been partially restored since the war. My father wrote that "men in top hats, the three rabbis on the *bimah* (the altar), families greeting each other—started to haunt me."

One afternoon, my parents visited the Palmengarten to hear a concert. My father wrote: "The band played familiar music and the setting was as I remembered it from my childhood. Nothing seemed to have changed, almost as if time had stood still." Yet, at that same time, these words, too, from my father: "I guess Thomas Wolfe was right when he said, 'You can't go home again.'"

On the last evening, my father was seated next to the mayor of Frankfurt. He wrote that "it took me seventy-six years to reach this 'place of honor.'" Ever comfortable with a microphone in his hand, Rudy delivered words of appreciation on behalf of the group's contingent from the United States. While his speech was a heartfelt thank you, my father recalled telling the mayor and the other German dignitaries gathered there that, "Maybe someday we can forgive because they have held out their hand in friendship and forgiveness, but we can never forget what they did to the community, my family, and me."

How essential was forgiveness to my father's ability to move forward in his life? Another Holocaust survivor, Eva Fahidi—a Hungarian Jew who was deported to Auschwitz, lost her parents and sister and forty-six other relatives in the Holocaust, and recently attended the trial of an Auschwitz guard—asserted in a *New York Times* article: "One of the biggest lies is that time could help. Time does not help. It only deepens the feeling that something is missing. One simply learns to live with such trauma. And if you don't get to the point where you can forgive them, then I think you can't go on living."[2]

29

Berlin, 2000, and Dallas, 2002 and 2005

He, however, always struggled against becoming embittered because of these memories.

FRIEDE SPRINGER | widow of Axel Springer, remembering Ernst Cramer of Axel Springer Verlag

My father had an ongoing willingness to return to Germany. In the fall of 2000, when he received an invitation to attend the dedication of the Abraham Geiger Kolleg in the Berlin suburb of Potsdam, he immediately accepted. The Kolleg is the first rabbinical school in Germany since the Holocaust and is named after my father's great-great uncle, Rabbi Abraham Geiger, one of the founders of Reform Judaism. Rudy, at the age of eighty-five, would attend as a living descendant of Abraham Geiger.

And, he would have the opportunity to reconnect with his old German Jewish army buddy Ernst Cramer, with whom he had maintained correspondence. But—unlike some of his other army buddies—my father had not seen Ernst in more than fifty years. So, yes, my father was going. And I decided to go with him.

It was November 10 when we arrived in Berlin, and immediately after we checked in to our hotel, we set out to take part in a 200,000-person march—a *Kristallnacht* commemoration that was a demonstration against Germany's far right, and in favor of tolerance and humanity. The march began at the bombed-out Neue Synagogue, guarded by a policeman with an army tank, where a brief service was conducted outside in the pouring rain, claps of thunder in the background. The march ended at the Brandenburg Gate, where the chancellor of Germany addressed the crowd. And, the conductor of the orchestra of the Berlin State Opera, Daniel Barenboim, born in Argentina to Russian Jewish parents, conducted a stirring version of Beethoven's Ninth Symphony. Along the way, we passed a large poster of a handsome black man wearing a t-shirt with the words "I'm proud to be a true German."

My father and I visited the two major Jewish cemeteries—the Schönhauser

Allee Cemetery, the site of Rabbi Geiger's grave as well as many desecrated gravestones, and the major Jewish cemetery, the Weißensee. With approximately one hundred acres, the Weißensee is the second largest Jewish cemetery in Europe, and has a section of more recent graves, a reminder of the small Berlin Jewish community that still exists. Policemen guard these cemeteries 24/7.

Rudy made plans for us to have lunch with Ernst Cramer at Axel Springer Verlag, the major publishing house at which Cramer was a top executive. Ernst had worked for an American news agency in 1958, when he met Axel Springer, the founder of Axel Springer Verlag, which by 2000, the year of our visit, was an approximately $2.5 billion newspaper, magazine, and digital publishing company. Ernst returned to Berlin and joined the company, where he would spend his entire professional career and rise to its highest ranks—as a managing director of the publishing arm, and then chairman of the firm's foundation, the "appointed guarantor of the core values for which the Axel Springer company stands." He was also the executor of Axel Springer's will and the namesake of the Ernst Cramer Fellowship, an exchange program for journalists in Germany and Israel.

After my father and I were escorted up to the nineteenth floor, to Ernst's office, Ernst rose from his chair to greet us from behind his big wooden desk, with its neat stacks of documents and books and an old typewriter. He was impeccably dressed in a custom-tailored navy blue suit. His eyes twinkled through gold wireframe glasses. After he and my father embraced, they were momentarily speechless. Here they were, reunited in the year 2000 in Berlin, with their shared memories and painful histories.

As we headed to lunch, Ernst asked if we would be willing to walk the stairs, rather than take the elevator, to the executive dining room. The eighty-seven-year-old, my eighty-five-year-old father, and I—all walked. The waiters treated Ernst like royalty as he and my father reminisced about their army buddies, their commanding officer, their losses, their lives. Ernst—I came to learn—was known for remembering horrors but seeming to live without bitterness or anger. Shortly after Ernst's death, Axel Springer's widow, Friede, wrote: "It was precisely his ability to remember things from the past which held much that was terrible. He, however, always struggled against becoming embittered because of these memories. Quite the opposite: being constructive was his way. He attempted to give reason to hope; helping to shape a today and tomorrow, that are better than yesterday was."[1] The Axel Springer CEO wrote that, "The trauma of the Holocaust, the uncompromising 'Never Again,' was the motive of Ernst Cramer's life."[2] Ernst Cramer and my father, so similar. Perhaps in more ways than I realized at the time.

For the Abraham Geiger Kolleg dedication, we took the short trip to Potsdam, which became known after World War II as the site of the Potsdam Agreement that disarmed and demilitarized Germany and destroyed the Nazi Party. We were also driven through the beautiful neighboring town of Wannsee. It had been the site of the fateful Wannsee Conference in early 1942, where high-ranking Nazi officials discussed "The Final Solution of the Jewish Question," the extermination of European Jews.

Upon arrival at the Kolleg, we were surprised to see a crowd of some five hundred people, including dignitaries from Berlin and the president and the minister of the interior of the province of Brandenburg. The ceremony was filled with pomp and circumstance, with ceremonial music from trumpets and cantors alike.

In my father's speech at the dedication ceremony, he said: "No one could have predicted eighty-five years ago that I would be standing here at the dedication of the Abraham Geiger College. I was born in Frankfurt, where Abraham Geiger was born in 1810. For me, life has been a remarkable odyssey." He recalled knowing Abraham Geiger's grandson, Dr. Rudolf Geiger, who lived near the Reuterweg apartment. He also recalled his grandfather August Geiger. My father then spoke of his and Gretel's emigration and his parents' journey to their death. He continued: "So, I have returned to Berlin, perhaps for the last time, as a representative of what is left of the Geiger family. . . . This is the story of a family that contributed so much and lost so much. By naming this institution the Abraham Geiger College, you not only honored his name but also honored his descendants. . . . The end of an odyssey."

* * *

But less than two years later, my father's personal odyssey would take him through his suicide attempt, in February of 2002. He nearly died.

But then, he recovered. Months later, I wrote to my father's psychiatrist: "Thank you for giving me my father back. . . . You gave him his life back, and you gave my family back our 'Dad.'"

The only people who were privy to this dark part of my father's odyssey were the widowed Ruth Heydemann (who met my grandparents in Germany after

Rudy and Hanne, July 2002.

my father had emigrated and later would become his confidante in Dallas); the Temple Emanu-El clergy—including his dear friend, Rabbi Klein, the Rabbi Emeritus; and Karl Kuby, the Mormon German who owned Kuby's, the popular German deli in Dallas.

Later in 2002, my parents finally chose to move from their home of fifty-two years, to Edgemere, the senior community complex that was just around the corner.

When Edgemere was built in 2000, my father refused to consider it; too fancy, not Jewish enough, probably too expensive, he said. Then, after his electroshock therapy and reentry to the world, when he seemed not only back to normal but also a bit more brazen, he and my mother took a tour of Edgemere and shortly thereafter moved into a small two-room apartment in its independent living wing.

* * *

Three years later, in 2005, Ruth Heydemann and I were in the parking lot of Edgemere after an eighty-fifth birthday party for my mother. I commented that I thought my mom was doing fairly well. Ruth agreed, but followed with an addendum: "You know, your mother was never the same after finding your father that day," she said, referring to my father's try at suicide. How so? I asked. Ruth said she had noticed my mom was losing her memory, becoming quieter. That she just wasn't the same.

My mom had mild dementia and was slowly deteriorating from lymphoma and congestive heart failure. She lived in Edgemere's skilled nursing unit, while my father continued to live independently in their apartment in Edgemere. My father visited her several times daily, often keeping her company for hours. She seemed happy. Although he seemed tethered to her, he seemed freer. Lighter. The electroshock therapy had eased his load.

And yet. I commented to Ruth that I couldn't imagine what it was like for my mom to discover my father after his suicide attempt. Had my parents ever talked about that? Ruth had an answer I won't forget. She said, in her heavy German accent, "No, no. You know, it was so deep. So underneath. I think it was all related to the Holocaust. Your father finally couldn't stand it anymore. I'm telling you."

Ruth was a confidante of my father, and she understood his dark place. It became clear to me then that Ruth knew more than my mother or anyone else would ever know about my father's psyche, whether it was from direct conversation with my dad or not. Because of my mother's less introspective nature and because she had emigrated at the age of fourteen with her immediate family and did not lose close relatives, she never was able to fully empathize with my father's struggle, although he had shared some of his wartime experiences with her. On the other hand, Ruth understood my father—the context, the roots, the loss, the guilt, the pain. Her belief stayed with me, that the underlying haunting shadow of the Holocaust in my father's soul was the seed of his depressions and the core of his suicide attempt.

It was like finding a key piece to a puzzle.

30

Dallas and Houston, 2008 and 2009

I am writing this to tell you that, whenever I depart this life, I will have been thankful for a good and long life that turned out far better than I could have hoped for. I had many joys and I was fortunate to overcome adversities—some with your help.

RUDY BAUM | a letter to his children

My mother died on April 5, 2007. In her last days, when her passing seemed imminent, we hoped that she would not die on my birthday, my brother's birthday, her caretaker Helen's birthday, or my father's birthday—all of which were between April 3 and April 11. She did us that favor.

My German Jewish mother died surrounded by her two Southern black caregivers, Helen and Eunice, and my father holding hands with her. Eunice, using her best Gospel voice, belted out "Amazing Grace." After the final words, my mother took her last breath.

Surrounded by black women—black women who, in my mother's home, were allowed only to use their own dishes, silverware, and glassware.

"Amazing Grace," a hymn of forgiveness and redemption.

Did I wish for a different mother at times? Yes. One that did not wear bobby socks and pedal pushers when they were not in style. One that got her hair and nails done and always looked her best. One that would dote on me when I was sick (she tended not to waste energy on empathy). One that was nurturing and kinder. One that seemed more interested in me. One that was a great cook, beyond her specialties of sauerbraten, goose, banana bread, and hard-as-a-rock matzo balls (yes, an acquired taste). One that did not drive miles to save a nickel on toilet paper.

Still, she was proud of each of her children and grandchildren, bragging when she could. She was proud of me for managing restaurants in my early twenties. She would be dismissive of waiters whom she perceived to be incompetent with the comment, "They could never work for Karen."

She taught me skills to thrive. To be organized. To be responsive. To "stay in touch." To remember birthdays (much like my grandmother); she had a small datebook with birthdays and anniversaries of family and friends and neighbors.

I did not make it easy for her. Once my brother and sister were out of the house, my mother and I were together one on one for much of the time. I sometimes barely spoke with her, entering the teenage mode.

Yet, some of my best memories are from that one-on-one time together. Belly-laughing with her while the two of us watched the comedic pianist Victor Borge or the TV comedy variety show Rowan and Martin's Laugh-In. Shopping for clothes—she was generous. "Buy it in a few colors, if you like it," she would say.

During her last months, I came to believe that my mother did her best. She did not have good role models in her own parents—a father who was a curmudgeon and both a mother and father who seemed somewhat parsimonious emotionally. Much of her married life, meanwhile, my mother was home alone raising three children, as my father, a traveling salesman, was out of town Monday through Friday for eight months each year. She never missed a beat to be right there, to be an anchor for my father through his episodic depressions. Until she couldn't be anymore.

For her last five years, she lived with the emotional aftermath, at whatever level it was present in her, of coping with my father's suicide attempt. A tremendous burden for her. My mother's mild dementia and her various mild medical conditions eventually advanced to the point that "Amazing Grace" called her home.

Eleven months after my mother's death, in March 2008, we unveiled her tombstone in the Temple Emanu-El Cemetery in Dallas. During that trip to Dallas, my father and I and my son Adam enjoyed an afternoon not only with Ruth, my father's confidante, but also with her daughter and my lifelong friend Lynnie and Lynnie's son, David, who were in town. Three generations of two families connected through their Frankfurt roots.

It was at the unveiling that I saw Ruth for the last time. Ruth was getting a ride home with friends. I leaned into the backseat of the car, made sure she was safely strapped in, gave her a kiss, and told her that I would be seeing Lynnie soon again. She said, in her inimitable voice, "You girls, your friendship is such a blessing."

"Yes, it is that." I leaned over to give her another kiss, then closed the car door and waved good-bye. She died suddenly six weeks later, on May 4, 2008

From left: Lynn Heydemann Brotman, David Brotman, Adam Gordon, Ruth (née Simon) Heydemann, Rudy, and Karen.

Rudy and Ernst Cramer, 2008.

(coincidentally, May 4, 1942, is the date of my grandmother's suicide). Those were the last words that she said to me.

Later that year, I once again had the honor of accompanying my father to visit Ernst Cramer, this time for dinner in Houston. Cramer, now ninety-five years old, had come to the US to attend his great niece's college graduation and my father, at ninety-three, was intent on seeing him. But my father had recently recovered from a torn rotator cuff and was not nearly as steady on his feet as he once was. These recent months of no longer being in caretaking mode for my mother brought a sense of newly found freedom for my father, but at a time when his own physical fragility had begun to define his limits.

Shortly after we arrived at Ernst's niece's home, a mansion tucked into suburban woodlands, Ernst shuffled toward us in his clunky black round-toed orthopedic shoes. He was not nearly as spry as he had been even eight years earlier.

After a warm hug and an exchange of niceties, the two old buddies sank into a crimson leather couch in the library. After an hour or so, they emerged and joined us for a drink, my father with his scotch and soda, Ernst with his cranberry juice. About the reunion in Houston with my father, Ernst would later write, "It was a reunion I shall never forget."

At dinner, these two wise men steered the conversation. About Zionism. About the presidential primaries. Hillary Clinton versus Barack Obama. Informed, insightful, articulate, passionate. And optimistic.

Ernst had a deep appreciation for life. He once wrote about it, in *Die Welt* in 2004, in an essay:

> What . . . makes my life worth living? There is no doubt of the fact that it is worth living. Perhaps, the fact that I survived, while millions of others were murdered? Yet is survival something worth living for? Is it not rather the cause of a recurring bad conscience?
>
> Or the love, the affection, the recognition, the understanding that I encountered over and over again? All that is certainly significant and important, and I cannot be thankful enough for it.
>
> But what really made and still makes my life worth living is beauty in all its facets, which I found everywhere and at all times. . . .
>
> Most moving of all however has always been the beauty in the people, that I have encountered everywhere, among the rich and poor; this beauty,

that is something quite different from glamour or make-up, namely charisma, decency, respectability, nobility of spirit, and refinement of attitude.

Time and time again I have found beauty. This beauty, which 'beautiful people' cannot understand, has made me happy.[1]

Yet much later, I would discover that Ernst also had written this, in instructions to his colleagues and family about handling his death: "I strongly urge that there should be no memorial service or anything similar. . . . 'No funeral feast' is my last grateful and melancholy tribute to my parents and my brother, for whom there was not only no funeral service, but rather no burial, no resting place, no gravestone; in whose murder I am even indirectly implicated, for believing for too long that the horror, the mass murder, could not happen in Germany; for this reason I emigrated much too late and no longer had time to organize the emigrations of my parents and my brother."[2]

* * *

Later in 2008, in September, the treasure of the translation of the first letter from my grandmother Julie to her son Rudy was in my handbag as I boarded the plane to make the journey to Dallas to spend time with my father.

To check up on him, accompany him to doctors' appointments, clean out his fridge, and take him shopping, his coupon stash in hand.

By then, finally, I had begun to get the letters from his parents translated. I remember my father giving them to me just over a decade earlier. One morning during a visit to New York, he had come downstairs clutching a fraying and faded green folder, onionskin paper peeking out of the edges. We had a full day planned, including coffee with someone my father had stayed in touch with for over fifty years—Arthur Samuels Jr., the sixty-something-year-old grandson of Mr. Heilbronn, the man who gave my father his first job in America.

But what was that folder? My father announced that he wanted to donate these letters—from his parents, he explained—to the Leo Baeck Institute the next day. I opened the folder. Touching the fragile pages was like handling ancient mortar that could crumble to the touch. Although the *Sütterlin* script, an ornate early twentieth-century form of German handwriting, was beautiful, it was illegible to me.

Nonetheless, I had a visceral reaction: I wanted to keep these onionskin sheets of paper touched by my father's parents, by *my* grandparents. My father

Rudy and Karen, 2007.

seemed pleasantly surprised to hear this; there was a joyful glimmer in his blue eyes. We agreed to go together to loan the institute the letters to make photocopies. When I went to retrieve the originals three weeks later, the institute's chief archivist did not want to return them, as he understandably wanted them for research and was concerned I would not store them properly. I successfully fought for those originals and later placed each in an archival sleeve, in an archival binder, after researching how to best keep them.

And now, while I could not have asked my father to translate the letters and re-live every word, I wanted to ask him questions that the translation raised. In fact, I was bursting to discuss this first letter word by word with my father as soon as I set foot in his apartment. But I knew better. Instead, I waited for just the right moment. As usual, we met for dinner downstairs in Edgemere's formal dining room.

We placed our order with the waiter. As my father sipped his low-sodium V-8 and I my iced tea, I gently broached the subject—that I was working on getting his parents' letters translated, that I had the first one translated already, and that I was curious about a few things.

First, a basic question: Who were Paula, Erich, and Eva Kahn?—to whom his mother asked that he give "best regards." He wasn't sure.

Then I asked him about the allusion his mother made in the letter to joining him: ". . . think about that your mother always thinks about you and will accompany you in your new home[land]." Did they have a likely affidavit sponsor for themselves just as he left? He said he didn't think so: "You know that letter was a lot of years ago."

I said that I had the translated letter upstairs, and he could look at, if he were interested. He was eager to do so.

After my dad polished off his regular dessert—one scoop of sugar-free chocolate ice cream—we headed upstairs. As we settled in to watch TV, he asked to see the letter. I couldn't jump up quickly enough to retrieve it from my bag. My father sat in his rattan chair, with his feet up on the ottoman, holding the letter in his left hand and his head with his right. At ninety-three, he was enveloped once more in the words of his parents.

I waited patiently, observing my father savor each line of the letter, yet showing no visible signs of emotion.

He then asked me what I wanted to know.

I asked if he had stopped in London on his way to the States. He confirmed that he had, and from there boarded the *Cunard White Star*.

I asked what his mother meant by the phrase, "and I will always accompany you in your new homeland."

My father said that maybe one day she would be here.

But how did that fit with the "last train" syndrome?

My father didn't know.

There were too many "I don't knows" coming from a man like my father, who was always certain, always knowing, always with a point of view. Was it, in part, the difficulty of remembering events of more than seventy years ago? Was it, in part, the pain of revisiting the words of his parents?

Four months later, my father suffered a heart attack, from which he never fully recovered. He died two months afterward.

* * *

I was fortunate in that I got to say goodbye. It happened on March 29, 2009, while I was having brunch with a girlfriend, Cathy, tucked away at a wobbly table for two in the back of a tiny, somewhat noisy, New Orleans-style restaurant on Atlantic Avenue in Brooklyn Heights. "So, how's your Dad doing?" Cathy asked.

"He's ready to go." I said, without hesitation, having visited my father in Dallas the week before, helping him move back into his apartment at Edgemere from the complex's adjacent skilled nursing unit—to live independently, but with daily assistance from a caregiver.

The very next second, my cell phone rang with the caller ID of Marina, my father's caregiver. I picked it up to hear Marina say, "Mrs. Karen, I'm with your daddy and . . ." He was not doing well, she said. She wanted to call 911.

I had just spoken to him a few hours earlier, to arrange Marina's visit. I asked her to put him on the phone.

Next, I heard my father's weakened voice, with only a glimmer of his signature intonation.

"Dad, Dad, Marina says she should call 911 for you and take you to the hospital. She wants to call and have an ambulance take you to Presbyterian. Do you want to go? Do you want to go to the hospital?"

"I'm OK. It's OK. I'm OK. It's OK." That's all he said, again and again.

I got it. I understood my father's wish: I'm OK to leave this life. It's OK. It's OK to let go of me.

"I love you, Dad, I love you very much." I let him know, it *is* OK.

"Love you, too," he said.

Marina called 911. The fragile electronic connection ended. And I knew my father had said good-bye to this life. All the passersby on Atlantic Avenue seemed so distant. It was as though I was in a fishbowl, insulated from the world. I took a seat on the wrought iron bench in front of the restaurant, coddling my cell phone. Only five minutes passed when it rang again.

It was Marina sobbing. "Your Daddy, he's gone."

Cathy came out to check on me. With one look, she knew.

"He's gone," I wailed.

My father was gone. It was weeks shy of his ninety-fourth birthday. He was ready.

Part Five

THE STUMBLING STONES

The stones . . . before you stumble, you stop in front of the stone and have a look at them and stumble with your eyes. You bend down to read the name, and this is a form of respect.

GUNTER DEMNIG | Cologne artist, creator of the Holocaust Memorial, *Stolpersteine*

31

My Search Begins, 2009

Date of death: Unknown. Cause of death: Murdered, killed by the Nazis.

YAD VASHEM CENTRAL DATABASE

And so my father came to the natural end of his life, a life he had attempted to end prematurely seven years earlier. In the days following his death, we opened that gray metal box containing my father's will and the envelope we had noticed at the time of his suicide attempt, with the words "Letter to My Children to be opened upon my death." In the letter, dated April 27, 1998, my father wrote: "Leaving home in 1936 and subsequently losing my parents in the Holocaust were the two most defining events in my life. Having to leave Germany changed the course of my life. The loss of my parents left me with a feeling of guilt that stayed with me throughout my life. Nothing can change what happened, but I do not want my parents to be forgotten. . . . I now ask you to observe the Yahrzeit of the grandparents you never knew, and yet who contributed so much to your lives."

His heavy and nearly insurmountable internal burden: the loss of his parents, and then that loss all the more searing when haunted by his parents' last written words, "But you will have to figure out how to master the difficulties, because it must happen . . . We place our hopes in you."

From a tiny scrap of paper in that same gray metal box, my siblings and I learned what my father had bequeathed to each of us. He had left me three items: the *Stammbaum der Familie Geiger* (the Geiger family tree), which tied me to my Frankfurt roots going back more than three centuries; his mother's gold bracelet, studded with tiny pearls and diamond chips, which tied me to my grandmother and miraculously found its way to my father (perhaps through one of the many visitors from Frankfurt); and his US Army ID bracelet, which tied me to my father's military service and my mother (whose name is engraved on the back).

The bound family tree, with its gold leaf lettering on the spine, had somehow made it from Frankfurt to my father's hands in America. It traces my paternal grandmother's family back to 1632, as the Geiger family lived in Frankfurt for generations and produced some notable individuals. In the introduction, dated "Spring of 1904," the genealogist Daniel August Worms wrote: "I herewith hand over this family tree to the person who commissioned this research with the hope that it will spark the interest of future generations and give them the incentive to live and work in the spirit of their great ancestors." He handed it over to my great grandfather August Geiger, who handed it over to my grandmother Julie Baum (née Geiger), who handed it over to my father, who handed it over to me.

My father did "live and work in the spirit" of his great ancestors. He was intellectually curious. He was an observant Reform Jew. He transitioned from being a German first and a Jew second to something else here in America. He told his story and his parents' story countless times, sometimes as a featured speaker, sometimes as a panelist, and always as a German Jewish refugee with painful memories of the Holocaust.

I, too, try "to live and work in the spirit of my great ancestors"—as I struggle to understand my father's story and how he came to be the man who, late in life, no longer wished to live; and as I struggle with the legacy of suicide in my family and to find some sense of peace with my grandparents' and my father's journeys.

Within weeks after my father died, I became determined to translate the remainder of my grandparents' letters to my father. Like the *Stammbaum der Familie Geiger,* these letters were a treasure of my history. Of my father's story. Of my grandparents' lives. I also became obsessed with resolving one of my father's lifelong unknowns. My father wrote, "There is no record as to when, where, or how my father died. He is simply listed in the records as missing." The obituary in 1942 stated that his parents died "in short order." My father always said that he assumed that his father, in all likelihood, had been deported to a death camp from the ghetto and died before his mother died by suicide. It was unimaginable to him that his mother would have taken her life if her husband were still alive.

That said, years later my father would attempt to take his life—while my mother was still alive.

So when, where, and how did my grandfather die? I began my search.

I trolled the Web, one website leading to another; made phone calls; drafted emails and letters. I joined ancestry.com. I typed *n.o.r.be.r.t. b.a.u.m.* and answered half a dozen basic questions. I hit "submit" and waited with strange anticipation. It was just my computer and me. The search wheel stopped turning and up popped the transmigration voucher that my father had filed with the American Jewish Joint Distribution Committee. That voucher was my first glimpse of my father's efforts on his parents' behalf.

I soon discovered the online Yad Vashem Central Database, an archive of the names and biographical details of three million Jewish victims of the Holocaust. About my grandparents, it reported: "Date of death: Unknown. Cause of death: Murdered, killed by the Nazis." Information submitted by my aunt. Nothing new. I joined jewishgen.org, but that website offered only the Yad Vashem information.

During those weeks, I continued reading *The Chronicle of the Lodz Ghetto,* hoping that the next paragraph, the next annotation, the next picture, the next footnote, would hold another clue to my grandfather's fate. I tried YIVO—*Yidisher Visnshaftlekher Institut*, or the Yiddish Scientific Institute—the preeminent center for the study of East European Jewry and Yiddish. People there encouraged me to reach out to the US Holocaust Memorial Museum. On the museum's website, I came across a 2007 panel discussion: "Voices from the Lodz Ghetto: Conversations with Survivors." I carefully read the bios and listened to the brief video clips of each of the four panelists. Perhaps one of them had searched for loved ones, and could give me some direction?

I took it from the top. The first panelist lived in DC. Using whitepages.com, I found his number, called him, and hung up when I got his answering machine, assuming that I would reach one of the panelists. On to the next: Salomea Kape in New York. She lived in Larchmont, was a retired anesthesiologist, and had written numerous short stories about her life in Lodz, before, during, and after the war. I read every one of her stories that I found, and after I was as informed about her as I could be, I called. An answering machine, with a male voice. This time, though, I left a message: *This is for Salomea Kape. I gather she was in the Lodz Ghetto. My grandparents were in the Lodz Ghetto. . . .* I was skeptical that I would hear back.

But the next day, she called. With her high-pitched, Julia Child–like voice and thick Polish accent, she said, "This is Salomea Kape. I got your message. How can I help you?" I could not believe I was in conversation with someone who walked the soil of the Lodz Ghetto. I told her more. *My father died, my grandparents were in the Ghetto, I have these letters, I found a translator. I want to find out about the fate of my grandfather. . . .*

She didn't miss a beat. "Let me tell you this. I can tell you about the German

Jews. They had an exceptionally hard time adjusting to life in the Ghetto. For the most part, they were old." Like my grandparents, I thought.

She said, "When they arrived, all of them were put in the cinema and the school, until they were placed elsewhere. I remember going there and staring at them. They, in their finery, looked down on us, as though to say, 'We will not end up so weak and looking like you.'" Salomea noted that she was fifteen years old at the time and, along with her girlfriend, asked the seventeen- and eighteen-year-old German Jewish boys about the current songs. "We were hungry to know about life anywhere outside the ghetto," she told me. Also, because the school was where the German Jews were held initially, there was no more school in the ghetto, she said, "and that was a sad day."

Salomea continued, "Let me tell you, *all* of the German Jews died. I remember the transports taking them away. That is, the ones who didn't die already of starvation or disease." Was my grandfather in one of those transports? Or did he wither away?

I didn't want my conversation with Salomea to end. I proudly told her that I had read her stories. I asked her about one of them, the one about when she was in medical school just after the war in Lodz—"Is that true that the cadaver in your anatomy class was the body of the commandant of the Ghetto?" Offended, she replied, "I want you to know that what I write is *all* facts. I never write otherwise. I don't have to make it up. I don't have to embellish."

Had I blown it? I sheepishly asked, "Could we meet one day? *If* it were appropriate, *if* you were interested, *if* it were possible, then I'd be willing to drive to Larchmont to meet you for coffee." She was willing not only to meet me, but to come into the city and meet me for lunch.

Before we hung up, I asked her my burning question—how could I find out more about my grandfather's death? She suggested that I call someone in the tracing department of the United States Holocaust Memorial Museum. I did so the next day.

I learned that the museum used the Red Cross International Tracing Service and that I should request the trace from both the museum and the Red Cross. I was told to not become disillusioned, as a tracing search might last months.

Only forty-eight hours later, I received an email with attachments from the Holocaust Museum. The email stated that the attached documents were from the Red Cross International Tracing Service, that no Lodz Ghetto worker card had been found for my grandfather, and that I should feel free to contact them again. I could not open the attachments because I was in the car, heading to our Vermont cabin with my husband and younger son, Adam. When we finally arrived, six hours later—it seemed like an eternity—I raced inside and turned on my laptop.

With tremendous anticipation, I opened each of the five attachments one-by-one, wondering what treasured information each one held, or didn't. I opened a document that was a list of people from Frankfurt who died in the Lodz Ghetto. There it was: my grandfather's name, *Norbert Baum*, the third name from the bottom of the list; his *gebursdatum* (birthdate); and then *gestorben an* (died on) February 22, 1942.[1]

And now I knew. At least the date.

But how did he die? I assumed he had likely succumbed to either starvation or TB. Starvation was a common cause of death of the frail and elderly inhabitants of the Lodz Ghetto. But also, an outbreak of TB had occurred there—and in February 1942. However, I later learned that my grandfather's recorded date of death coincides with the date of the second wave of deportations from the Lodz Ghetto to nearby Chelmno, the killing center where victims were gassed and then buried in mass graves. Was that my grandfather's fate?

At the least, I finally knew that my grandfather had died—or was taken to his imminent death—ten weeks before my grandmother took her life. But I still had many questions: When were my grandparents deported to Lodz? Were they deported from Frankfurt or taken elsewhere first? Were there death certificates? I circled back to the Holocaust Museum, the YIVO, and the Red Cross. I wrote to the *Institut für Stadtgeschichte Frankfurt am Main*, the Institute for Frankfurt City Archives. One month later, an oversized thick envelope arrived from the *Stadtgeschichte*. They sent a biography compiled by the Jewish Museum Frankfurt with mostly basic information that I already knew about each of my grandparents—date and place of birth, profession, spouse, marriage date.

But the biography also had information that was new to me—date of deportation: October 19, 1941. That was the date of the first major deportation of the Jews in Frankfurt—four days after my grandparents had written their last letter to my father. And four months before my grandfather's death and six months before my grandmother's suicide. Because the Westend section of Frankfurt was a desirable place to live, the Nazis wanted to reside there during their tour of duty. Consequently, it was one of the first neighborhoods in Frankfurt from which Jews were deported.

For my grandfather's *Todesdatum*, his date of death, the document stated

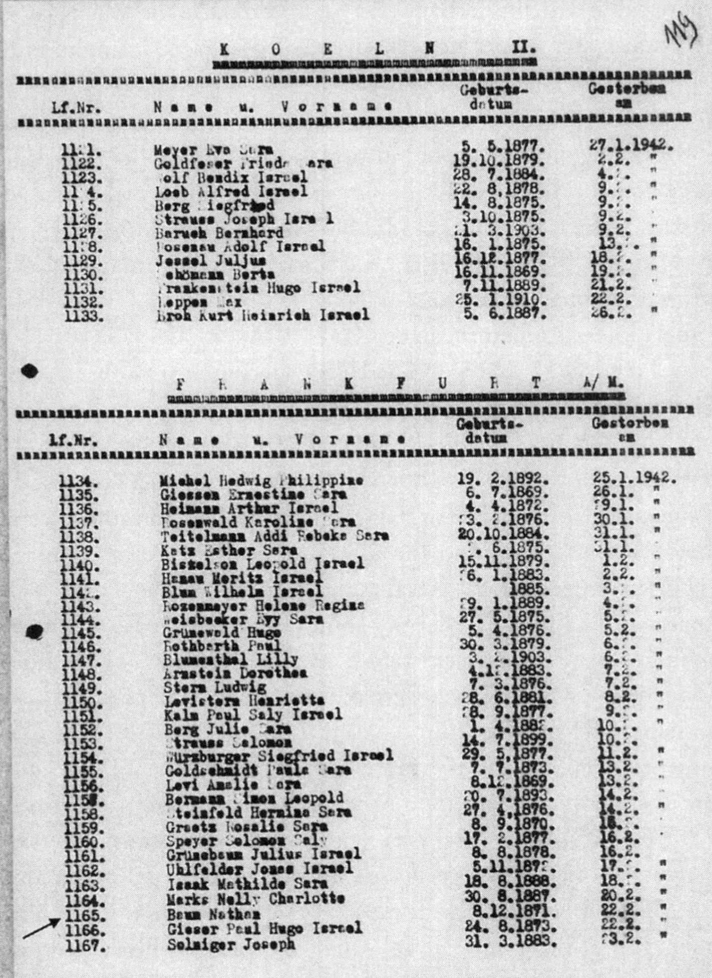

119

K O E L N II.

Lf.Nr.	Name u. Vorname	Geburts-datum	Gestorben am
1121.	Meyer Eva Sara	5. 5.1877.	27.1.1942.
1122.	Goldfeser Frieda Sara	19.10.1879.	2.2. "
1123.	Wolf Bendix Israel	28. 7.1884.	4.2. "
1124.	Loeb Alfred Israel	22. 8.1878.	9.2. "
1125.	Berg Siegfried	14. 8.1875.	9.2. "
1126.	Strauss Joseph Israel	3.10.1875.	9.2. "
1127.	Baruch Bernhard	21. 3.1903.	9.2. "
1128.	Rosenau Adolf Israel	16. 1.1875.	13.2. "
1129.	Jessel Julius	16.12.1877.	18.2. "
1130.	Schömann Berta	16.11.1869.	19.2. "
1131.	Frankenstein Hugo Israel	7.11.1889.	21.2. "
1132.	Leppen Max	25. 1.1910.	22.2. "
1133.	Broh Kurt Heinrich Israel	5. 6.1887.	26.2. "

F R A N K F U R T A/ M.

Lf.Nr.	Name u. Vorname	Geburts-datum	Gestorben am
1134.	Michel Hedwig Philippine	19. 2.1892.	25.1.1942.
1135.	Giessen Ernestine Sara	6. 7.1869.	26.1. "
1136.	Heimann Arthur Israel	4. 4.1872.	29.1. "
1137.	Rosenwald Karoline Sara	13. 2.1876.	30.1. "
1138.	Teitelmann Addi Rebeka Sara	20.10.1884.	31.1. "
1139.	Katz Esther Sara	[illegible]. 6.1875.	31.1. "
1140.	Bitzelson Leopold Israel	15.11.1879.	1.2. "
1141.	Hanau Moritz Israel	16. 1.1883.	2.2. "
1142.	Blum Wilhelm Israel	1885.	3.2. "
1143.	Rozenmayer Helene Regine	29. 1.1889.	4.2. "
1144.	Weisbecker Evy Sara	27. 5.1875.	5.2. "
1145.	Grünewald Hugo	5. 4.1876.	5.2. "
1146.	Rothbarth Paul	30. 3.1879.	6.2. "
1147.	Blumenthal Lilly	3. 2.1903.	6.2. "
1148.	Arnstein Dorothea	4.12.1883.	7.2. "
1149.	Stern Ludwig	7. 3.1876.	7.2. "
1150.	Levistern Henrietta	28. 6.1881.	8.2. "
1151.	Kaln Paul Saly Israel	28. 9.1877.	9.2. "
1152.	Berg Julie Sara	1. 4.1882.	10.2. "
1153.	Strauss Salomon	14. 7.1899.	10.2. "
1154.	Würzburger Siegfried Israel	29. 5.1877.	11.2. "
1155.	Goldschmidt Paula Sara	7. 7.1873.	13.2. "
1156.	Levi Amalie Sara	8.12.1869.	13.2. "
1157.	Bermann Simon Leopold	20. 7.1893.	14.2. "
1158.	Steinfeld Hermine Sara	27. 4.1876.	14.2. "
1159.	Graetz Rosalie Sara	8. 9.1870.	15.2. "
1160.	Speyer Salomon Saly	17. 2.1877.	16.2. "
1161.	Grünebaum Julius Israel	8. 8.1878.	16.2. "
1162.	Uhlfelder Jonas Israel	5.11.1872.	17.2. "
1163.	Isaak Mathilde Sara	18. 8.1888.	18.2. "
1164.	Marks Nelly Charlotte	30. 8.1887.	20.2. "
1165.	Baum Nathan	8.12.1871.	22.2. "
1166.	Gieser Paul Hugo Israel	24. 8.1873.	22.2. "
1167.	Selmiger Joseph	31. 3.1883.	23.2. "

Jews from Frankfurt who died in the Lodz Ghetto.

AUFSTELLUNG

der in der Zeit vom 23. Februar bis 1. März gemeldeten Todesfälle

250

Nr.	Name	Vorname	Adresse	Beruf	Geburts-datum	Ort	Todes-datum	Todesursache
1.	Antmann	Abraham-I.	Bolzengasse 26	Kaufmann	1872	Przemysl	22.2.	Dementia
2.	Altgenug	Lina-Sara	" 26	ohne	1865	Norden	19.2.	Dementia senilis
3.	Abraham	Adelbert-I.	Alexanderhofstr.45	Kaufmann	1870	Pinne	21.2.	Zuckerkrankheit
4.	Akin	Mordka	Sulzfelderstr. 7	Schneider	1907	Lodsch	21.2.	Verschüttung
5.	Amsel	Riwka	R Str. 6	Kind	1939	"	20.2.	Unterernährung
6.	Brabetz	Oskar-I.	Siegfriedstr.101	Handelsagent	1878	Prag	22.2.	Entkräftung, Erfrierun
7.	Blumental	Rudolf	T. Str. 11	Tischler	1901	Breslau	20.2.	Tuberkulose
8.	Borensztein	Symcha-Binem	V. Str. 7	Schlosser	1891	Kielce	23.2.	Erschöpfung, Inanitio
9.	Bursztajn	Moszek	Kirchplatz 8	Arbeiter	1921	Lodsch	25.2.	Tbc. pulm.
10.	Birencwajg	Rojza	D. Str. 2 a	ohne	1870	Szydłowiec	23.2.	Herzinsuffizienz
11.	Biedak	Frajndla	A Str. 6	"	1899	Lodsch	22.2.	Unterernährung
12.	Birgier	Icko-Majer	Am Quell 5	Kaufmann	1873	Grodno	23.2.	Insuff.m.cordis
13.	Berger	Chemja	Telegrafenstr. 9	"	1884	Nowe Miasto	23.2.	Unterernährung
14.	Berger	Wolf	Neustadtstr. 32	"	1881	Lodsch	21.2.	"
15.	Bessermann	Estera	Kirchplatz 5	ohne	1878	Opatów	22.2.	Herzschwäche
16.	Berliner	Moszek-A.	16. Str. 31	Arbeiter	1878	Przedbórz	23.2.	Polyavitaminosis
17.	Białystok	Fajga	5. Str. 8	Wäschenäherin	1907	Radomsko	21.2.	Lungenentzündung
18.	Baum	Nathan	Hohensteinerstr.70	Kaufmann	1871	Hasselbach	22.2.	Unterernährung
19.	Czerny	Itta	O. Str. 32	ohne	1904	Brzeziny	21.2.	Schwindsucht
20.	Caspary	Anna-Sara	Brunhildstr. 25	"	1879	Schlochau	23.2.	Erschöpfung, Hirnblutu
21.	Fajtlowicz	Berek	Am Quell 1	Scherer	1874	Lodsch	20.2.	Herzschwäche
22.	Finkelsztajn	Elia	C Str. 3	Schneider	1912	Włocławek	22.2.	Avitaminosis
23.	Flumbaum	Dwojra	O. Str. 29	ohne	1880	Hawa Maz.	22.2.	Herzschwäche
24.	Fürst	Arthur-I.	Bolzengasse 26	Apotheker	1874	Königsberg	22.2.	Marasmus
25.	Fuks	Mascha	10. Str. 33	ohne	1882	Petrikau	22.2.	Herzschwäche
26.	Gelbard	Tauba	Bolzengasse 26	"	1855	unbek.	22.2.	Inanitio
27.	Goldstein	Rachela	25 Str. 2	"	1865	Nowy Korczyn	22.2.	"
28.	Gernbach	Cyrla-Laja	7. Str. 1	Arbeiterin	1912	Lodsch	24.2.	Tbc. miliaris
29.	Gotesgnaden	Szulim-Hersz	15. Str. 20	Scherer	1875	Zgierz	23.2.	Herzmuskelentartung
30.	Gieser	Paul-I.	Hohensteinerstr.70	Jurist	1873	Frankfurt	22.2.	Herzschwäche
31.	Gielnowski	Caler	Alexanderhofstr.35	Schuster	1906	Klwów	21.2.	Inanitio, Erschöpfung
32.	Grubstein	Bajla	O. Str. 5	Friseur	1896	Lodsch	21.2.	Herzmuskelschwäche
33.	Gotesgnade	Chana	10. Str. 40	Schneiderin	1897	"	20.2.	Lungenschwindsucht
34.	Guthere	Sura	26. Str. 3	ohne	1890	Kowal	2122.	Hungerödem
35.	Gerson	Maks	Z. Str. 18	Tapezierer	1901	Lodsch	21.2.	Unterernährung
36.	Herz	Albert	2. Str. 5	Kaufmann	1882	Lombahm	23.2.	Blutvergiftung
37.	Jacob	Simon-I.	Brunhildstr. 25	Dekorateur	1878	Köln	22.2.	Multiple Hirnblutunge
38.	Joachimsthal	Bertha-S.	Ottilienstr. 18	ohne	1893	Berlin	21.2.	Carcinoma d.Rectums
39.	Kon	Majer-Hersz	Sulzfelderstr.74	Händler	1890	Zgierz	22.2.	Tuberculosis pulm.
40.	Kilbert	Majer	Packerstr. 14	Angestellter	1892	Zychlin	23.2.	Lungentbc.

Lodz Ghetto Hospital Death Records from March 1 to February 23, 1942.

that it would "be fixed at December 31, 1945"—date "fixed," or assigned, to be the last day of the year in which WWII ended. I sent an update to the Jewish Museum Frankfurt—a twist in the roles of information provider and information seeker.

Eight weeks later, on March 29, 2010—the one-year anniversary of my father's death and, coincidentally, the first night of *Passover*—I was preparing Seder when I received a call from a woman from the Red Cross International Tracing Service. With a heavy French accent, the woman reported, "So sorry to tell you this news. So sorry." She continued: the Lodz Ghetto, my grandparents' dates of death, date of deportation. I already knew.

It would not be until six years later that I would learn my grandfather's fate. A Lodz Ghetto Hospital record, forwarded to me by the Holocaust Museum, stated *Todesursache: Unterernährung*, Cause of Death: Malnutrition.[2]

Still, even then, and certainly before that, I wanted more.

* * *

But going to Poland to learn more was not what I, as a *German* Jew, had envisioned.

It was during my lunch with Salomea, back in October 2009 that the idea came up. "If graves for your grandparents are there, maybe you will go," she said. Without missing a beat, I replied, "If there are graves there, I *will* go!" For these grandparents I've never known. For these tombstones my father never knew existed. For my father's sentiments: "*Nothing can change what happened, but I do not want my parents to be forgotten. . . .*"

Salomea was eighty-three at the time. She is barely five feet tall and has wispy strawberry blonde hair that frames her rosy cheeks and endearing smile. Toward the end of our three-hour lunch, she made a surprise offer: "And if you go, I will go with you. It will make it easier for you."

Easier for *me*? I quickly transitioned from amazement to gratitude. I told her that I would be honored. Salomea is one of eight hundred people who survived the Lodz Ghetto, which had 250,000 inhabitants over time.

She dutifully followed through with Marek Szukalak, the administrator and record keeper of the historical Jewish Cemetery of Lodz. Within a week, she learned from Szukalak that there were no cemetery records for my grandparents. A few weeks later, we spoke again. "Look, mine dear, Szukalak researched your grandparents," she explained. "It seems seven months of records are missing and it is just in those seven months that your grandparents died."

I tried not to let my disappointment cloud my gratitude for this new information. She went on to explain that I could place a memorial plaque on the wall of the cemetery as a way to permanently memorialize my grandparents. I was eager to do so. Together, we designed the plaque, with its last line: "Remembered by Family.'" Salomea and I planned to travel to Lodz in a few months, in June 2010. But I didn't want this connection with my grandparents to stop with me. My sons, Matthew and Adam—twenty-one and seventeen at the time—agreed to accompany me. I began to make the arrangements and, at Salomea's request, coordinated on her behalf with her high-energy forty-six-year-old son, John. He had never been to Poland and said he intended to go, eventually. I pointed out the irony that my two sons and I were going with his mother before he had been with his mother. The next week, John announced that he would join us.

We barely knew one another, but we had agreed to embark on a seven-day journey to Poland together. We German Jews and Polish Jews. We three generations.

32

A Trip to Frankfurt, 2010

Look, mine dear, I am Polish. I am American. And, I am a Jew. Why must I choose what I am first, second, and third? This makes no sense. None at all. I am all of these.

SALOMEA KAPE | a survivor of the Lodz Ghetto

In the interim, I was invited to Frankfurt to attend a symposium in May 2010, to commemorate the two hundredth birthday of my great-great-great uncle Rabbi Abraham Geiger, for his achievements in helping to found Reform Judaism. I wanted to represent the Geiger family after my father's death. My brother and sister chose not to go, so I invited a dear friend, Lauren Glant, to meet me in Frankfurt after the symposium, to support me in retracing steps in the lives of my grandparents and my father.

Sitting in the crowded gate area in Newark, waiting to board my direct Lufthansa flight to Frankfurt, I was spooked by being surrounded with so many thirty- and forty-somethings conversing in German. I was wondering about their grandparents. How old would their grandparents have been in, say, 1940? I was unnerved by this blanket of everything German around me: German language, English with a German accent, German fashion, German books, German passports. I'd been to Germany twice before, and I'd often worked with young German professionals. Why was I having such a visceral reaction now? Perhaps because I was about to step into those places where my father and grandparents lived, worshipped, walked, and struggled.

With all things German all around me, I reflected upon the spiritual journey talk that I had delivered at our synagogue six months earlier. I had addressed it to my grandparents:

> September 28, 2009
>
> *Dear Grandma Julie and Grandpa Norbert—*
>
> I want to share with you that I have been given the honor today on Yom Kippur to stand here on the *bimah* at my synagogue to talk about

my spiritual journey. Although we've never met, I do feel that our lives are inextricably woven together. While I know only pieces of the fate that befell you during your suffering in the Holocaust, the strong family ties and the emotional burden that both you and my father carried are very much a part of who I am. L'dor v'dor (from generation to generation).

I think you'd be interested to know that, at the Museum of Jewish Heritage, your son's (i.e., my father's) voice declares what most German Jews felt, "We were Germans first and Jews second." Knowing the atrocities you all suffered, I now declare that I am a Jew first and an American second. . . .

Grandma Julie and Grandpa Norbert, I love you, and my spiritual journey as a Jew first and an American second continues with my husband and my sons, with my brother and sister and extended family members, and with my dearest friends by my side and it continues with you at its core. L'dor v'dor.

Hugs and kisses,

Your granddaughter,

Karen

I remembered asking Salomea, "Do you think of yourself as a Jew first?" I was shocked by her response. "And why do you ask such a question? I do not like such a question. Look, mine dear, I am Polish. I am American. And, I am a Jew. Why must I choose what I am first, second, and third? This makes no sense. None at all. I am all of these."

If *she* doesn't think of herself as a Jew first, then how could I?

And yet . . . How could I *not*? It was because my father was a Jew that he felt compelled to leave Germany. And it was because my grandparents were Jews that they were forced from their home, deported, and perished.

For the sake of my children, how could I *not*? For their Jewish identities. Otherwise, might the very part of their heritage that painfully shaped my father's and grandfather's destinies be diluted? In the course of only one or two more generations, might that part of their heritage be forgotten, washed away like a shoreline weathered by changing tides?

It was time to board the plane.

* * *

The symposium took place at the University of Frankfurt, in a building that was formerly home to I.G. Farben, the chemical industry conglomerate, the one that produced the Zyklon B. It was seventy-three years earlier that my grandmother wrote of having a view of that building.

Day one of the International Symposium Celebrating the 200th Birthday of Rabbi Abraham Geiger had come to a close. I had listened to several lectures in German, each one relevant to the intellectual challenges voiced by Rabbi Geiger. Struggling with my German, I occasionally nodded to signal that I was able to follow along. But I felt like an outsider looking in. An American among mostly Germans. A Jew, a businesswoman, among mostly non-Jewish religious scholars, academics studying Geiger. Near the lecture podium was a larger-than-life poster of him—my great-great-great uncle. He resembled my father to a great extent—the profile, jawline, soft eyes, long smile lines, and sharp nose belied the three generations separating them. I felt my father's presence.

After the last lecture, an informal group gathered to have dinner. The agreed-upon restaurant was on the corner of Wolfsgangstraße and Hansaallee. Wolfsgangstraße—the street of the last residence of my grandparents. During the half-hour walk to the restaurant, I spoke with one of the many scholars. It was dusk, and the sky was a soft dark blue curtain spotted with glaring fluorescent streetlights. Suddenly, a blue and white street sign: "Wolfsgangstraße"; the restaurant was at #84 Wolfsgangstraße. I announced I would be back shortly, as my new acquaintance and I walked further, to #132—my grandparents' final address.

It was a white stucco building, a boxy three-story affair with a bright yellow fluorescent outdoor porch light, an unsightly architectural interruption in a stretch of aesthetically charming residences, most of which seemed original to times past. The original building at #132 had been bombed in 1945.

Still, it was from here that my grandparents had been roused early, pulled from their home, and, along with 1,100 other Frankfurt Jews, herded through the streets in front of the peering eyes of neighbors and countless strangers. As Monica Kingreen, author of *Forcibly Dragged Out of Frankfurt: The Deportation of the Jews in the Years 1941–1945*, recounted: "They were awakened on Sunday morning, October 19, 1941, between 6–7 a.m., without forewarning. The police armed with weapons came to the front door. 'You have to leave in two hours. Pack and clean the house and leave the apartment in order and to go to the assembly point. On your neck you must wear a badge with your name and birthday and an i.d. number. You have to do exactly this way, otherwise you will be punished by the most severe methods.'"

* * *

After the two-day symposium, Lauren met me at the University of Frankfurt. Armed with our umbrellas against the drizzly day and prepared with our camera, video, and dictaphone, we began our trail of discovery. Unlike when I had been in Frankfurt with my parents in 1972 and only briefly seen some places, on this trip I was on a mission. Having been immersed in my grandparents' letters and steeped in primary and secondary research, I was driven to get close to, to experience, places of significance to my father and grandparents. To walk the streets, to touch and feel objects, to use my imagination to take me back in time.

The first stop for Lauren and me would be Reuterweg, to find the apartment where my father grew up.

As we knew from studying the maps, Reuterweg was a main north-south thoroughfare—busy with two-way traffic and crowded with pedestrians on its cobblestone sidewalks. While largely residential, it had its share of storefronts, restaurants, and bistros interspersed among its multistory brownstone-like houses, some of which were original nineteenth-century architecture and some of which were rebuilt after being destroyed during WWII. It did not have the charm of the narrow nearby interconnecting residential streets, the one-way streets that changed direction willy-nilly and were lined with pastel-colored five-story attached homes, like a box of watercolors, one façade more grand than the next.

As we walked down Reuterweg, I asked Lauren, who is so knowledgeable about history and architecture, if the sidewalk was the original sidewalk. Probably not, she explained, given the seam in the bluestone. I asked about the curb. Probably not. *That gate? This street sign? That storefront? This door?* I was desperate to see, to be in the presence of, *something* that existed when my father and my grandparents walked these streets.

We finally came upon the blue street sign announcing "Reuterweg 71–83." There was #73, a drab brown stucco building, with black water stains framing most of the windows, some rounded, some square, some multi-paned, some single-paned, some with balconies, some with window boxes full of red geraniums.

My grandparents' apartment had been bombed during the war. It has been rebuilt, with an additional floor above it.

After a few minutes of huddling in the rain and gazing at #73 from across the street, Lauren was ready to move on. But I was compelled to ring the apartment buzzers to see if someone would let us in—that is, someone other than the two residents I had tried to reach by phone last week. One had seemed receptive, and we had agreed that I would call him upon my arrival to confirm a visit on Monday or Tuesday. But the day before my departure, he emailed: "I am sorry to tell you that there will be no possibility to visit our private apartment at Reuterweg 73. It is not an official office open for public visits, so I hope you will understand, I regret." I understood that he did not trust me. I wanted to visit this place, now his place. Perhaps he viewed me as someone trying to reclaim property? The unspoken: I am Jewish. The outcome: I was shut out.

The other resident spoke English well and initially responded with "*ja*" or "yes, I see" comments. But then he suddenly switched into speaking only German. When the call abruptly ended, I questioned if we had been disconnected or he hung up. I called back immediately: voicemail.

I wasn't giving up. I was going to ring the buzzers. Lauren said, "You're going to do *what*? Oh, no. Oh, no!" I explained that I had to do it.

The entrance was on the side of the house, with a buzzer keypad with eight bells, signifying that each floor had two apartments. I rang the first bell: No response. Second bell: Simm. Skipped that one, as he was the one with whom I had the email exchange. Third bell: no response. Fourth bell: no response. Fifth bell: the sound of victory, the buzz of someone letting me in.

I turned the doorknob that my father couldn't turn. I was in. A bit shaky, feeling like a sleuth, worried I could be interrogated. At the same time, I began to take in the moment, the space.

A small simple entryway. Grungy walls painted an institutional beige. An oak staircase, with well-worn stair treads, sagging in the middle and showing decades of black scuff marks. Only six shallow steps up to the first floor. An arched and rounded thin oak handrail atop white iron spindles with decorative interstitial scrollwork. All seemed original. The staircase on which my father learned to climb stairs; the banister he would have slid down (*if* that were allowed under his rigid German upbringing); the landings on which he would have crawled. The stair treads worn, in part, by my grandparents' comings and goings during their twenty-two years here, by my father's comings and goings.

Suddenly, a voice from the top floor interrupted my dreamlike state, with "*Ja? Was wollen sie?*" Looking up, I saw an unshaven man with black hair. Dressed in a t-shirt and sweatpants, he stood with his hands on his hips, a trash bag just outside his open door. I rushed to answer in my broken German, announcing my name and explaining that my father had been born in this apartment building, and I only wanted to see it briefly. He agreed. I then asked if I could go inside his apartment. He replied, *"Nein, nein,"* as he signaled *no* with his pointer finger.

I thanked him and heard his apartment door close. I snapped pictures as quickly and unobtrusively as I could. The railing, the stairway, the doors. And the short white door to the basement, probably the laundry room. I walked up to the next floor, and then to the next. The apartments had white double doors, opaque glass on the upper portion and plain black doorknobs.

I propped open the door with some paper so that I could go across the street to urge Lauren to come and see. She gazed at the entryway and confirmed that it all seemed original. I'm satisfied.

Lauren and I then walked from Reuterweg 73 in search of Eysseneckstraße 20, where my grandparents and father had moved to in 1934. We headed south on Reuterweg to Grüneburgweg, where we turned left. We spotted a makeshift stand with a handwritten sandwich board sign announcing "*Spargel*" (asparagus), scrawled in thick red marker, in front of a makeshift food stand over which a stout German *Frau* with a broad grin proudly presided. It was *Spargelzeit*, the country's two-month asparagus festival, and six woven vegetable baskets sat side by side at a tilt, each offering its own variety of white asparagus of a specified length and thickness, each from a designated region and for a given price. Unlike the jarred or canned versions that I grew up on, these were the real thing. One evening on this trip, Lauren and I would have our fill of white asparagus, enjoying it with hollandaise sauce; another evening, rich creamy white asparagus soup.

As we continued on our way in a thin veil of continuous drizzle, we juggled our cheap umbrellas and half-torn maps and struggled to read the street signs. We meandered along, marveling at the rainbow-colored rows of elegant mansions, each white, but each with a different accompanying color trim of pink, blue, yellow, or beige. And then we stumbled upon a lush forest green blanket, the Holzhausen Park. Just on the other side of it, we entered a wide street with its breathtaking allée—a fifty-foot grass carpet rolled down the middle, symmetrically lined with trees more than one hundred years old. Checking the map, we realized we were *on* Eysseneckstraße.

Like well-preserved grand dames, Eysseneckstraße's majestic homes reflected the time and attention they had received over the years. We arrived at #20, pale pink with four cherub friezes on its façade. Lauren and I puzzled over which floor belonged to my grandparents. Seemingly out of nowhere, a drenched young woman on a bicycle approached the front gate. I quickly shifted from a relaxed picture-taking mode to determined detective. In my poor German, I asked if I could accompany her to meet whomever buzzed her in.

The next minute I was chatting with a forty-something dark-haired man, handsome and slight, who not only grew up in this house but also was the current owner. "Alex Zahn," he said by way of introduction, "Zahn, as in teeth in German." And, yes, I could come in.

Upon entering, I noticed the polished mahogany banister, with its countless nicks and scratches, some of them from cherished wedding bands they wore, maybe, or from sharp-edged packages they moved in or out.

As we walked upstairs to the duplex apartment, I savored each step. On the third floor, I met Alex's elderly mother, who explained that she and her husband bought the house from the children of the original owners. That would have been the Herrmanns, from whom my grandparents rented.

We proceeded to the fourth floor. The apartment's entryway was relatively large, and the bathroom off the entryway was huge. What would have been my grandparents' kitchen was now a clothing storage room. I peered out the small window in the "kitchen," imagining my grandmother doing so as she cooked her famous *grüne Soße* (green sauce). Alex then showed me the large master bedroom, with its window overlooking the allée. Then the sitting room, with a desk. I pictured my grandmother sitting at such a desk, gazing out and writing those cherished letters to my father.

Then we entered what must have been my father's bedroom. It was small, but with two windows—one looking out on the allée and another on the airshaft. It was there that my father slept his last night under the same roof as his parents, that he dreamt his last dreams in Frankfurt.

* * *

We arrived in the early afternoon at the Jewish Museum Frankfurt to meet with the archivist, Herr Lenarz, whose focus is the nineteenth and twentieth centuries. The museum was housed in the nineteenth-century Rothschild mansion and an adjacent building overlooking the Main River. Its grand neoclassical façade belied its small functional lobby, with a tiny café, one-counter gift shop, and four-rack "bookstore."

We met Herr Lenarz in his office, which was filled with stacks of books, old periodicals here and there, and scattered boxes of various sizes. He methodically addressed the questions I had emailed. He provided the exact location of the Unterlindau Synagogue, the Orthodox synagogue that my father had occasionally attended with his father. That synagogue was only five minutes from the Westend Synagogue. My father became a *bar mitzvah* at the Unterlindau Synagogue, under the tutelage of Rabbi Jakob Horovitz, whose father had been the rabbi of both the Unterlindau and the Bockenheim synagogues. Lenarz searched the Internet and then printed a black-and-white photograph of Horovitz, who was mostly bald and had a beard and full mustache and gentle eyes. He wore a *yarmulke* and jacket and tie.

The archivist explained that the Westend Synagogue was the only one of Frankfurt's eleven synagogues to survive the two days of anti-Semitic riots the Nazis called the *Kristallnacht*. That said, the synagogue's interior was damaged extensively because it was used as storage for the Nazi's tanks and other armaments. It was partially renovated in the early 1950s, and then fully renovated in the early 1990s. Lenarz noted that today the synagogue serves a fledgling Orthodox community and, on occasion, an even smaller liberal Jewish contingent, which is relegated to one small classroom. The Orthodox community has its origins in the Eastern European Orthodox Jews who had immigrated just before, during, or after WWII. The synagogue is open only on Shabbat and holidays.

I also asked what he knew about Jews renting apartments in the late 1930s and early 1940s, as my grandparents had moved twice in a short period of time. He said, "There were many evictions and a kind of self-ghettoization. So it wouldn't be surprising that your grandparents moved. Probably to save money."

Who were my grandparents' landlords? Could Gentiles knowingly rent to new tenants who were Jews? To answer that, Herr Lenarz went to the adjoining room to retrieve a tall stack of twelve-by-eighteen-inch books, each three inches thick with gold-leaf lettering on their torn spines. He plopped down the stack on his desk, explaining that the books were *Adreßbuchs* [address books] and that my grandparents probably bought one every year. The stack contained the 1933, 1935, 1938, and 1942 volumes, with well-worn brown covers embossed on the front with black print "*Frankfurter Adreßbuch für das Jahr* __." Herr Lenarz handled these volumes with great command, though Lauren and I felt somewhat tentative as we touched and turned the delicate yellowed pages.

They were organized by address, and Herr Lenarz, looking down his nose through his thick glasses, leafed through the 1933 *Adresßbuch* to find the Reuterweg 73 listing. The onionskin pages were filled with names and addresses, typed in small print of an old serif font. Reuterweg 67, 69, 71, and then, yes, 73. Listed as the owner was Trier, J., Dr. (America). So an American? Then the tenants by floor, including "Baum, N., Kfm., T, 3."—indicating that my grandfather, Norbert Baum, was a *Kaufman* (salesman) who had a telephone and lived on the third floor. That was where my father was born and raised, the largest of the three apartments that Norbert and Julie lived in. And my grandfather's business was listed under his company's name, Harff: "Norbert Harff, Futterstoffe, Kaiserstraße 44. T. 33702."

We searched the 1935 *Adreßbuch* for Eysseneckstraße 20, my grandparents' second apartment. The owner was "Herrmann, F.W., Fabrf, T. Erdg." My grandfather was listed as a tenant on the third floor. We then looked up Herrmann in the back section of the book, arranged alphabetically by name. A boxed entry with large print: "Friedr. Wilh. Herrmann, *Bleckwrfbk* (manufacturer of metal objects)." Next we searched for my grandfather's business listing. The business had a new address, Große Kornmarkt 18, probably not by choice of my grandfather and his partner.

Lenarz showed us other entries in which buildings that had been owned by Jews were listed with a dash mark—not a name.

We searched the 1938 *and* 1942 book for Wolfsgangstraße 132, their third apartment. Both had a listing for my grandfather on the second floor, although my grandparents were deported in October 1941. The January 1942 *Adreßbuch* did not take into account the deportations. Lenarz described those deportations as "totally chaotic." He said people were led in small groups by the SS to the *Großmarkthalle*, once Frankfurt's largest wholesale produce market, with 140,000 square feet located next to the railroad tracks for convenient transport of freight; the cavernous hall had been converted by the Gestapo into a depot to process Jews for convenient transport out of German society.

We spent two and a half hours with Lenarz, who proved to be not only incredibly thorough, but also patient and kindhearted. Lauren and I then wandered through the museum's permanent exhibition and viewed a detailed floor plan of the *Großmarkthalle*, which described the flow of the processing of the deportees through the areas once used as market stalls.

* * *

Lauren and I entered the Musterschule, the school where my father had received the last bit of his formal education—from nine to sixteen, 1924 to 1931. As we entered the silent hallways of the original building, we noticed that the original doors, handrails, and floor tiles were still in place. We found our way to the administrative offices, where the administrative secretary was accommodating and gave us permission to walk through and see a few classrooms. When I inquired about pictures from the time period, she called over the principal, who offered to look in the files. The unspoken was obvious. My father was Jewish, attending this school at a time when dark winds were gathering in Germany's history.

The principal gave me a fifty-page booklet from 2008. Its cover was a sepia photo that bled into a color photo. In the sepia photo, a dozen boys—it was boys only at the time—peered from a balcony that overhung rows of beautifully carved wooden chairs. I searched for my father in that group, only to realize the picture was from 1903. Suddenly the hallways came alive with teenage German voices and several students stopped into the office, forming an orderly line to ask questions, get passes, and turn in notes. I imagined my father, a skinny kid with red hair and blue eyes, dressed in *lederhosen* or breeches. Under what circumstances did he come to this office? Who were his friends? How lively were the hallways?

Later I thumbed through the booklet from the principal. An article entitled "Visit to Auschwitz and Birkenau," caught my attention. Written by a high school senior about students visiting the camps, the article's epigraph quoted the Polish journalist Mieczyslaw Kieta, from the forward to the survivor Wieslaw Kielar's book about Auschwitz, *Anus Mundi*: "No one will be in the position later to say the full truth about Auschwitz when the last witnesses are gone. This truth is not conceivable. It goes beyond the imagination of every man who has not witnessed this."

These Musterschule students had come face to face with their history.

* * *

I knew when I visited Frankfurt that I must connect with the eighty-five-year-old photographer-cum-cemetery administrator, Klaus Meier-Ude. I hoped he would escort Lauren and me through Frankfurt's Old Jewish Cemetery on Rat-Beil-Straße, where my great-grandparents were buried. To me, his melodic name was only that, a name, though I knew that he had befriended my parents and my aunt after escorting them through this cemetery numerous times. He had been the cemetery's administrator for nineteen years, living in the little nondescript house onsite.

Lauren and I picked up Herr Meier-Ude by taxi at his current home, an assisted living residence. He wore a beret atop his full head of white hair and carried his umbrella like a walking stick. We entered the cemetery through a wooden gate next to the locked iron gate between the white neoclassical columns. Above the portal, in Hebrew, were the words:

יָבוֹא שָׁלוֹם יָנוּחוּ עַל־מִשְׁכְּבוֹתָם הֹלֵךְ נְכֹחוֹ׃

> He shall enter into peace: they shall rest in their beds, each one walking in his uprightness. (Isaiah 57.2)

As we began our trek through the wet cemetery grass, along the path lined with linden trees, our dialogue with Klaus Meier-Ude commenced. He explained that although this was not the oldest Jewish cemetery in Frankfurt, it was indeed old, filled to capacity with graves from 1828 to 1928. It is nearly 174 acres and has approximately thirty-thousand to forty-thousand graves, including those of many famous people: Bertha Pappenheim—the founder of the League of Jewish Women, who had the pseudonym of Anna O. when described in a case study by the psychoanalysts Sigmund Freud and Joseph Breuer; Paul Ehrlich—the Nobel Prize–winning physician and scientist who discovered the cure for syphilis; the Rothschild family, of the financial dynasty, with several grand sarcophagi.

Klaus was only seven years old in 1934 when he "became a young man who marched" in the *Hitler Jugend* (Hitler Youth) in World War II, "not as a soldier, but as a working soldier without a gun." He described it as a terrible time, asserting, "What could we do? We were young people. We were not interested in politics."

Fast forward to 1982, when he photographed the cemetery's tombstones of famous people at the request of Frankfurt's *Institut für Stadtsgeschichte,* the Institute for City Archives. As he wrote in a book of those photographs, "As a contemporary of the Nazi years I also considered myself responsible for what happened at that time. I now had an opportunity to turn my attention to the Jews in our city and, as part of the reconciliation and normalization process, take on an assignment." That same year, the cemetery's administrator died suddenly of a heart attack. He asked the cemetery director to appoint him as

August Geiger,
circa 1922.

the administrator—on the condition that he would not accept payment. He promised to serve as a guide to visitors and to protect the premises.

We continued our walk to Block 92, to the six-and-a-half-foot-tall polished black granite tombstone of my great-grandparents, Rosalie Geiger (1853–1908) and August Geiger (1843–1924). While Rosalie died at a relatively young age before my father was born, my father knew his grandfather August, and wrote in *A Son of a Respectable Family*: "My mother's father . . . was the patriarch of the family, a man about town, cutting a dashing figure with his mustache and goatee. One of my treats as a little boy was to have Friday night dinner at my grandfather's house, a meal prepared by his housekeeper. Although I always complained about the combination of items on her menu, I always looked forward to these visits. My grandfather died of throat cancer in 1924 at the age of 81. I remember going to his funeral, which was my first encounter with death."

We continued walking until we come upon three uniform rows of approximately twenty simple, unadorned gray granite stones each. Those stones, erected after the war by the City of Frankfurt, marked buried urns of ashes. The ashes were sent from the Buchenwald crematorium and randomly apportioned among the urns. Each stone was inscribed with a name, some with a date of death, all with these three lines of Hebrew text that translates as:

He died for God's name;
He was a martyr; and,
Now he is allowed to be buried in ashes.

That text had accompanied a special Jewish law that made special dispensation for the cremation, which is against Jewish law in most circumstances. Some tombstones had a five-letter Hebrew abbreviation ת.נ.צ.ב.ה. *tav, nun, tsadi, bet, hey*–for תהא נפשו/ה צרורה בצרור החיים *teheye nafsho/ah tsrurah b'tsror haChayyim* (May his soul go to heaven, in paradise. May his soul be bound up in the bounds of eternal life.).

After the cemetery, we three took a taxi to Börneplatz, to see the Holocaust Memorial Wall. We first saw a square with T-shaped sycamore trees, with no branches on the trunks and green-blooming flattened tops. These trees were planted methodically, equidistant apart in eight rows of eight, forming a roof of green in late summer. They were planted in a bed of basalt gravel on which it is difficult to walk, reminding visitors of the cruelty of unknown deaths. The square is the site of the destroyed Börneplatz Synagogue.

The trees and the nearby Holocaust Memorial Wall are for the Frankfurt Jews like my grandparents, who died in concentration camps, ghettos, or sanitoriums, and have no graves. The wall runs along either side of Frankfurt's oldest Jewish cemetery, the Battonnstraße Cemetery, which has tombstones dating from 1272 to 1828. Before World War II, the cemetery had approximately seven thousand tombstones. The Nazis intended to use the stones to build streets, but their efforts were interrupted in 1944 by heavy bombing from the Americans and the British. Instead, the Nazis used many of the stones to build a blockade. Only about two thousand gravestones are in place today.

The Holocaust Memorial Wall, spanning more than three hundred yards, has almost twelve thousand small iron blocks, arranged alphabetically in five long rows, which seemed endless.

We walked along the wall in reverse alphabetical order, past the block for Anne Frank, past many blocks with the last name *Baum*, including a block for Hedwig Baum, who was mentioned often in my grandmother's letters. Then we saw: Julie Baum *geb.* (*geboren*, born) Geiger, 3.11.1883–3.5.1942, Lodz. Nathan Norbert Baum, 8.12.1871—the dates written in the European fashion, with the day before the month. The dates were incorrect, but because the blocks are made of iron, incorrect and incomplete information remains in place. We knew that Julie died on 4.5.1942 and that Norbert's date of death was 22.2.42.

Klaus Meier-Ude and Lauren Glant, Frankfurt, May 2010.

Klaus reached into his breast pocket and pulled out a bag of pebbles. According to Jewish tradition, a visitor to a tombstone places a pebble on the stone. One interpretation is that such an act symbolizes continuing love and memory—as strong and enduring as rock. We placed a pebble on top of the iron blocks of Julie and Nathan.

My father never saw this wall with these blocks for his parents, except in a photograph. I saw it for him. I saw it for me.

* * *

When Lauren and I realized that the Jewish holiday *Shavuot*—the harvest festival as well as a holiday commemorating the giving of the Torah at Mount Sinai—fell during our stay, we knew we might be able to go inside the Westend Synagogue.

As we turned the corner on Freiherr-vom-Stein-Straße, we were awed by the monumental building—its multitiered structure, its red-shingled rooftops, and its myriad windows in all shapes and sizes. It loomed like a proud parent, scarred by the deep sadness of having lost a child. I wanted a photo, but as I readied my camera, a security guard shouted, "No pictures! No cameras allowed!" The guards checked our bags, and we entered the grand courtyard, with its pristinely polished stone, laid in a circular pattern, and its three-tiered fountain.

As women entering an Orthodox synagogue, we were relegated to the balcony, and not allowed to sit with the men in the sanctuary's main space on the first floor. The balcony was empty except for two women—a stark comparison to my grandparents' days, when the balcony brimmed with the lively spirit of well-dressed men, women, and children alike, all seated and worshipping together. A nearly twenty-foot teardrop chandelier bathed the gold walls with light reflected off of the blue and gold mosaic-domed ceiling. The *bimah* was in a huge alcove with blue-green granite flooring, a blue and gold mosaic backdrop, and gold Hebrew lettering above.

We peered over the balcony's ledge, feeling like voyeurs as we observed fifteen middle-aged and older men, all wearing hats or *yarmulkes* and *tzitzit*, some *davening*, some wandering about whispering to one another. I fumbled to find my camera. Though I knew picture-taking was *verboten,* I felt entitled to do so. I turned off the flash and snapped away: the chandelier, the domed ceiling, the *bimah*, the side balconies, the organ.

I imagined my grandmother, in all her finery, and my grandfather, with his stern gaze, entering the synagogue and searching for seats in a sanctuary overflowing with congregants. My father, all of ten years old, with his flaming red hair, and his sister, all of twelve, both petite for their age, each with their prominent Geiger profile. What was it like for them to participate in a Reform congregation, replete with its organ music, which had come about, in large part, thanks to Rabbi Abraham Geiger, their relative of only a few generations back? What was their worship experience like, as they identified as Germans first and Jews second?

And I thought about all that had occurred here since then.

33

A Trip to Poland, 2010

Remembered by Family.

PLAQUE AT THE JEWISH CEMETERY OF LODZ

It was mid-June 2010 when Matthew, Adam, and I took our nine-hour redeye to Warsaw and were greeted at the baggage carousel by the sign, "Nowy Jork JFK, 09:30, LO 007." We were in Poland for our own 007 mission: to investigate my grandparents' lives in the Lodz Ghetto.

With $200 worth of Polish *zlotys* in hand, we arrived at the rundown, 1970s-style *Warszawa Centraina*, the main rail station, and looked for Salomea and her son, John. Though they had never met, Matthew easily spotted John, with his red baseball cap. He was standing next to his short mother in the ticket line, obviously looking around in search of someone. He motioned us to come quickly, and we learned that we had only three minutes to make the next train to Lodz. No time for introductions.

Matthew and Adam grabbed Salomea's bright orange luggage so that the spry eighty-four-year-old could focus on keeping up with the rest of us. We bolted down a long staircase as if in a chase scene in a movie—five of us, loosely connected, each with fierce determination to make this train. We clumsily mounted the train's steep steps and took the first compartment: John and Salomea on one side of the booth and my boys and me on the other, two moms and our boys. The train began to roll.

Taking a deep breath, we settled in. John jumped right in and asked the boys if they were Yankees or Mets fans. The high-fives and the banter about recent games began. We were off to a good start.

I expressed my amazement to Salomea that here we were, with our sons, on a train to Lodz, just six months after first meeting over lunch at Sarabeth's Kitchen. She replied, "Yes, mine dear, we did it! Hard to believe." Her signature expression of "mine dear" comforted me, somehow. We were with Salomea, who was at home, in a way.

Later, on our self-guided tour, we reoriented under our umbrellas with our maps and video camera. We set up a wireless video mic on Salomea to begin our walk through the former ghetto.

First, we walked through a small park with scraggly trees and a significant amount of litter, and then stumbled upon the words *Litzmannstadt Ghetto*, stenciled in white on the sidewalk. We had crossed several borders: from rich to poor, from clean to dirty, from freedom to where freedom once didn't exist.

Salomea's high-pitched voice and thick Polish accent guided us. She described where barbed wire had defined the ghetto's border. She recalled where there had been a footbridge that she crossed daily to her job to sew coats for the Gestapo, passing the armed guards that were stationed every two meters. "Every day I was afraid for my life," she said.

Adjacent to the footbridge was St. Mary's Assumption Church, used by the Gestapo as a warehouse for the piles of valuables they stole from the Jews. The church's statues and crosses had been desecrated during the war. Nearby, the dreary gray day was a monochrome backdrop for dreary, graffiti-covered tenement buildings, seedy bars, and dirty storefronts. Of the few people we passed, the adults seemed joyless and the adolescents seemed like hoodlums scavenging for their next no-good adventure.

We came upon an abandoned corner storefront with a large empty lot behind it. Salomea explained that there the Gestapo had distributed the food rations—"Frozen potatoes in the winter and moldy potatoes in the summer."

The only time I saw Salomea become choked up was in front of the Red House, an old Gestapo building now used as a busy church rectory, with

Dr. Salomea Kape,
Lodz, June 2010.

people coming and going. In the basement of that building, Salomea's father had been tortured. "I think we should go," she stammered. "This is the most . . . the cellars . . . let's go . . . I cannot even look at it."

The sign in front made crystal clear what had happened inside: "The Red House—location of the Criminal Police Station. Site where Jews were submitted to torture, maimed, and usually murdered." The Gestapo often sent dead bodies back to their families, claiming that the victim had a heart attack. Sometimes they didn't even send the dead back. Salomea's father was one of the lucky ones: he returned to their tenement badly beaten, but alive.

As we walked along the east-west thoroughfare, Wojska Polskiego Street, I noted that the map indicated we were near the former cinema that initially housed the Frankfurt deportees. There, the likes of my grandparents slept on the floor or in the theater seats until they were placed in a crowded tenement. This was where the fourteen-year-old Salomea and her friends had come to gape at the new inhabitants from Germany and to talk with the young German boys about music. Now the cinema had been converted into a Tesco grocery store, a glaring white fluorescent-lit space filled with customers and their shopping carts.

After Salomea briefly spoke with the Tesco store manager, we left. She explained that people were suspicious of us, concerned that we came to reclaim property. She reassured them that we are not here to take anything, only to remember.

We visited the Radegast Train Station in Lodz, finally standing on the platform from which my grandparents had descended the train from Frankfurt. The inside of the station is now a museum in which we discovered the original papers listing those deported to Lodz, including my grandparents. More than twenty-thousand Jews—from Germany, Austria, Czechoslovakia, and Luxembourg—arrived around the same time as my grandparents, adding to the nearly 155,000 Jews already inhabiting the ghetto.

We hopped into a cab, heading to 70 Zgierska Street, the building that housed the Jews from Frankfurt, and, as we drove, our taxi traversed the 4.13 kilometers of the ghetto, past rundown tenements. The only distinctions from one to the other were where the neglected water stains or black soot marks appeared, or where the utility cables intruded.

From 1941 to 1944, these buildings provided little beyond shelter from the elements. The bone-chilling winters in those years had been as life-threatening as hunger. Sometimes seven to ten people lived in two small rooms with a single

VI Transport B. 185

Liczba porz.	Nazwisko i imię	Data urodzenia	Zawód	Skąd przyb.	
1	✓ Bacharach Selma	21.7 1895	Hausangest.	Frankfurt.	
2	Bakenheimer Salomon	3.10 1873	Kaufmann	"	
3	✓ " Mathilde	31.7 1885	ohne	"	
4	Badmann Ludwig	3.5 1893	Vertreter	"	
5	✓ " Fanny	22.8 1894	Arbeiterin	"	
6	✓ " Max	1.11 1866	Bankbeamter	"	Gnesenerstr. 26
7	✓ " Mimi	10.9 1875	ohne	"	"
8	Bamberger Sally	3.3 1891	Viehhändler	"	
9	Bablschewski Rose	15.11 1885	ohne	"	
10	✓ Bamberger Ida S.	13.3 1899	"	"	
11	✓ " Else	28.6 1927	Praktikantin	"	
12	✓ Baer Friedrich	2.9 1890	Angest.	"	
13	✓ " Klara S.	4.4 1894	Pflegerin	"	
14	✓ Bär Margarete	15.6 1897	ohne	"	
15	✓ " Edith S.	13.6 1932	Sprechstd.	"	
16	✓ " Siegfried	5.10 1906	Hausangest.	"	
17	✓ " Elba S.	[illegible] 1881	Sekretärin	"	
18	✓ Bauer Ella S.	[illegible] 1881	ohne	"	
19	✓ " Clara	12.5 1887	Verkäuferin	"	
20	✓ " Klara	9.9 1883		"	
21	Bauernfreund Johanna	15.6 1902	ohne	"	
22	✓ " Heinrich	16.10 1890	Kaufmann	"	
23	✓ " Fred	23.9 1925	ohne	"	
24	✓ " Hans	21.2 1926	"	"	
25	✓ Baum Gustav	18.1 1881	Kaufmann	"	
26	✓ " Meta	15.9 1887	Köchin	"	
27	✓ " Nathan	8.12 1871	Kaufmann	"	

do przeniesienia

VI Transport B. 186

Liczba porz.	Nazwisko i imię	Data urodzenia	Zawód	Skąd przyb.	
	z przeniesienia				
28	Baum Julie	3.11 1883	ohne	Frankfurt	
29	✓ " Salomon	29.7 1875	Kaufmann	"	
30	✓ " Klara S.	23.3 1884	ohne	"	
31	✓ " Käthe S.	7.5 1927	Schülerin	"	
32	✓ " Klara	10.2 1878	ohne	"	Gnesener 26
33	✓ " Marta S.	3.9 1881	Lab.	"	
34	✓ Baumann Max	4.12 1891	Kaufmann	"	
35	✓ " Selma	16.3 1904	Schneiderin	"	
36	✓ Baumblatt Isidor	26.7 1870	Kaufmann	"	Gnesenerstr. 26
37	✓ " Emma S.	16.9 1874	ohne	"	"
38	✓ Becker Martha	31.1 1885	"	"	
39	✓ Beckhardt Arthur	7.10 1889	Kaufmann	"	
40	✓ Bender Luise S.	17.11 1892	ohne	"	
41	✓ " Selma S.	15.8 1877	Angest.	"	
42	~~Bentheim Felice~~	~~8.9 1882~~	~~Lehrerin~~	"	gest. [illegible]
43	✓ " Emmi	19.5 1884	Angest.	"	
44	✓ " Ida S.	27.7 1893	Hausang.	"	
45	✓ Benditt Fanny S.	30.7 1879	"	"	
46	✓ Berberich Moses	31.11 1888	Kaufmann	"	
47	✓ " Erna	12.5 1896	ohne	"	
48	✓ Berg Julie	1.4 1881	"	"	
49	~~Bergen Max~~	~~16.9 1874~~	~~Kaufmann~~	"	gest. [illegible]
50	✓ Bergen Hedwig	21.12 1887	ohne	"	
51	✓ Bergenthal Nathalie S.	11.12 1868	"		Gnesener 26
52	✓ " Elsa	17.9 1896	Kindergärtn.	"	
53	✓ " Ernst	21.10 1891	Angest.	"	
54	✓ Bergmann Karl	23.5 1895	Dienstellender	"	

TRANSPORT LIST: Transport number VI (Frankfurt) that arrived at the Radegast railroad station in Lodz on October 21, 1941. Provided by the State Archives in Lodz. Series: Head of the Jewish Council of Elders. Signature: Name lists of foreign Jews brought into the ghetto, number 997.

bed. One outhouse for one hundred inhabitants. Consequently, disease, such as tuberculosis, was rampant and spread quickly.

We turned onto Zgierska, and then there was number 70, a dilapidated beige tenement like all the others, five stories high. But this one had become a landmark with a metal sign out front that said in Polish, Hebrew and English: "Quarters for Deportees from Frankfurt (Collective 'Frankfurt')." Peeling maroon paint coated the windowpanes in front of cheap lace curtains. Then, in December 1941, Chaim Rumkowski, the Jew who presided over the Jewish administrative bureaucracy that was accountable to the Germans, announced that twenty-thousand Jews from Germany must be deported from the ghetto.

I spotted the doorway to number 70, adorned with maroon and black graffiti. To the right of the door, more graffiti—"the R✡S," a symbol drawn by a soccer team to denigrate its competition, the RS. I walked toward this sketchy entrance as though pulled by a some force, against the protests of Matthew and Adam. I just nodded and waved my hand high. As if walking into a haunted house, I gently pushed the door open and entered.

Sunlight pierced one window, but the institutional stairs were otherwise dimly lit. They had railings with chipped black paint, exposing specks of yellow and orange underneath, railings that provided support for my grandparents to trudge up and down in their prison-like existence. Graffiti covered the walls of the stairway, but the faintest hint of a pale blue flower design peeked through. The first stairway landing had a new cherry wood double door on the left but an old blue-green painted metallic door on the right. Could the one on the right have been my grandparents' entrance?

The next landing had a window with a view of the nearby tenements. Was that a view that my grandmother took one last look at before hanging herself?

* * *

On a sunny seventy-degree spring day, we took a taxi to the historical Jewish Cemetery of Lodz, at the far end of the Ghetto. The last quarter mile of the drive was down a remote, narrow street lined with high cement walls. The cemetery administrator, a tall, chain-smoking man, Marek Szukalak, greeted us. He and Salomea had a warm exchange; they had never met despite a six-year email correspondence. Szukalak did not speak English, so Salomea translated as much as possible. Although he is not Jewish, he is steeped in knowledge of the cemetery and Jewish traditions surrounding death and burial and remembrance, much like Klaus Meier-Ude at my great-grandparents' cemetery.

This cemetery is the largest Jewish cemetery in Europe, 105 acres with 160,000 people buried there, including 43,000 in the Ghetto Field. We passed the tombstones of the famous and the philanthropic, such as the textile magnate Poznanski and the parents of the pianist Arthur Rubinstein as well as the infamous, such as once well-known gangsters. We saw three enormous tombstones in a row, for three of the most famous rabbis who lived during the late 1800s. The one buried in the middle had been the peacemaker between the other two, who led congregations that were always in conflict with one another.

We trounced through weeds for three and a half hours. Toward the end, Salomea explained that, in 1944, everyone in the ghetto was sent to Auschwitz, except for the eight hundred who were chosen to clean the ghetto. Of those eight hundred, some were forced to dig six mass graves—for the rest of the eight hundred, including themselves. Salomea matter-of-factly pointed to the still-visible six large dug-out areas and observed, "Yes, one of those was meant for me."

Next we saw the wall with the memorial plaques. The granite plaque for my grandparents that we had designed and ordered was perfect: Julie and Norbert Baum with their dates of birth, death, and deportation, and "Remembered by Family." After the obligatory picture of Matthew and Adam and me beside the plaque, I overheard Salomea ask the boys if they thought that they would ever come back to Poland. Their answer was "Nah, probably not, except when we have kids one day, to bring them here." My work with them about this part of their roots was done.

* * *

The five of us piled into the *See Krakow* tours' minivan, along with twenty other tourists and a young blond German-speaking Polish woman who served as our tour guide on the ride to Auschwitz.

At the Auschwitz Visitor Reception Center, we became part of a large crowd of confused tourists. The sheer force of the crowd prodded us outside. We then heard "Everyone English-speaking, over here," from a young female tour guide. As the English-speakers formed an amoeba-like mass, we heard, "Form two lines. English-speakers, two lines now!" I yanked Matthew and

Karen and her sons Adam and Matthew with memorial plaque for Norbert and Julie Baum at the Jewish Cemetery of Lodz, June 2010.

Adam and told Salomea and John to be in *this* line, having a gut sense that the seemingly gentler tour guide with the British accent would be kinder, more connected, than her brusque, loud colleague. It seemed like the right line, whatever the "right line" meant at the moment.

"Two lines now" . . . Salomea remembers the SS ordering a group of deportees, ghetto inhabitants, concentration camp inmates—to divide them into those going to one place versus those going to another, she tells me.

> It all happened so fast, too, for the eighteen-year-old Salomea during the liquidation of the Lodz Ghetto in 1944. Salomea's mother grabbed her and her father's hand and, when the commandant turned his back for a split second, invisibly moved from the long line to the short line. Two lines. Two different outcomes. Death and Life. The Ghetto's Nazi commandant, Biebow, forced the ghetto inhabitants to form two lines; one very long line

> of those who would be sent to their death at the concentration camps of Auschwitz and Chelmno, and one very short line of those who would clean the Ghetto and then be shot in a mass grave. The short line of people cleaned . . . and lived because Soviet forces liberated the ghetto before they could be shot. Salomea and her parents were in the short line, in the right line.

We advanced toward the official entrance of Auschwitz, under the infamous sign *Arbeit Macht Frei* [Work Makes (You) Free]. We made our way on that beautiful spring day—from one building to the next, from one display case to another, from Auschwitz to Birkenau—viewing one inhumanity after another.

We had seen all we came to see.

34

The Stolpersteine *at Reuterweg 73, 2011*

We are now building a circle around these stones in order to take their souls in our midst which once existed. From now on they shall be in our midst as they were before they have been forced to start their life of suffering.

ELLEN HOLZ | member of the Initiative *Stolpersteine* Frankfurt

In June, 2011, I went to Frankfurt again, this time with my cousin Noam to witness the setting of what are called the *Stolpersteine* (Stumbling Stones) for my grandparents in front of Reuterweg 73. Noam is the second of three sons of my first cousin Micha, my Aunt Gretel's son; hence, my grandparents are Noam's great grandparents. This trip provided us the welcomed opportunity to spend time together beyond holidays and events.

I first learned about the *Initiative Stolpersteine* when Lauren and I were in Frankfurt in May 2010. Herr Klaus Meier-Ude, the cemetery administrator we had befriended, had pointed out the glistening four-by-four brass blocks—inlaid in the sidewalks in front of the homes of persons who had been deported and subsequently perished in the Holocaust. The victims are eternally memorialized by these *Stolpersteine,* which are inscribed with a name, date of deportation, and date of death, and placed at the site where the people once enjoyed life. These stones, throughout Europe, are initiated by descendants of the victims and paid for by local donors.

The *Stolpersteine* for my grandparents were among fifty-eight *Stolpersteine* to be set in Frankfurt over that June weekend. The first evening was an event for all of the descendants, donors, and volunteers associated with that weekend's stones. The petite and gentle Ellen Holz, a key Initiative *Stolpersteine* Frankfurt member with whom I had talked by phone, greeted us, and was eager to introduce us to others. She pointed out the artist Gunter Demnig, in his well-worn tan fedora, who had had the vision for the *Stolpersteine* nine years earlier as well as Hartmut Schmidt, the coordinator of the Initiative.

Because Noam and I were to deliver speeches that evening, we took seats at a table near the front, joining Ellen, Meier-Ude, and the evening's musician—the eighty-five-year-old Emil Mangelsdorff and his wife. A short blonde woman in her late thirties or early forties, Lissy Thomé, approached me to say that she was one of a few donors. I was glad to meet her and surprised that only a few donors had supplied the required funds for this weekend's fifty-eight stones.

By a show of hands, we learned that of the 125 people gathered, only four or five of us were from the States. Six were from Mexico City, one from the UK, two or three from Israel, and the remainder from Germany. Most were from Germany, somehow connected to the Initiative *Stolpersteine* Frankfurt.

Gunter Demnig addressed the audience:

> In 1993, when I started the project, it was only a project for the file [an idea]. Then I had a talk with a Protestant pastor and he encouraged me. "You never make a billion stones, but why not just start?" he told me. After next week I will have laid 30,000 stones in ten European countries. And last week I laid stones in a small village, this was the 649th village in Germany with the stones. . . . It is a completely different approach, not just written manuscripts and books and all theoretical, but this is something that goes very close. . . . The stones . . . before you stumble, you stop in front of the stone and have a look at them and stumble with your eyes. You bend down to read the name, and this is a form of respect.

After Noam and others spoke, I slowly walked to the lectern to deliver my carefully composed speech. After describing a bit of my grandparents' lives and my father's journey, I ended with these words: "My grandparents' desperate pleas and their deaths are forever woven into the fabric of our family. With the setting of this stone we have a permanent marker, ensuring that future generations of our family will know where these lives once thrived. This marker will also inform the casual passers-by, give them pause, cause them to 'stumble' into knowing that Julie and Norbert Baum lived here and to know the truth, that Julie and Norbert Baum suffered unspeakable horrors inflicted by the Nazis and were taken from this earth too soon."

My tears moistened the pages of my speech. Afterwards, strangers and new acquaintances embraced me. I was, in a strange way, at home.

* * *

The next day, Noam and I set out to explore parts of Frankfurt. We began at the Rat-Beil Cemetery, once again with the guidance of Klaus Meier-Ude. As always, Klaus was ready with his handful of pebbles to place on the tombstones we visited.

Noam and I then walked along the right bank of the Main River in Frankfurt, where we saw one of our key destinations—a massive building with fifteen arches, the *Großmarkthalle,* the large market hall, to which Lenarz had referred.

Monica Kingreen, the renowned expert on the deportations, described what happened after my grandparents were pulled from their home on that Sunday morning, October 19, 1941: "They march to the assembly point of the *Großmarkthalle*. They wait and stand there for hours. They give the list of their possessions and hand over their Wolfsgangstraße apartment keys, writing down their address and giving up their food card, I.D. card, and any money. They sleep on mattresses on the floor. Early the next morning they are forced to board the third class of a passenger train that takes them directly to Lodz, passing through Berlin and Posen, arriving on Oct. 22 at the Lodz train station of Radegast."[1]

This imposing structure, with its checkered history, was now part of a construction site complex, soon to be the bustling new headquarters for the European Central Bank. I gaped from behind a twelve-foot aluminum chain-link fence. The setting now was one of yellow cranes, orange-ribboned black netting, and safety signs; and the site was quiet. Because it was a holiday, the Day of the Ascension, I confidently walked farther into the site, camera in hand. Suddenly, a fit, white-haired sixty-something-year-old man emerged from a tiny prefabricated building, walked toward me, waving his hands and shouting in German. Entry was *verboten*. Rules were rules.

I grudgingly left the area and continued on, discovering the once-functional railroad tracks where my grandparents boarded their "last train."

* * *

The next morning, Noam and I were joined by a recently discovered distant Geiger cousin, Andrea Lissner, who lives in Berlin and is Christian, due to intermarriage along the line. We began our day with fresh buttermilk and berries and a tall iced café latte at an outdoor market, and then strolled along the Zeil, the pedestrian shopping mall. I was walking twenty steps behind the other two, taking in the people, the stores, a Saturday morning in Frankfurt. I heard a street musician in the distance playing *Que Sera, Sera*, the Doris Day song that my father occasionally sang and quoted.

Klaus Meier-Ude and Noam Ramati, Frankfurt, June 2011.

Soon we arrived at Reuterweg 73. On the sidewalk to the right of the outdoor gate, about a foot from the house, were two recently dug square openings.

Suddenly, a mustached forty-something-year old, bicycled up the driveway. After parking his bicycle inside the gate, he asked me if I was Karen Gordon. I knew instantly who he was—the gentleman with whom I had spoken the year before and asked for permission to go inside the building, before our call disconnected. He explained that Ellen had contacted him to allow us to enter the apartment today after the ceremony, and he and his wife had agreed.

A small group began to gather. A few of the Initiative *Stolpersteine* volunteers held a large six-by-ten-foot banner that read *"Steine Gegen das Vergessen"* (Stones Against Forgetting). Then, Lissy Thomé from the opening event appeared. I had since learned that she, along with Klaus Meier-Ude, were the two donors—neither of them Jewish—for my *grandparents'* stones alone, not for all fifty-eight stones of the weekend. When I asked her why these particular stones, she explained, "I wanted to do this *Stolpersteine* and I wanted it to be for a stone near my house, to be one I pass by every day. So every day I think of it."

A van pulled up on the sidewalk and out jumped Gunter, the artist, along with his assistant, equipped with all sorts of tools and implements and, of course, with the stones for my grandparents. Just as he began his work, bending down on one knee, an intense downpour began.

Gunter worked in the rain. With his chisel and mallet he made the square openings deep. His assistant stood nearby, cradling the two stones in his hands, waiting for the artist's signal. With a small trowel, Gunter scooped out more dirt, and then, first, placed the stone for my grandmother. The space was not deep enough, so he shoveled out more dirt, then placed the stone again. The implements hitting the sidewalk as Gunter switched between them—the trowel, the chisel, the mallet. Klank. Ping. The mallet pounding the stones in place. The sound like the pounding of shovels of dirt on to a casket.

Gunter then poured a thin stream of water at one edge of the newly laid stones. Next, he scooped two trowels full of fine gray-colored sand onto the stones, to fill in the surrounding crevices. Then he brushed off the sand and alternately pounded the stones in place with the mallet, placing them just so.

The artist's work was done. It was time to give life to these engraved names. I spoke first, stating my gratitude to those who had made this a reality and acknowledging Reuterweg 73 as the place where my grandparents' lives flourished. I noted that weather's turning gray and rainy symbolically reflected that my grandparents' lives had "turned" from lives of freedom to lives of restriction and emotional torture while at Reuterweg 73.

In German, Ellen read excerpts from my grandparents' letters and my father's autobiography. It seemed perfect to have their German words voiced in front of what was once their home. Next we recited the familiar mourners' *Kaddish*, the Jewish prayer recited in memory of the deceased but with no mention of death. It is directed to the living, affirming God's justice, addressing the value of life.

Stolpersteine for Norbert and Julie Baum at Reuterweg 73, Frankfurt.

We formed a circle, and Ellen read prepared remarks in her less-than-perfect English, including the following: "In remembrance of those who are not with us anymore, they shall now belong to us again. After they have once been chased away brutally from here. We are now building a circle around these stones in order to take their souls in our midst which once existed. From now on they shall be in our midst as they were before they have been forced to start their life of suffering. We are mourning for them and for the loss which we have caused to ourselves by their exclusion and by forgetting."

The circle broke up, and people left. The *Stolpersteine* for my grandparents were set.

Then five of us—Noam, Andrea, Klaus and Klaus's dear friend, Inge, and I—went to the first-floor apartment. We admired the fifteen-foot ceilings, the original decorative ceiling medallions from which the light fixtures hung, an antique ornate brass door handle above an old-fashioned keyhole. The large rooms were sunny and bright with front windows overlooking the street and back windows overlooking a courtyard. Assuming that the layout was the same as my grandparents' apartment on an upper floor, where was my grandparents' big eat-in kitchen? Which room had been the library? Which room was my grandparents' bedroom?

We joined the couple for coffee in their tiny kitchen. A mix of generations, of Jews and non-Jews, of different nationalities—together chatting about coffee, the weather.

As we left, the rain stopped, and it was a beautiful day once again.

35

The End of One Journey and the Beginning of the Next, 2013

If it is bitterness and anger you hold in your heart, it will kill you.
SALOMEA KAPE | a survivor of the Lodz Ghetto

The trips to Germany, the *Stolpersteine*, the deep research into my grandparents and their deaths—all highlighted a personal question: what is the impact of the long shadow of the Holocaust on me?

The "Jewish part" is clear.

The keeping of traditions feels like my direct and tangible connection to my history, to my parents' Jewish heritage, and certainly to the spirit and memory of my grandparents. But it feels like a fragile connection that is in danger of being frayed or weakened if I were to let go of those traditions.

Since our sons Matthew and Adam were toddlers, on most Friday nights, as a family we recited the Shabbat blessings: the kindling of the Shabbat candles, the *Kiddush* (sanctification of the Sabbath with wine), and the *Hamotzi* (blessing over the bread, the challah). Even if recited quickly, even if the meal was thrown together, even if—in later years—we were all headed in different directions. To this day, my husband Bob and I recite those blessings every week. Now I often attend Friday night services, remembering as a little girl sitting next to my father, holding his hand, during such services. I can still hear my father reciting the prayers and singing the melodies in a Hebrew that sounded "different." Perhaps it was his German accent.

Beyond attending holiday services, gathering with family is my anchor to making those times meaningful. As it was for my father, Passover is my favorite holiday, with its symbolic foods, traditional menu items, ancient storytelling, and traditional songs. The storytelling often serves as a catalyst for table conversation about contemporary issues of social justice or politics.

Yahrzeit candles. I always have them on hand. That flickering light that my father explicitly asked us to kindle in memory of his parents. That tradition of lighting a candle on the anniversary of a death. Now, for both of my parents, my grandparents, my in-laws, and a handful of dear friends. I never forget a *yahrzeit*. The glow of that light as it sits on the kitchen counter is a reminder of a life gone by, of a spirit, of a soul. They're here.

It is no coincidence that, over time, I became actively involved in, and eventually president of, our synagogue, the Brooklyn Heights Synagogue. Not only to be part of a formal community of Jews, but also to lead, in partnership with others, that community. To engage more families, to foster relationships between members, especially intergenerational relationships. To strengthen others' ties to a Jewish community, to their Jewish heritage.

I rarely, if ever, miss observance of *Yom HaShoah*, the Holocaust Day of Remembrance. I put the date in my calendar well in advance. The service I attend is a collaboration of six local synagogues. Sitting in a sanctuary surrounded by others, all of us devoted at that one moment to the remembering—hearing cantors sing, in Yiddish or Hebrew, songs of struggle—and sometimes of hope—written by victims, hearing stories of survival and loss.

Hearing Holocaust-related stories is always captivating to me. Furthermore, I am always interested in hearing from others—where they grew up, what it was like, what their "story is." I'm particularly intrigued by any reference to a generation of their family that emigrated from one place to another. I want to know more, to hear about those ancestors, to understand what it all means for that descendant in front of me.

Another impact of the Holocaust on me is that I sometimes play a strange head game with myself. I reflect on my grandparents having their souls tortured, experiencing loss and humility, and on and on; I reflect on my father making a life for himself at a young age, miles away from home, after leaving–and then losing–his parents. In comparison, I think: surely I can handle or manage whatever is thrown my way—I can overcome this seemingly impossible hurdle, deal with an overwhelming anxiety, make my way to the other side of this or the other challenge.

And our sons? It seems poetry provided each of them a vehicle to express their Jewish roots.

A precursor to our older son, Matthew, majoring in creative writing and poetry in college was his high school senior thesis, a portfolio of original poems written in 2006 when he was seventeen years old. The first in the portfolio was *A Child of Influences,* which references his Japanese-style karate and opens this way:

I am a child of the Americas
German, Russian, and Hungarian melted together to create this American
A student of the students of Japan
The open hand flowing across 11 years of dedication
The Holocaust survivor carrying Germany with him to his American children and grandchildren.

Yes, "this American," our son Matthew is, indeed "the final result of these influences." It was no surprise when Matthew observed *Tashlich* in his own way during college. *Tashlich*, which occurs on Rosh Hashanah, is a customary "casting away of your sins," as represented by throwing breadcrumbs into a body of water. He took bread from the cafeteria and threw the breadcrumbs into a campus pond. That was a mindful choiceful action of this Jewish warrior.

Around the same time, our younger son, Adam, also wrote a poem that provided me insight into his Jewish identity, a poem that he wrote in 2005, at the age of twelve, for *Yom HaShoah,* after visiting the Boston Holocaust Memorial. That's when I knew he "got it."

Bob, Karen, Matthew, and Adam at tombstone of Rosalie and August Geiger, 2013.

Vacation in Massachusetts,
Fun fun fun!
Then we arrive at the Holocaust Memorial,
I see the glass prisms of the ones who had passed,
Inscripted in horrid black,
Thousands, millions, too many for my mind to handle,
Going further, moving on, seeing the fog rising,
Flashbacks of the Jews standing, sweating,
You can see they're scared in their eyes,
Bang! A shot, gunsmoke . . . you turn around, you see some screaming, some wounded,
The smoke disappears, like the fog does,
Going further, moving on, seeing young children putting stones on a marble tablet,
Trying to remember their loved ones,
Each one representing a member of their family, a member of their love,
Now it's my turn, I put one up,
Imagining what they went through,
Love, pain, sorrow,
My relatives,
I love, them . . .

In his college years, in 2013, Adam studied abroad at the University of Freiburg, in conjunction with his double major in German and computer science. That December, at the end of his semester, we chose to have a family vacation in Germany.

We spent time in Freiburg and Berlin, and then ended our trip with a few days in Frankfurt. It was an opportunity for me to share with my sons and husband the places of importance to my father and grandparents: the Westend Synagogue; Café Laumer, for a quick lunch; a walk along the Zeil; Reuterweg 73, inside and outside, including of course, the *Stolpersteine*; and, the Jewish cemetery where my great-grandparents are buried.

My husband, Bob, had been living this, in many ways, as I had spent the last number of years on my journey of searching. He had supported me through the frustrations, the research, the travels, and the challenges as I sought answers.

At Reuterweg 73, I recalled the email and photos that I had received on November 10, 2013, the seventy-fifth anniversary of *Kristallnacht*, from Lissy

Thomé, one of the donors for my grandparents' *Stolpersteine*. She wrote, "During these days, my thoughts are with you and your family," with photos of her kneeling down and lighting votive candles at the *Stolpersteine* for my grandparents.

Also in the fall of 2013, I decided to apply for German citizenship. That is, restored German citizenship. According to German law, "former German citizens and their descendants who were persecuted on political, racial, or religious grounds between January 30, 1933 and May 8, 1945 shall on application have their citizenship restored. . . .This applies to descendants provided that the following hypothetical question can be answered with a 'yes': Had the primary claimant of the naturalization claim not been deprived of his/her German citizenship, would his/her descendants have acquired citizenship by birth according to the applicable German law of citizenship?"[1]

Yes, that's me.

The thought of becoming a German citizen had been disturbing and almost repulsive to me. How do I claim to now be a citizen of a country that was responsible for driving my grandparents to their death, a country that held such deep hatred of the Jews and caused mass destruction on the world stage?

Yet my sons, when they learned of this law, were eager to have German citizenship, which would enable them to have EU passports, allowing them to travel and work more easily throughout Europe. But they could not become German citizens unless I became a German citizen first.

I grappled with the concept for a year. How do I reconcile that with this long shadow of the Holocaust that I live under? The mere mention to some family and friends that I was considering "becoming a German citizen" was often met with expressions of shock with a subtext of disgust: *Really? Why?* and, *How could you?* My lifelong friend Lynnie (Ruth Simon Heydemann's daughter), while not judgmental of me, was not inclined to "restore" German citizenship for herself. And I remembered the sentiment of her mother, Ruth—she refused to purchase anything made in Germany.

Yet, I kept hearing the voice of my father, who was extremely pragmatic, and who would have been in favor of this restored citizenship. He would have said who knows what kinds of doors it could open for my boys one day.

And there was something larger to think about than pragmatism and opportunity. I considered Salomea's comment of a few years earlier: "If it is bitterness and anger you hold in your heart, it will kill you."

I needed a salve for the lingering scars of the anger I've had. I concluded that becoming a German citizen might lighten that long shadow of the Holocaust. It felt like a concrete way for me to live what my father came to believe: collective guilt is not the right approach. And, at the same time, I can reclaim my German roots, roots entangled with many complicated feelings—distrust, outrage, and pride.

I began the application process for my German citizenship.

Two of the required documents for the application were difficult for me to attain. I needed my father's certificate of naturalization. As I did not have it and it seemed to require excessive red tape to get it, I requested that other documents be accepted in the certificate's stead, namely, his petition for naturalization and a June 13, 1942, *Denver Post* article naming my father as one of five soldiers who had been naturalized on June 12, 1942.

I also needed my father's birth certificate from the archives in Frankfurt. The archives could send it to me or I could pick it up in person when I was there in December. But the office would not be open during the holiday dates when I would be in Frankfurt, so I asked Monica Kingreen, the historian whom I had befriended in the course of my research and whose office is only a few blocks from the archives, to pick it up for me. When I met her for coffee and proceeded to pay her the 10€ fee for the birth certificate, she refused my money. She felt synchronicity in the 10€ fee, reminiscent of the 10 RM limit on the funds with which the likes of my father could leave Germany in 1936.

A few weeks later, back in New York City, Adam and I went to the German consulate to file our applications, along with Matthew's. And after a short wait and a few pieces of paper, it was done.

As a result of my German citizenship, I have my German passport. My sons have their German passport. If they have children, those children—my grandchildren, my father's great-grandchildren, my grandparents' great-great-grandchildren—will be allowed to be German citizens. The journey of a citizenship stripped away had been "restored" to the next generations.

My hope is that this simple act—of becoming a German—opens a door to the future. I hope that it helps me break the link to my father's internal burden and liberates future generations.

It was time for something good to come from my grandparents' journey, my father's journey, and my journey.

Time to let go. Time for healing. Time for forgiveness.

Karen's *tallit* made from Julie's and Norbert's monogrammed pillow sham. Photo by David Arky.

Coda

At the age of fifty-nine, along with eight other women ranging in age from thirty-something to eighty, I chose to become a *bat mitzvah*, as I had not done so at the age of thirteen, the traditional age for such a milestone. Thus, on October 31, 2015, I was called to the Torah and chanted a selection from the *parsha*, the Torah portion for the week.

In preparation, I made my own *tallit* (prayer shawl) from a monogrammed white linen pillow sham that had belonged to my grandparents, Julie and Norbert, in Frankfurt. I do not know how that fabric came into my father's possession here in the US. Did he bring it in his big trunk? Did one of my grandparents' friends or acquaintances who visited here or immigrated to the US bring it from Frankfurt?

Wrapped in my *tallit*, I addressed the congregants, family members, and friends:

> Today we, as nine women, are weaving together our individual life experiences to make a stronger, more diverse, richer fabric not only for ourselves, but also for our synagogue, and for the broader Jewish community.
>
> As for my life experience, my thread in this fabric, this moment for me is like coming home.
>
> You see, I have roots in Reform Judaism that go back a few centuries to the movement's founding in Germany *and,* more recently, go back to the reform congregation in which I grew up—Temple Emanu-El in Dallas, Texas—where, at my father's insistence, my sister and I studied Hebrew, but *not* with the intention of becoming a *bat mitzvah*, a rite of passage not offered at the time.
>
> It took the burgeoning of Jewish feminism in the 1970's for the *bat mitzvah* ceremony to be adopted broadly here in the States. That said, each congregation chose if and when to offer it.
>
> This moment for me is also about exercising my right as a woman to have a voice and stand up and be counted in the Jewish religion. About taking a step to address the injustice of Jewish women NOT having a strong voice. I do so in the memory of my own mother and my maternal grandmother.

And I do so as I wrap myself in my *tallit* made from fabric from my paternal grandmother, a woman I feel I've grown to know in recent years after translating and studying letters she wrote to my father, and after tediously piecing together her life and my grandfather's life before they perished together in the Holocaust.

So this moment is about having a voice denied to my ancestors and solidifying and celebrating a core part of my history and of my identity.

And now, on behalf of the strong women in our history—Sarah, Rebecca, Rachel, Leah—and on behalf of each of the nine of us, let us say: *L'dor Vador.* From generation to generation.

1 2a (3) Frankfurt/M 11.5.37.

Mein lieber Rudolf, gerade erhalte ich Deinen Brief v. 3.5. Als ich Dir gleich beantworte, dass er noch rechtzeitig zum Fest kommt. Also, bei euch ist es schon richtig Sommer geworden, ich kann mir denken, dass es doch gleich etwas [illegible] wie hier es mal vorwärts, hoffentlich hast Du mit Deinem [illegible] Sonnenbrand keine unangenehme Nachwirkung. Beim Behandlung [illegible] ja – bei Deiner Haut, ich glaube doch ist es noch zu warm zu beachten. Hier ist es immer noch sehr abwechselnd, es waren schon schöne Tage, aber immer wieder kühl u. Regen dazwischen. Auch über Deine [illegible] habe schon nachgedacht, wie die [illegible] — hoffentlich ist der Rock keine zu große Anschaffung – u. es belastet dich nicht zu sehr. Ich hörte schon, dass die [illegible] die Sachen viel leichter gearbeitet sind u. zwar weniger. Was die mich der Sache doch so [illegible], [illegible] aber vielleicht findet ihr doch noch etwas besseres [illegible] – das sollte es in solch [illegible] doch geben. Auch Haushalt u. Zimmer[illegible] ich leider nicht meine schon – aber zu zweit geht es immer noch besser – Ich denke man sollte [illegible] – aber es wird mir anders auch nicht besser gehen u. das ist ein Trost. Hier gibt es wieder anderes was schwer ist; [illegible] hast Du auch Hedwig gesprochen. Ich freue mich dass sie so [illegible] ist – also scheint es bei [illegible] zu klappen. Genau [illegible] ich es noch nicht.

Dass es eine [illegible] in einer Branche so [illegible] ist, [illegible] vor [illegible], dass kann man sich hier gar nicht denken. Natürlich nicht schön, wenn man zu wenig [illegible] hat, aber ich bin schon froh, dass Du doch [illegible] – bis Du andere Sache [illegible] ist. Das ist eine große Beruhigung, dass Du da wieder in eine Tätigkeit kommst – die Dir liegt u. [illegible] Dich weiter

Page 1

Appendix

Frankfurt/M May 11, [19]37

My dear Rudolf, just now I received your letter of 5/3, which I am answering right away so it gets in the mail on time. So it has turned really summer over there, I can imagine that its effects are much more intense there than here, be careful, hopefully you won't have any unpleasant aftereffects from your first sunburn. You know how to treat your skin here, I believe over there you have to be even more exacting. Here it's still very changeable, there were some nice days already, but in between cool and rainy again. I have been thinking about your wardrobe, how you manage with it. I hope the frock is not too big a purchase and doesn't constitute too great a burden. I heard that clothes over there are made much better and more suitable. That you are so dissatisfied with the laundry is very sad, but perhaps you will find somewhat better opportunities—that should be possible in such a giant city. Managing a household and washing socks etc. aren't always very pleasant either, but it is easier with the two of you. I think a lot about you—but the others are probably not any better off and that is a consolation. Here there are other things that are difficult; by now you will have talked with Hedwig. I am happy that she is so enamored—it appears to be working out at Paula's. Please give them all my best regards.

That business is so quiet even in your industry sector now before Pentecost is difficult to imagine over here. It's not nice, of course, when there is so little work, but I am glad that you can stay there—until the other matter is ready. It is very reassuring that you will start a job that suits you and advances you.

[*page 2*] Surely it'll be better not to be in N.Y., because the crowd of acquaintances is too big—or would you prefer to stay there? It's very nice that you are making good progress with the language—that is very important. I hope very much that you'll get a few days vacation—but not if it costs you. For I imagine life over there to be quite stressful, the large distances and purchases etc. Be sure to eat right and well—do you eat your big meal at home or only in the evening. White asparagus season is starting here, do they have that over there, too, or do they have other delicacies. They must put on quite a spread for the Friday evenings at the Keller's, a record meal apparently. But very pleasant that F.N. always invites you, which is understandable. Of course,

Page 2

Inzwischen wirst Du auch Ella W. gesehen haben – was sich alles N.Y. ansieht. Ich wünsche Dir recht schöne Feiertage, was hast Du vor – ich warte noch auf Aufnahmen, jetzt bei dem schönen Wetter – hoffe mal Bilder von Dir. Viele herzl. Grüsse u. innige Küsse Deine Mutti

Page 3

one worries a lot here, you can't completely avoid that. You know that I take things a bit hard—it takes time, then it gets better. Don't worry about it—but I have to write to you about it, then I feel better. As for the Hertha issue, I would not make any efforts—one can forget, but her conduct was so ugly—and its form so especially hurtful—especially that Hans [is supposed to have] gambled it away, whereas it was definitely Hertha who failed. You wrote that she has a cousin over there—I shall never forget the letter from Hans—I would not write that to her. Perhaps she'll have a chance to make amends. One should not be too nice [to her].—I just got various things ready for Hirschberg who will bring you greetings. Other than that there's not much new to report from here—Papa is still out of town until tomorrow, Wednesday—today for lunch I go to Berta Jeidel's—things haven't worked out for Curt yet—Marta has 3 pupils—but she's not not enthused yet.

[page 3] By now you will also have seen Ella W.—[amazing] who all is sightseeing in N.Y. I wish you really nice holidays, what are you planning to do—I am still waiting for photos, now with the nice weather I am hoping for pictures from you. Many affectionate regards and heartfelt kisses, Your Mutti

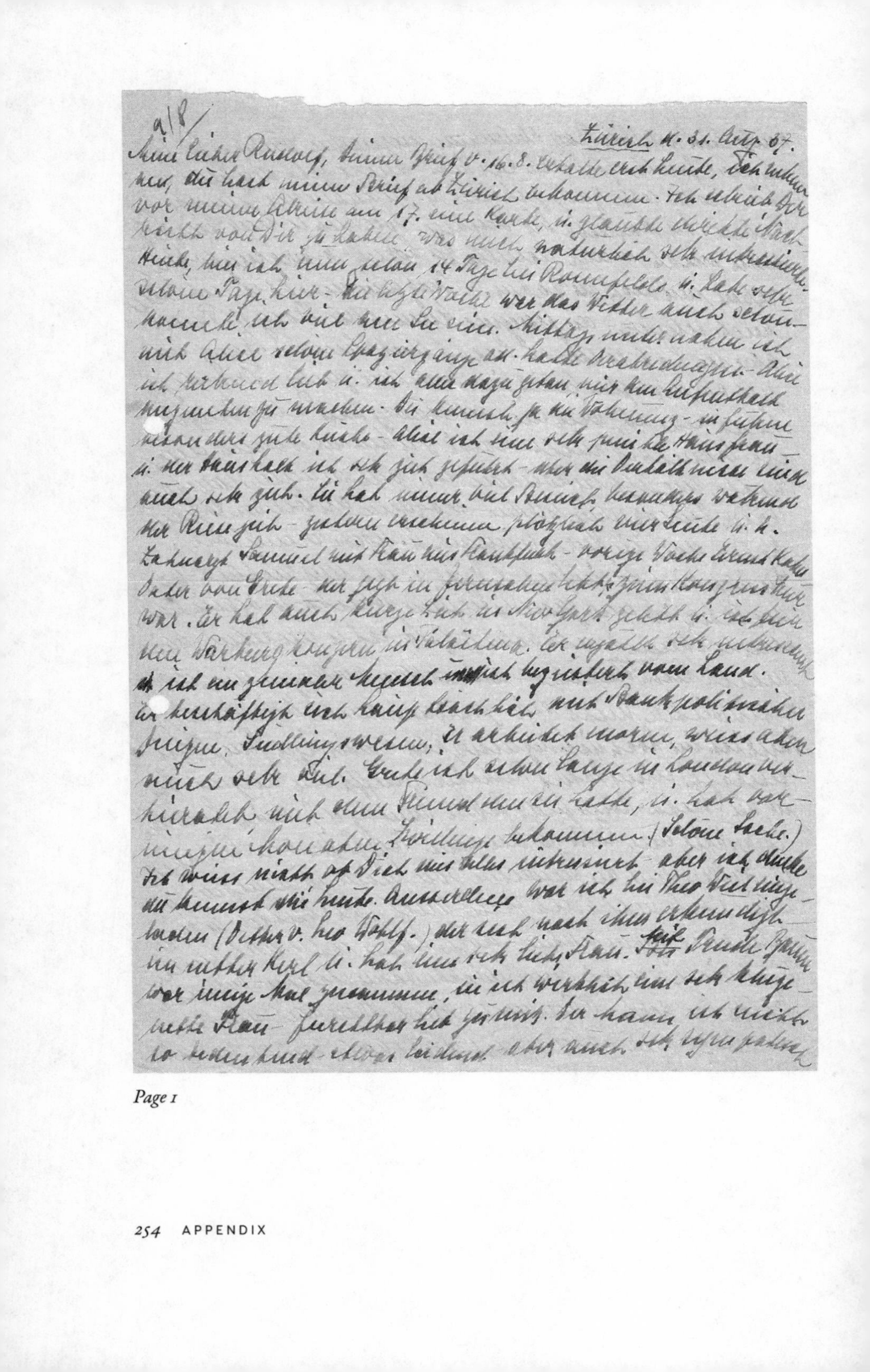

9/8

Zürich d. 31. Aug. 67.

Mein lieber Rudolf, deinen Brief v. 16.8. erhalte ich heute, [illegible]

Page 1

Zurich, 31 August 1937

My dear Rudolf, received your letter from August 16 only today, I suppose you got my letter from Zurich, I wrote a card to you before my departure and believed to have a direct message from you, which I was very interested in, of course. Today I have been already 14 days with Rosenfelds and have very nice days here—last week the weather also was nice. I was able to be at the lake a lot. In the afternoon I took nice walks with Alice and had engagements. Alice is touchingly dear and has done everything to make my stay pleasant. You know the apartment, they eat especially well, Alice is a very exacting housekeeper and her household is managed very well, but they also have the means. She always has many visitors, especially during vacation time. Yesterday suddenly four people appeared, among them the dentist Samuel and his wife from Frankfurt, last week Ernst Kahn, the father of Grete, who now lives in Jerusalem, and had been here for the Congress [of Zionists]. He also lived in New York for a short time and works for the Warburg Company in Palestine. He tells very interesting stories and is a genius and is enthusiastic about the country [i.e., Palestine]. He is mainly occupied with bank politics, settlement affairs. He works enormously hard, but also knows a lot. Grete has been married for a long time in London to the boyfriend she had and had twins a few months ago (nice lot). I don't know if you are interested in all this--but I think you know these people.

Besides this I was invited at Theo Weil's (cousin of Leo Wohlf[arth]), who inquires about him, a nice guy and has a very dear wife. I got together with Trude Baum a few times, she is really a very smart, nice woman, terribly sweet to me. Her husband is not so distinguished—somewhat ailing—but also very likeable.

[page 2] Today I am invited at Frau Abelmann (formerly in Frankfurt) who has a fabulous villa here—so people here are still quite well off and they have a comfortable life. You can imagine how good I feel here—not to hear always the same things, and to have cheerful people around me. Yet Alice still makes it hard for herself, you know the boys, Franz and Paul, they don't make it easy for her. Franz is now finishing his last paper before the Dr. [Ph.D.] and is only intellectual, Paul on the contrary refuses everything, only wants to be independent. He has no need for any amenities etc. and is at the same time a fervent Zionist. Also Lotte, who is now in London wants to become a governess/au pair, although her parents wish for her to take courses and study. She lives the simplest of lives and is unhappy—when her father sends her a larger amount—and she wants to be sure that it is not a burden for them. Such is life—Alice is very worried about it, also, the siblings don't get along, everyone has a different attitude. Paul is a highly intelligent, but difficult boy, he works in his father's business (as a partner) from morning until night. Rosenfelds travel on Tuesday, Sept. 7, to London via Paris in order to visit Lotte. I'll go from here to St. Gallen, in order to visit Ruben's sister,

Page 2

she seems to be very nice and I am looking forward to it. Would have also liked to see the mother in Gailingen, but I cannot do this with my ticket, there is not train station, maybe I'll see her there. Alice would like to keep me here over the holidays, I don't know yet how it will work out.

[page 3] I don't want to leave Papa alone for all these days, but he wrote that I should enjoy it and four days is a long time—I would feel bad about it, because it is Monday and Tuesday.

Page 3

Wir wären sehr glücklich, wenn wir [illegible] hätten – ich höre
hier vielleicht die Eröffnungsvorstellung v. [illegible] Meistersinger. Das ist mir ein Ereignis, nach so langer Zeit.
Schicke mir den nächsten Brief nach Frankfurt –
da ich spätestens Anfang September hin [illegible] fahre –
Also, ich küsse Dich herzlich u. halte [illegible] Feiertage
mit innigen Grüssen Deine Mutter

Von uns allen herzliche Grüsse. Ich freue mich sehr mit der l. Mutter und wir sind sehr vergnügt. Es freut mich auch sehr von der l. Mutter zu hören daß es Ihnen gut geht. Nochmals beste Grüsse

Alice Rosenfeld

Page 4

At any rate I wish you very good holidays and a very good New Year and continued all best for everything. I hope job and prospects will develop according to your wishes, next year you will be much further along. Above all stay healthy and we are happy to have good reports from you. I hope you will get an invitation for the holidays and see some of the family. Give our greetings to all and I wish them all best. I live here in the land of plenty. I eat so well and so much—whipped cream, chocolate, cake—wonderful. I sent you a package, chocolate from here, besides I put in a letter from Curt, in the last letter, send it back to Frankfurt. I received a letter from Friedel she meets [her son] Hans in Italy, she asks about you very much. As of late, Fritz [Friedel's husband] again has not been feeling well. I hear from Heddy that Paul has been transferred to the town with the highest altitude of all—, Potrisi, 4000m, she won't be delighted.

I am glad you heard a good concert, that's very sensible. I have already heard that one can hear music over there even for free and wanted to write to you about it.

[page 4] We would also be happy if we had a chance, perhaps I will hear here the opening performance of the opera, Meistersinger. This will be an experience for me, after such a long time.

Just write the next letter to Frankfurt, because I'll leave here at the beginning of September at the latest. So, I kiss you heartily and have good holidays, with heartfelt greetings, Your Mutter

From all of us cordial greetings. I am very happy with your dear mother and we are very cheerful. I am also very glad to hear from dear mother that you are well. Once again best wishes,
Alice Rosenfeld

Full translation on pages 79–80.

GRAND HOTEL STAAR

LUXEMBOURG-GARE

LUXEMBOURG, le 5. Mai 1938.

Mein lieber Rudolf!

Page 1

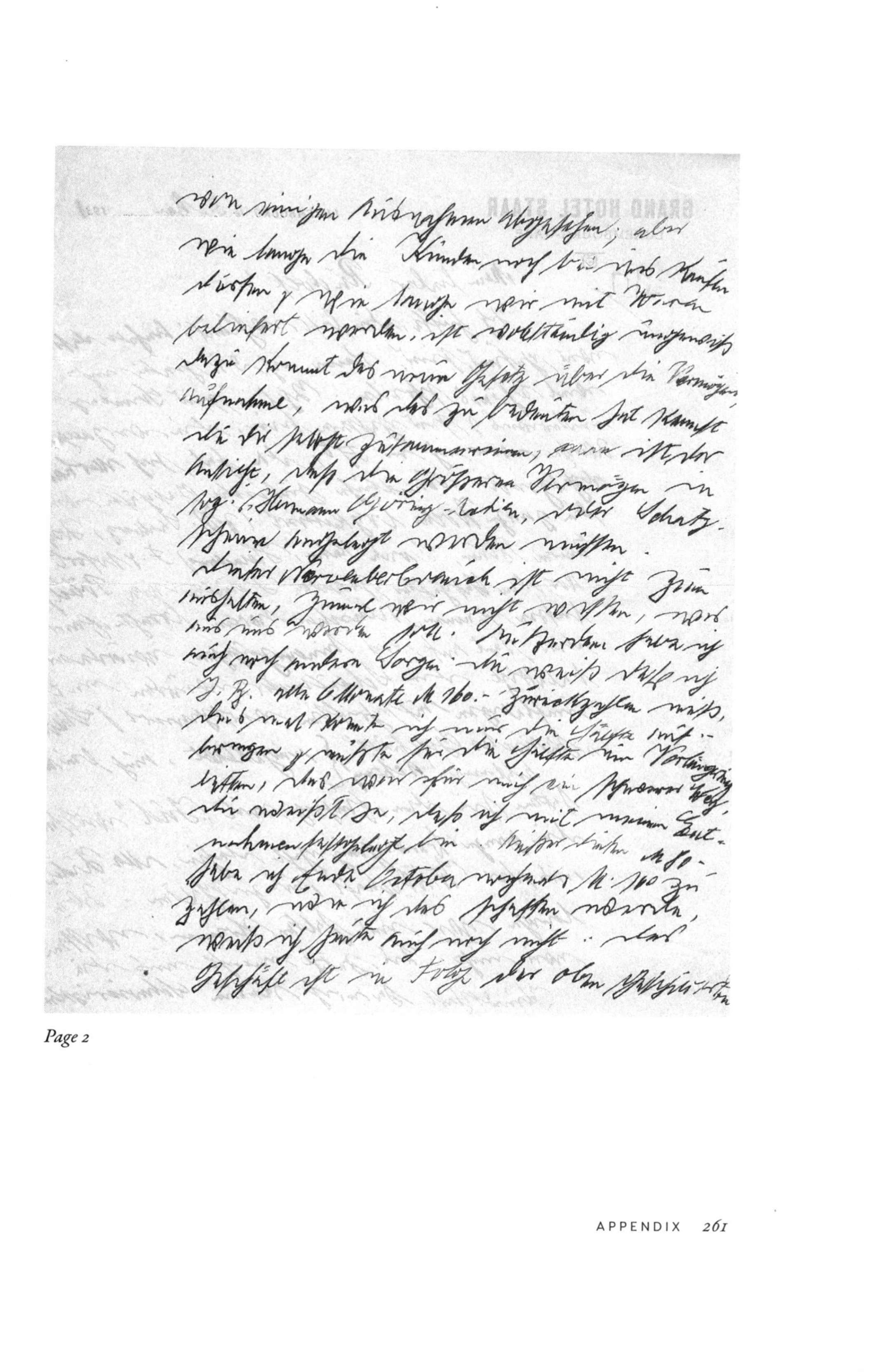

Page 2

GRAND HOTEL STAAR

LUXEMBOURG-GARE

LUXEMBOURG, le .... *193* .

Zustände auch nicht gut, denn haben
wir infolge der politischen Zustände auch
nicht gut erhalten können. Doch Mutti
und ich verlieren den Mut nicht. Es ist ein
Glück, dass Mutti gesundheitlich wieder
einigermaßen auf der Höhe ist, denn es ist
mehr als fraglich, ob wir in Deutschland
bleiben können. Was aus uns werden
soll, weiss ich allerdings nicht.

Es tut mir leid, dass ich dir nichts
Schöneres schreiben kann, aber du bist
doch unterrichtet. Wie [illegible] von [illegible]. Kann
man das nicht schreiben. Frau Marx wird
dir wohl [illegible] [illegible] wird dir noch
Einzelheiten erzählen. Besteht für uns
irgend eine Möglichkeit in America?

Morgen Abend komme ich wieder
nach Hause. Heute sende ich dir ein Päckchen
Schokolade, lasse sie dir [illegible]

Page 3

Page 4

Acknowledgments

Years ago my neighbor Nat Lamar said to me, "You have a book inside of you," after he had read a talk about my spiritual journey that I delivered on Yom Kippur at our synagogue. Our rabbi, Serge Lippe, suggested that talk before either of us knew where it would take me. The talk was in the form of a letter I had written to my late grandparents Julie and Norbert, after I had read—multiple times—the eighty-eight letters they had written to my father as they struggled to survive Nazi Germany. Shortly thereafter, as I began to delve deeper into their story, I wrote more. I would slip the pages into Nat's mail slot and eagerly await their return, adorned with his thoughtful comments in pencil. It was his encouragement in those early days that inspired me to continue writing.

At the same time, I had the encouragement of my college mentor and dear friend Phyllis Markowitz (†), who taught me how to push my way past the blank page, to get my thoughts out, and edit only later. In the early days of this endeavor, she lovingly pushed me with probing questions. Early on, Elizabeth Cohen helped me find my writer's voice.

Given that I wrote this book after my father died, my father's sister, Gretel Merom (†), served as a source to confirm details and family history. We had those conversations when she was in her late nineties, and even when she was over one hundred years old. I also had helpful conversations with my second cousin, Ernst Stevens (†); Arthur Samuels (†), the grandson of my father's first employer in America; and Klaus Meier-Ude (the administrator of Frankfurt's Rat Beil-Straße Cemetery). All helped round out specific elements of my father's and grandparents' journeys.

Ruth Heydemann (†), a dear friend and confidante of my father, the mother of my lifelong friend Lynn Heydemann Brotman, and someone whom I trusted, was the one person who said that the Holocaust was the underlying driver of my father's suicide attempt, a conviction I came to share. Multiple conversations with Michael Shapiro, a professor at Columbia's Graduate School of Journalism, enabled me not only to figure out the arc of my story, but also to learn about how to bring a book into the world. And early on I gathered a group of close friends—Lynn Heydemann Brotman, Lauren Glant, and Janet Keefe—to read and discuss my grandmother's letters, helping me to further develop my sense of her as a person, of her letters' impact on my father, and of her worries—expressed and not expressed. These friends, along with Sharyn Taylor, read an early draft of the manuscript and provided feedback through the lens of their closeness to my grandmother's sentiments. Melanie Danielsen also read an early draft and became an unrelenting cheerleader. Each of these friends provided invaluable support as the manuscript evolved.

Dietlinde Hamburger (†) translated, with great care and curiosity, my grandparents' letters from the German (written in Sütterlin) as well as many documents from the Hessian State Archives. Andrew Verner, meanwhile, translated the first and last letters in the early days before I knew this project would become a book. And he stayed with it. Throughout the project, Andy and I often ruminated together about the nuances of a word choice here or a meaning there. Andy became a friend who was truly invested in the story I was telling.

There are many others to thank, including the researchers, archivists, and museum staff members who provided material. Monica Kingreen (†), of the Pedagogical Center of the Fritz Bauer Institute and the Jewish Museum Frankfurt, shared her deep knowledge of the deportations and her love of *Handkäse mit Musik*. Michael Lenarz, the deputy director and an archivist of the Jewish Museum Frankfurt, answered many a question about Frankfurt Jews back in the day, and took time to delve through those fragile 1930s Frankfurt *Adreßbuchs* with me. Thank you to the Hessian State Archives for providing the files of my grandparents. Ellen Holz, a member of the Initiative *Stolpersteine* Frankfurt, helped make the *Stolpersteine* for my grandparents a reality.

I also wish to thank the Dallas Holocaust and Human Rights Museum—more specifically, David Bell (past president), Felicia Williamson, and Sara Abosch—and the United States Holocaust Memorial Museum—more specifically, Michlean Amir, Steve Vitto, Kyra Shuster, Lindsay Zarwell, and Nancy Hartman—all of whom were right there when I was in search of more documents and pictures. Independent of the museums, Blake Sell served as an amazing detective to help solve some photo-related mysteries and provided invaluable design guidance, as did Ann Harakawa. Photographer David Arky so artfully captured my *tallit*. Jay Brotman applied his passion for genealogy to help me fill in some family tree details.

Dr. Salomea Kape (†), a survivor of the Lodz Ghetto, became my living link to uncovering as much as possible about the ghetto where my grandparents spent the last months of their lives. Her lifelong dedication to sharing her experiences and knowledge of the Lodz Ghetto was the perfect match for my thirst to know as much as I could about it. Traveling to Lodz with Salomea and her son John and my sons somehow closed part of an unfinished circle. It is a gift to have gotten close to Salomea, who became a part of our family. Also integral were Katherine and Ben Marinucci for their support as I addressed the emotional challenges that emerged during this project, as was Ann Cheng in the early stages of writing.

I would like to extend a special thank you to Lauren Glant and Mike Hoyt, as this book would not be what it is without either of them. Any single word or phrase to describe their efforts would be an understatement. A testimony to their efforts is how deeply they each came to "know" and care about my grandparents.

Lauren served as an anchor to me throughout the project—in countless phone conversations, coffees, and lunches, even accompanying me on one of my trips to Frankfurt. She was always there—to solve puzzles of history, ensure accuracy, address stylistic questions, and make this the best book it could be. Her love of history, her in-depth reading of innumerable Holocaust-related books, her rich intellectual curiosity, her passion for exploring mysteries of the past—all served to support me from my earliest days of writing straight through until the finish. Lauren unquestionably made this book better.

Mike Hoyt, a member of the adjunct faculty at Columbia's Graduate School of Journalism and the twelve-year executive editor of the *Columbia Journalism Review*, where he worked for over two decades, helped me structure the story and then edited the book through its several drafts. His devotion to helping me tell the story was essential to my writing process and to the substance and final shape of the book. His collaborative style, his listening, his methodical and thorough consideration of words and phrases—all contributed. His gift of being able to hold the whole of the book while at the same time focus on the details was extraordinary. Mike was core to how this book reads.

Thank you to my agent, Susie Cohen of PearlCo Literary Agency, who believed in this story and its impact and so found it a home. Her enthusiasm and easygoing way made her a true joy to work with. And thank you to Thomas Wells and the University of Tennessee Press for recognizing how this Holocaust-related book is different from others and for giving it its place in Holocaust literature and, more broadly, among the legacies of war. I appreciate Annalisa Zox-Weaver for her copyedits on the final draft. I felt I had true partners in Thomas and the staff of the press.

I am in appreciation of both my mother and father for being the best parents they knew how to be and for giving me the grounding of an excellent education and the strength of my Jewish roots, such that I had it "in me" to write a book such as this. And I appreciate the support that my mother gave to my father during his struggles along the way.

Thank you to my brother, Dick, and my sister, Diane, who are the two people who, literally, have been there for me since day one. They put up with my endless reporting related to our family history. In addition, thank you to my sister-in-law, Robin Baum, for her careful reading and to my brother-in-law, Clive Martin, who read an early draft with his scholarly eye and gave me important editorial comments.

My husband, Bob, accompanied me on all aspects of my journey in writing this book. In the winter, he knew just when to bring up more wood for the fireplace, as so much of my writing occurred in the wee hours of the morning accompanied by the mysteries of a warm fire. He was a pillar of support, and uncomplaining about the significant time that this project demanded and of my many sojourns abroad. The emotional toll was a continuous thread of this endeavor—and Bob never swayed from being right there with me, listening to my twists and turns as I struggled with parts of the journey, and being there for my literal twists and turns when the project would keep me up at night.

Throughout this process, my sons, Matthew and Adam, were unwavering and attentive; they were participants in many a conversation about a latest discovery or turn in my story—ultimately their story. They didn't miss a beat in agreeing to travel with me to Lodz to learn more about that chapter. Their interest in my ongoing efforts made the process all the more meaningful for me. Along the way, Matthew made copious editorial notes and suggested revisions on a draft; he asked probing questions and helped me realize how some phrases were not accessible to his generation. Adam spent countless hours touching up and, dare I say, bringing back to life, old pictures that had been compromised with the time they had spent in photo albums. He also spent days single-handedly creating a user-friendly version of the relevant parts of our family tree. His eye for detail, his diligence, and his artistic sensibility combined to make the photos and the family tree just right. Matthew and Adam each got close to the story in their own way, for which I am grateful.

And to countless others—family, friends, and colleagues—who encouraged me throughout the process and whose connection enabled me to keep going until the book was finally born, thank you.

Notes

CHAPTER 2

1. Hanna Eckhardt, "Martha Wertheimer," in *Frankfurter Biographie* 2, 1996, pp. 552n for Frankfurter Personenlexikon, https://frankfurter-personen lexikon.de/node/1724; Trude Maurer, Part IV: "From Everyday Life to a State of Emergency: Jews in Weimar and Nazi Germany," in *Jewish Daily Life in Germany 1618–1945*, ed. Marion Kaplan (New York: Oxford University Press, 2005), 330; George Duncan, "The Nazi Party: Women of the Third Reich," https://www.jewishvirtuallibrary.org/women-of-the-third-reich.
2. Saul Friedländer, *The Years of Extermination: Nazi Germany and the Jews, 1939–1945* (New York: Harper Perennial, 2008), 5.
3. Rudy Baum, autobiographical essay, April 20, 1993.

CHAPTER 3

1. Rudy Baum, "Jewish Was Our Religion." essay, February 6, 2000.
2. Friedländer, *The Years of Extermination*, xvii.
3. Ibid., 7.
4. "Nazi Party Platform," *Holocaust Encyclopedia* last edited October 15, 2020, https://encyclopedia.ushmm.org/content/en/article/nazi-party-platform.
5. Friedländer, *The Years of Extermination*, 9.
6. Laurel Leff, *Buried by The Times* (New York: Cambridge University Press, 2006), 13.
7. Ibid., 22.
8. Ibid., 25.
9. Ibid., 31.
10. Ibid., 30.
11. Ibid., 5.
12. Friedländer, *The Years of Extermination*, 9.
13. Saul Friedländer, *Nazi Germany and the Jews,* Volume I, (New York: Harper Perennial, 1998),167.
14. David Bankier, "Jewish Society Through Nazi Eyes 1933–1936," *Holocaust and Genocide Studies 6, no. 2* (1991):113-14.

15. Maurer, Part IV: "From Everyday Life to a State of Emergency," 336.
16. Hershel Edelheit and Abraham J. Edelheit, *A World in Turmoil: An Integrated Chronology of the Holocaust and World War II* (Westport, CT: Greenwood Press, 1991), 39.
17. Maurer, Part IV: "From Everyday Life to a State of Emergency," 341.
18. Friedländer, *Nazi Germany and the Jews*, 1:66.
19. Maurer, Part IV: "From Everyday Life to a State of Emergency," 341.
20. Hillary Reder, "Max Beckmann.," https://www.moma.org/artists/429?locale=en.
21. Report in the *Frankfurter Zeitung* (March 31, 1933), in *Dokumente zur Geschichte der Frankfurter Juden 1933-1945*, 22ff, ed. Kommission zur Erforschung der Geschichte der Frankfurter Juden, Frankfurt (1963).
22. Rudy Baum, "A Son of a Respectable Family," in *Children of a Respectable Family* edited by Erhard Roy Wiehn (Konstanz: Hartung-Gorre Verlag, 1996), 135.
23. Rudy Baum, Speech for 50th Anniversary of the Liberation of the Camps., Dallas, TX, February 12, 1995.
24. Baum, "Jewish Was Our Religion."
25. Gretel Baum-Merom, "A Daughter of a Respectable Family," in *Children of a Respectable Family*, 107–08.
26. Baum, Speech for 50th Anniversary of the Liberation of the Camps.
27. David Wyman, *Paper Walls*, (New York: Pantheon Books, 1985), 3–4.
28. United States Holocaust Memorial Museum, *Jewish Refugees from the German Reich, 1933–1939*, http://www.ushmm.org/exhibition/st-louis/teach/supread2.htm.
29. Wyman, *Paper Walls*, 221.
30. Ibid., 5.
31. Baum, autobiographical essay, April 20,1993.
32. Ibid.
33. Abstract of log of the Cunard White Star *R.M.S. Berengaria*, Southampton (via Cherbourg) to New York, November 1936.
34. Friedländer, *Nazi Germany and the Jews*, I:178–79.
35. "The Nazi Party: Hitler Youth." Jewish Virtual Library [a Project of American-Israeli Cooperative Enterprise], http://www.jewishvirtuallibrary.org/jsource/Holocaust/hitleryouth.html.
36. Michael Berenbaum, "Nürnberg Laws," *Encyclopedia Britannica*, last edited May 13, 2020, https://www.britannica.com/topic/Nurnberg-Laws.
37. "Anti-Jewish Legislation in Prewar Germany," United States Holocaust Museum, https://encyclopedia.ushmm.org/content/en/article/anti-jewish-legislation-in-prewar-germany.

38. Edelheit and Edelheit, *A World in Turmoil*, 90.
39. "2000 Books by Jews on New Nazi Blacklist," Jewish Telegraphic Agency, *Daily News Bulletin*, Vol. II, No. 94, November 24, 1936, http://www.jta.org/1936/11/24/archive/2000-books-by-jews-on-new-nazi-blacklist.
40. Simone Ladwig-Winters, "The Attack on Berlin Department Stores (Warenhaeuser) after 1933," Yad Vashem, Shoah Resource Center, the International School for Holocaust Studies, http://www.yadvashem.org/odot_pdf/Microsoft%20Word%20-%205622.pdf.
41. Friedländer, *Nazi Germany and the Jews*, I:224–25.
42. "Concentration Camps, 1933–39," last edited June 27, 2019, http://www.ushmm.org/wlc/en/article.php?ModuleId=10005263.
43. Eric Lichtblau, "The Holocaust Just Got More Shocking," *New York Times*, March 1, 2013, 3.
44. Friedländer, *Nazi Germany and the Jews*, I:181.
45. David Margolick, *Beyond Glory: Joe Louis vs. Max Schmeling* (New York: Knopf, 2005), 164.
46. Friedländer, *Nazi Germany and the Jews*, I:180–81.
47. "Germany Recognizes 1936 High Jump Record by Jewish Woman," World Jewish Congress, last edited November 25, 2009, https://www.worldjewishcongress.org/en/news/germany-recognizes-1936-high-jump-record-by-jewish-woman?print=true.
48. Rudy Baum, speech at Congregation Beth Shalom, Arlington, TX, March 9, 1997.

CHAPTER 4

1. "Law Justice, and the Holocaust—Part I: Documents Relating to the Transition from Democracy to Dictatorship," United States Holocaust Memorial Museum, last edited 2009. Translated from *Reichsgesetzblatt* I, 1933, p. 83. https://www.ushmm.org/m/pdfs/20091123-ljh-dictatorship.pdf.

CHAPTER 5

1. Edelheit and Edelheit, *A World in Turmoil*, 102; "Labor Democracy is Bar to Fascism, Lewis Says Here," *New York Times*, March 16, 1937, 1–2, https://timesmachine.nytimes.com/timesmachine/1937/03/16/118964747.html?pageNumber=1.

CHAPTER 6

1. Edelheit and Edelheit, *A World in Turmoil*, 103.
2. "The Holocaust: Timeline of Jewish Persecution (1932–1945)," Jewish Virtual Library, http://www.jewishvirtuallibrary.org/jsource/Holocaust/chron.html#37.

CHAPTER 7

1. Edelheit and Edelheit, *A World in Turmoil*, 99–110.
2. "1937 Munich Exhibition of Degenerate Art"; "'Degenerate' Art," United States Holocaust Memorial Museum, https://www.ushmm.org/collections/the-museums-collections/collections-highlights/julien-bryan/nazi-germany-1937/1937-munich-exhibition-of-degenerate-art; "'Degenerate' Art," United States Holocaust Memorial Museum, last edited June 8, 2020, https://encyclopedia.ushmm.org/content/en/article/degenerate-art-1.
3. "Mussolini Meets with Hitler in Germany," UCLA Film and Television Archive. United States Holocaust Museum, http://www.ushmm.org/wlc/en/media_fi.php?MediaId=200.
4. Edelheit and Edelheit, *A World in Turmoil*, 111.
5. "Buchenwald," United States Holocaust Memorial Museum, http://www.ushmm.org/wlc/en/article.php?ModuleId=10005198.

CHAPTER 8

1. "Zionism: World Zionist Organization (WZO)," Jewish Virtual Library, https://www.jewishvirtuallibrary.org/world-zionist-organization-wzo.
2. "Weizmann Advises Partition Be Accepted As 20th Congress Opens in Zurich," ," Jewish Telegraphic Agency, Daily News Bulletin, Vol. III, No. 4, August 4, 1937, https://www.jta.org/1937/08/04/archive/weizmann-advises-partition-be-accepted-as-20th-congress-opens-in-zurich.
3. "Zionist Congress: Zionist Congresses During British Mandate (1923–1946)," Jewish Virtual Library, https://www.jewishvirtuallibrary.org/zionist-congresses-during-british-mandate-1923-1946
4. "The Holocaust: Timeline of Jewish Persecution (1932–1945)," Jewish Virtual Library, http://www.jewishvirtuallibrary.org/jsource/Holocaust/chron.html#37.

CHAPTER 9

1. Institut für Stadtgeschichte Frankfurt am Main, https://www.frankfurt1933-1945.de/nc/chronologie/.
2. "October 5, 1937: Quarantine Speech," Presidential Speeches Franklin D. Roosevelt Presidency, University of Virginia Miller Center, https://millercenter.org/the-presidency/presidential-speeches/october-5-1937-quarantine-speech.
3. Kaplan, *Between Dignity and Despair*, 46.

CHAPTER 10

1. Kaplan, *Between Dignity and Despair*, 51.
2. Ibid., 117.
3. Ibid, 51–52.
4. "Nazi Conspiracy and Aggression Volume 2 Chapter XVI Part 4: Wilhelm Keitel," The Avalon Project, Yale Law School, http://avalon.law.yale.edu/imt/chap16_part04.asp.
5. "Peace and War: United States Foreign Policy, 1931–1941," Publication 1983. U.S. Department of State, Washington, D.C.: U.S., Government Printing Office, 1943, 403–5, https://www.mtholyoke.edu/acad/intrel/interwar/fdr11.htm.
6. "War Refugee Board: Background and Establishment," United States Holocaust Memorial Museum, https://encyclopedia.ushmm.org/content/en/article/war-refugee-board-background-and-establishment.
7. "The Nuremberg Laws: Background & Overview," Jewish Virtual Library, https://www.jewishvirtuallibrary.org/jsource/Holocaust/nurlaws.html.
8. "The British War Blue Book: Reichstag Speech, February 20, 1938," The Avalon Project," Yale Law School, http://avalon.law.yale.edu/wwii/blbk05.asp [full page accessed in 2015 is no longer accessible].
9. Edelheit and Edelheit, *A World in Turmoil*, 122.
10. Ibid., 120.
11. Giles MacDonogh, *1938: Hitler's Gamble* (New York: Basic Books, 2011), 94.
12. "Recession of 1937–1938," Federal Reserve History, last edited November 22, 2013, https://www.federalreservehistory.org/essays/recession_of_1937_38.

CHAPTER 11

1. Wyman, *Paper Walls*, 3.
2. Ibid., 168–69, 221.

3. "History Lesson 5: U.S. Immigration Policy and the Holocaust," Constitutional Rights Foundation, http://crfimmigrationed.org/index.php/lessons-for-teachers/144-hl5.
4. Wyman, *Paper Walls*, 168.
5. "Franklin Delano Roosevelt," United States Holocaust Memorial Museum, http://www.ushmm.org/wlc/en/article.php?ModuleId=10007411.
6. Wyman, *Paper Walls*, 221.
7. "Timeline of Events, 1938, Evian Conference," United States Holocaust Memorial Museum, http://www.ushmm.org/learn/timeline-of-events/1933-1938/evian-conference.
8. Wyman, *Paper Walls*, 169.
9. Deborah Dwork & Robert Jan Van Pelt, *Flight from the Reich,* W.W. Norton & Company (2009), 100–01.
10. Edelheit and Edelheit, *A World in Turmoil*, 123.
11. Wolf Gruner, "Poverty and Persecution: The Reichsvereinigung, the Jewish Population, and Anti-Jewish Policy in the Nazi State, 1939–1945," Yad Vashem, Shoah Resource Center, The International School for Holocaust Studies, https://www.yadvashem.org/odot_pdf/Microsoft%20Word%20-%203214.pdf, 4n8.
12. "Unit One: The World Before," USC Shoah Foundation, Center for Initiatives in Jewish Education, IWitness, 25 https://iwitness.usc.edu/SFI/Documents/CIJE/Curriculum/Unit%201.pdf.
13. "Jewish Transmigration Bureau Deposit Cards, 1939–1954 (JDC)," Jewish Transmigration Bureau Files and Index, American Jewish Joint Distribution Committee Archives: New York, https://www.ancestry.com/search/collections/1355/.
14. Maurer, Part IV: "From Everyday Life to a State of Emergency," 356, 358; Wyman, *Paper Walls*, 28.

CHAPTER 12

1. Institut für Stadtgeschichte Frankfurt am Main, www.frankfurt1933-1945.de [page accessed in 2015 is no longer accessible].
2. Friedländer, *Nazi Germany and the Jews*, I:259.
3. Kaplan, *Between Dignity and Despair*, 28.
4. "The Holocaust: Timeline of Jewish Persecution (1932–1945)," Jewish Virtual Library, www.jewishvirtuallibrary.org/jsource/Holocaust/chron.html#38."
5. Maurer, Part IV: "From Everyday Life to a State of Emergency," 355–56.

CHAPTER 13

1. *Das Sonderrecht für die Juden im NS-Staat*, ed. Joseph Walk, Müller Juristischer Verlag (1981), 232; Raul Hilberg, *The Destruction of the European Jews* (Chicago: Quadrangle Books, 1961), 83-4; Edelheit and Edelheit, *A World in Turmoil*, 127.
2. Ino Arndt and Heinz Boberach, "Deutches Reich," in *Dimension des Völkermords: Die Zahl der Jüdischen Opfer des Nationalsozialismus*, ed. Wolfgang Benz, Oldenbourg, (1991), 28.
3. "Nazi Germany and Anti-Jewish Policy," Anti-Defamation League [Sources: Echoes and Reflections—Anti-Defamation League, USC Shoah Foundation, Yad Vashem, www.echoesandreflections.org], https://www.adl.org/sites/default/files/documents/assets/pdf/education-outreach/nazi-germany-and-anti-jewish-policy.pdf.
4. Kaplan, *Between Dignity and Despair*, 27–28; "Unit One: The World Before." USC Shoah Foundation, Center for Initiatives in Jewish Education, IWitness, 24.
5. Edelheit and Edelheit, *A World in Turmoil*, 126, 131.
6. "The Holocaust: Timeline of Jewish Persecution (1932–1945)," Jewish Virtual Library, http://www.jewishvirtuallibrary.org/jsource/Holocaust/chron.html#38.
7. Friedländer, *Nazi Germany and the Jews*, I:254.
8. Ibid., 254–55.
9. "Timeline of Events, 1938, German Jews' Passports Declared Invalid," United States Holocaust Memorial Museum, http://www.ushmm.org/learn/timeline-of-events/1933-1938/reich-ministry-of-the-interior-invalidates-all-german-passports-held-by-jew.
10. Susanne Heim, "'Deutschland muss ihnen ein Land ohne Zukunft sein': Die Zwangsmigration der Juden 1933–1938," in *Arbeitsmigration und Flucht: Vertreibung und Arbetiskräfteregulierung im Zwischenkriegseuropa (Beitrage zur Nationalsozialistischen Gesundheits- und Sozialpolitik* 11), Verlag der Buchläden (1993), 56.
11. Alfred J. Kutzik, "Kristallnacht Was the Name the Nazis Gave It," *The New York Times*, November 25, 1988, Section A, 30, https://www.nytimes.com/1988/11/25/opinion/l-kristallnacht-was-the-name-the-nazis-gave-it-681188.html; Michael Berenbaum, "Kristallnacht," Encyclopedia Britannica, last edited February 13, 2020, https://www.britannica.com/event/Kristallnacht.
12. Joseph B[enjamin] Levy, *Mein Leben in Deutschland vor und nach dem 30. Januar 1933[1939–1940]*, Leo Baeck Institute, 70, 72.
13. "Synagogues," United States Holocaust Memorial Museum, https://www

.ushmm.org/information/exhibitions/online-exhibitions/special-focus/kristallnacht/synagogues.

14. Friedländer, *Nazi Germany and the Jews*, I:286.
15. Edelheit and Edelheit, *A World in Turmoil*, 139; "Jewish Businesses—Atonement Fee," United States Holocaust Memorial Museum, [Source: Reichsgesetzblatt], https://www.ushmm.org/information/exhibitions/online-exhibitions/special-focus/kristallnacht/jewish-businesses/atonement-fee.
16. Edelheit and Edelheit, *A World in Turmoil*, 138, 139.
17. Lara Daemmig and Marion Kaplan, "Juedischer Frauenbund (The League of Jewish Women)," Jewish Women: A Comprehensive Historical Encyclopedia, February, 27, 2009, Jewish Women's Archive, http://jwa.org/encyclopedia/article/juedischer-frauenbund-league-of-jewish-women.
18. Maurer, Part IV: "From Everyday Life to a State of Emergency," 336.
19. Friedländer, *Nazi Germany and the Jews*, I:281–82.
20. Kaplan, *Between Dignity and Despair*, 146.
21. Gruner, "Poverty and Persecution," 4–5.
22. Wyman, *Paper Walls*, 33, 37.
23. SD [Sicherheitsdienst—Security Service—intelligence service of Nazi SS] Section II 112 [Jewish section], 15.6.1939, SD-Hauptamt, microfilm MA 554, IfZ, Munich.
24. Gruner, "Poverty and Persecution," 10–11; Kaplan, *Between Dignity and Despair*, 173.

CHAPTER 14

1. "The Fight of the Century: Louis vs. Schmeling," NPR, http://www.npr.org/2006/11/25/6515548/the-fight-of-the-century-louis-vs-schmeling.
2. "Louis Destroys Schmeling in Rematch," International Boxing Hall of Fame, last edited 2000, http://www.ibhof.com/pages/archives/louisschmeling.html; James P. Dawson, "Louis Defeats Schmeling by a Knockout in First," *New York Times*, June 23, 1938.
3. Deborah E. Lipstadt, *Beyond Belief: The American Press and the Coming of the Holocaust 1933–1945*, Touchstone (1986), 99.
4. Wyman, *Paper Walls*, 73.
5. Carey McWilliams, *A Mask for Privilege: Anti-Semitism in America* (Nabu Press, 2011), 45.

CHAPTER 15

1. "Adolph Hitler, Man of the Year," *Time Magazine*, January 2, 1939, http://content.time.com/time/covers/0,16641,19390102,00.html.
2. "Adolph Hitler: Man of the Year, 1938," *Time Magazine*, January 2, 1939, http://content.time.com/time/magazine/article/0,9171,760539,00.html.
3. "Extract of the Speech by Hitler, January 30, 1939," Yad Vashem, Shoah Resource Center, The International School for Holocaust Studies [Source: The Speeches of Adolf Hitler, I, edited by N.H. Baynes, London, 1942], https://www.yadvashem.org/odot_pdf/Microsoft%20Word%20-%201988.pdf, 3.
4. Friedländer, *Nazi Germany and the Jews*, I:312.
5. "The Establishment of the Reichsvereinigung, July 1939," Yad Vashem, Shoah Resource Center, The International School for Holocaust Studies [Source: "Documents on the Holocaust, Selected Sources on the Destruction of Germany and Austria, Poland, and the Soviet Union," edited by Y. Arad, Y. Gutman, and A. Margaliot—Yad Vashem, 1981], http://www.yadvashem.org/odot_pdf/Microsoft%20Word%20-%205389.pdf.
6. Friedländer, *Nazi Germany and the Jews*, I:307.
7. Wyman, *Paper Walls*, 29.
8. *Das Sonderrecht für die Juden im NS-Staat*, ed. Walk, Müller Juristischer Verlag (1981), 275.
9. Kaplan, *Between Dignity and Despair*, 173.
10. Edelheit and Edelheit, *A World in Turmoil*, 149.
11. Kaplan, *Between Dignity and Despair*, 146.
12. Friedländer, *Nazi Germany and the Jews*, I:291.
13. Kaplan, *Between Dignity and Despair*, 150.
14. Erna Albersheim, memoir, Harvard University: Houghton Library (1940), 21, 28, 37.
15. Kaplan, *Between Dignity and Despair*, 151–52.
16. Edelheit and Edelheit, *A World in Turmoil*, 152; "Nuremberg Trial Defendants: Alfred Rosenberg," Jewish Virtual Library, https://www.jewishvirtuallibrary.org/jsource/Holocaust/Rosenberg.html.
17. "Ford's Anti-Semitism," PBS, https://www.pbs.org/wgbh/americanexperience/features/henryford-antisemitism/.
18. Friedländer, *Nazi Germany and the Jews*, I:299; "The Evian Conference," United States Holocaust Memorial Museum, http://www.ushmm.org/outreach/en/article.php?ModuleId=10007698.
19. Wyman, *Paper Walls*, 95.
20. Leff, *Buried by The Times*, 43–44.

21. Ibid., 2–3.
22. Wyman, *Paper Walls*, 152.
23. Ibid., 37.
24. Ibid., 152.
25. Ibid., 37.
26. Ibid.

CHAPTER 16

1. H.S. Linfield, "Statistics of Jews—1929," *American Jewish Year Book Vol. 34: Statistics of Jews and Jewish Organizations in the United States: An Historical Review of Ten Censuses, 1850–1937* (American Jewish Committee and Springer, 2008), 248; http://www.ajcarchives.org/ajc_data/files/1930_1931_7_statistics.pdf.
2. Franklin D. Roosevelt, "Fireside Chat, September 3, 1939," The American Presidency Project, https://www.presidency.ucsb.edu/documents/fireside-chat-13.
3. "Jewish Transmigration Bureau Deposit Cards, 1939–1954 (JDC)," Jewish Transmigration Bureau Files and Index, American Jewish Joint Distribution Committee Archives: New York, https://www.ancestry.com/search/collections/1355/.

CHAPTER 17

1. Kaplan, *Between Dignity and Despair*, 147, 151, 153.
2. Gruner, "Poverty and Persecution," 16, n. 48.
3. Maurer, Part IV: "From Everyday Life to a State of Emergency," 339.
4. Hermann Glaser, "Film," *Enzyklopädie des Nationalsozialismus*, eds. Benz, Graml, and Weiss, Deutscher Taschenbuch Verlag (1997), 175.
5. Friedländer, *The Years of Extermination*, 35, 38.
6. *The Chronicle of the Lodz Ghetto 1941–1944*, edited by Lucjan Dobroszycki, translated by Richard Lourie, Joachim Neugroschel, and others (Yale University Press, 1984), xxiii-xxiv.
7. Friedländer, *The Years of Extermination*, 104.
8. Ibid., 38.
9. "Warsaw," United States Holocaust Memorial Museum, http://www.ushmm.org/wlc/en/article.php?ModuleId=10005069.
10. James M. Lindsay, "TWE Remembers: FDR's 'Stab in the Back' Speech," Council on Foreign Relations, June 10, 2013, http://blogs.cfr.org/lindsay/2013/06/10/twe-remembers-fdrs-stab-in-the-back-speech/; "The Presidency:

Tenth of June," *Time Magazine*, June 17, 1940, http://content.time.com/time/subscriber/article/0,33009,789854-2,00.html; "June 10, 1940: 'Stab in the Back' Speech," Presidential Speeches Franklin D. Roosevelt Presidency, University of Virginia Miller Center, https://millercenter.org/the-presidency/presidential-speeches/june-10-1940-stab-back-speech.

11. Charlie Chaplin, final speech from *The Great Dictator*, 1940. https://www.charliechaplin.com/en/articles/29-the-final-speech-from-the-great-dictator-.
12. Louisa Thomas, "America First, for Charles Lindbergh and Donald Trump," *The New Yorker*, July 24, 2016, https://www.newyorker.com/news/news-desk/america-first-for-charles-lindbergh-and-donald-trump.
13. Alden Whitman, "Lindbergh Says U.S. 'Lost' World War II," *New York Times*, August 30, 1970, https://archive.nytimes.com/www.nytimes.com/books/98/09/27/specials/lindbergh-lost.html?_r=1&oref=slogin; "Ford's Anti-Semitism," PBS, https://www.pbs.org/wgbh/americanexperience/features/henryford-antisemitism/.
14. Charles A. Lindbergh, "Aviation, Geography, and Race," *Reader's Digest*, November 1939, Volume 5, 64–67.
15. "America First Committee," *Encyclopedia Britannica*, last edited March 28, 2019, http://www.britannica.com/EBchecked/topic/19247/America-First-Committee; Lynne Olson, *Those Angry Days: Roosevelt, Lindbergh, and America's Fight Over World War II, 1939–1941* (Random House Trade Paperbacks, 2014), 224.
16. Friedländer, *The Years of Extermination*, 86.
17. Wyman, *Paper Walls*, 172.
18. Friedländer, *The Years of Extermination*, 92.
19. Kaplan, *Between Dignity and Despair*, 143.
20. Elisabeth Freund, Elisabeth Freund Collection: Autobiographical Notes, Leo Baeck Institute, 29–30, 49–50, 74.
21. "Adolf Hitler: Speech at the Berlin Sports Palace (January 30, 1941)," Jewish Virtual Library [a Project of American-Israeli Cooperative Enterprise]. [Source: ibiblio.] http://www.jewishvirtuallibrary.org/jsource/Holocaust/hitler013041.html; text of Speech by Chancellor Adolf Hitler, At Berlin Sports Palace, January 30, 1941—recorded by the Monitoring Service of the British Broadcasting Corporation, courtesy of the Research Project for Totalitarian Communication, New School for Social Research, http://www.ibiblio.org/pha/policy/1941/410130a.html."
22. Martin Gilbert, *The Routledge Atlas of the Holocaust*, (Routledge, 2009), 42.
23. Friedländer, *The Years of Extermination*, 38–39.
24. Gilbert, *The Routledge Atlas of the Holocaust*, 55.

25. John Weiss, *The Ideology of Death: Why the Holocaust Happened in Germany* (Ivan R. Dee, 1997), 335.
26. Ibid., 337.
27. "Killing Centers: An Overview," United States Holocaust Memorial Museum, https://encyclopedia.ushmm.org/content/en/article/killing-centers-an-overview.
28. "Auschwitz," United States Holocaust Memorial Museum, last edited March 16, 2015, https://encyclopedia.ushmm.org/content/en/article/auschwitz.
29. Jürgen Steen, "Air War Damage as a Sensation," Institut für Stadtgeschichte Frankfurt am Main, last edited January 1, 2003, https://www.frankfurt1933-1945.de/nc/beitraege/show/1/thematik/der-luftkrieg-1940-1942/artikel/luftkriegs-schaeden-als-sensation/.
30. Friedländer, *The Years of Extermination*, 131.
31. McWilliams, *A Mask for Privilege*, 43.
32. Alyn Brodsky, *The Great Mayor: Fiorello LaGuardia and the Making of the City of New York* (Boston: Truman Talley Books, 2003), 4. https://www.nytimes.com/2003/06/29/books/chapters/the-great-mayor.html.
33. Daniel Greene and Frank Newport, "American Public Opinion and the Holocaust," last edited April 23, 2018, https://news.gallup.com/opinion/polling-matters/232949/american-public-opinion-holocaust.aspx.
34. Charles Herbert Stember and others, *Jews in the Mind of America* (New York: Basic Books, 1966), 121 [Opinion Research Surveys, October 1941 and June 1945].
35. Wyman, *Paper Walls*, 192–95.
36. Ibid., 198; Albert Einstein, "Letter to Mrs. Franklin D. Roosevelt, July 26, 1941," Franklin D. Roosevelt Presidential Library and Museum: FDR's Papers as President: President's Personal File 7177, https://fdrlibrary.tumblr.com/post/141047307759/i-have-noted-with-great-satisfaction-that-you.
37. "1941: The Atlantic Charter," United Nations, https://www.un.org/en/sections/history-united-nations-charter/1941-atlantic-charter/index.html.
38. James M. Lindsay, "TWE Remembers: Charles Lindbergh's Des Moines Speech," Council on Foreign Relations, September 11, 2012, https://www.cfr.org/blog/twe-remembers-charles-lindberghs-des-moines-speech.
39. Friedländer, *The Years of Extermination*, 251.
40. Ibid., 255.
41. Michael H. Kater, *The Twisted Muse: Musicians and Their Music in the Third Reich* (Oxford: Oxford University Press, 1997), 103.
42. Kaplan, *Between Dignity and Despair*, 194–95.
43. Ibid., 132.

CHAPTER 18

1. "Frankfurt am Main," Yad Vashem, Shoah Resource Center, The International School for Holocaust Studies, http://www.yadvashem.org/odot_pdf/Microsoft%20Word%20-%205861.pdf.
2. "Communication, News & Censorship," PBS, last edited September, 2007, http://www.pbs.org/thewar/at_home_communication_news_censorship.htm.
3. Herbert Strauss, "Jewish Emigration from Germany, Part I", *Leo Baeck Institute Year Book* (1980), 317–18, 326–27).
4. "List of Jews from Dresden Who Perished During the Holocaust," Item ID 7710741, Central Database of Shoah Victims' Names, Yad Vashem, https://yvng.yadvashem.org/nameDetails.html?language=en&itemId=7710741&ind=1, accessed on September 15, 2020.

CHAPTER 19

1. "Timeline of Events, 1942–1945," United States Holocaust Memorial Museum, http://www.ushmm.org/learn/timeline-of-events/1942–1945.
2. Rabbi Akiva Males, "Jewish GIs and Their Dog-Tags," Hakirah Press, last edited 2013, 271-287, www.hakirah.org/Vol15Males.pdf; Paul Lippman, "Letter to the editor: In World War II, Many Jewish GI.'s Left Religion Off Dog Tags," *New York Times*, June 22, 1994, 20, https://timesmachine.nytimes.com/timesmachine/1994/06/22/470333.html?pageNumber=20.
3. Christian Bauer, *The Ritchie Boys: A Film by Christian Bauer* (Tangram Productions, 2004).
4. Ibid.
5. "Timeline of Events, 1942–1945: D-Day," United States Holocaust Memorial Museum, http://www.ushmm.org/learn/timeline-of-events/1942–1945/d-day.
6. Laurence Rees, "Hitler's Invasion of Russia in World War Two," BBC, last edited March 30, 2011, http://www.bbc.co.uk/history/worldwars/wwtwo/hitler_russia_invasion_01.shtml

CHAPTER 20

1. Rudy Baum, interview by Steven Spielberg's USC Shoah Foundation, 1998.

CHAPTER 21

1. Rudy Baum, essay, March 19, 1991.

CHAPTER 22

1. Harry J. Herder, Jr., "Liberation of Buchenwald," http://www.remember.org/witness/herder.html.
2. Ibid.
3. "U.S. Policy During WWII: U.S. Army & the Holocaust," Jewish Virtual Library, http://www.jewishvirtuallibrary.org/jsource/Holocaust/usarmy_holo.html.
4. Rudy Baum, interview by Dallas Holocaust and Human Rights Museum, 1991.

CHAPTER 23

1. Baum, interview by Dallas Holocaust and Human Rights Museum.
2. Rudy Baum, "A Son of a Respectable Family," 145–46.
3. Rudy Baum, interview at home, 1999/2000.

CHAPTER 24

1. "Saul Kagan, Architect of Holocaust Restitution," Claims Conference, http://www.claimscon.org/about/history/saul-kagan/.

CHAPTER 28

1. Rudy Baum, interview at home, 1999/2000.
2. Alison Smale, "A Holocaust Survivor Tells of Auschwitz at 18 and, Again, at 90," *New York Times,* March 13, 2015.

CHAPTER 29

1. "Farewell to Ernst Cramer, 28 January 1913—19 January 2010," *inside.mag, Special Edition of the Axel Springer AG Staff Magazine,* January, 2010, 3.
2. Ibid., 8.

CHAPTER 30

1. "Farewell to Ernst Cramer, 28 January 1913—19 January 2010," *inside.mag, Special Edition of the Axel Springer AG Staff Magazine,* January, 2010, 16–17

[Previously published in *Die Welt*, December 8, 2004 and in the book *I Was There* by Ernst Cramer, 2008].

2. Ibid., 8.

CHAPTER 31

1. Jews from Frankfurt Murdered in Lodz, Record Number 1202255 1202227 4 1.1.22.1/0003A/0028 65/Arolson Archives in Bad Arolson Germany, accessed at the United States Holocaust Memorial Museum Digital Collection on August 18, 2015.
2. Lodz Ghetto Hospital Death Records, RG 05.008M.0009.00000257 (Record Group 05.008M, Reel 9, page 257)/Polish State Archives, accessed at the United States Holocaust Memorial Museum Archives in October, 2009.

CHAPTER 35

1. "Restoration of German Citizenship—Article 116 par. 2 of the Basic Law (Grundgesetz)," German Missions in the United States, German Consulates General in the United States, https://www.germany.info/us-en/service/03-Citizenship/restoration-of-german-citizenship/925120

Bibliography

MEMOIRS, ESSAYS, INTERVIEWS, AND SPEECHES

Albersheim, Erna. Memoir. Harvard University: Houghton Library, Cambridge. 1940.

Baum, Rudy. "A Son of a Respectable Family." In *Children of a Respectable Family*, edited by Erhard Roy Wiehn, 55–81, 129–152. Konstanz: Hartung-Gorre Verlag, 1996.

Baum, Rudy. Autobiographical essay. April 20, 1993.

———. Essay. March 19, 1991.

———. Interview at home. 1999/2000.

———. Interview by Dallas Holocaust and Human Rights Museum. 1991.

———. Interview by Steven Spielberg's USC Shoah Foundation. 1998.

———. "Jewish Was Our Religion." Essay. February 6, 2000.

———. Speech for 50th Anniversary of the Liberation of the Camps. Dallas, TX. February 12, 1995.

———. Speech. Congregation Beth Shalom, Arlington, TX. March 9, 1997.

Baum-Merom, Gretel. "A Daughter of a Respectable Family." In *Children of a Respectable Family*, edited by Erhard Roy Wiehn, 16–54, 89–128. Konstanz: Hartung-Gorre Verlag, 1996.

Freund, Elisabeth. Elisabeth Freund Collection: Autobiographical Notes. Leo Baeck Institute, New York.

Levy, Joseph B[enjamin]. *Mein Leben in Deutschland vor und nach dem 30. Januar 1933[1939–1940]*. Leo Baeck Institute, New York.

BOOKS

Brodsky, Alyn. *The Great Mayor: Fiorello LaGuardia and the Making of the City of New York*. Boston: Truman Talley Books, 2003.

The Chronicle of the Lodz Ghetto 1941-1944. Edited by Lucjan Dobroszycki. Translated by Richard Lourie, Joachim Neugroschel, and others. New Haven: Yale University Press, 1984.

Dwork, Deborah, and Robert Jan Van Pelt. *Flight from The Reich*. New York: W.W. Norton & Company, 2009.

Edelheit, Hershel, and Abraham J. Edelheit. *A World in Turmoil: An Integrated Chronology of the Holocaust and World War II.* Westport, CT: Greenwood Press, 1991.

Friedländer, Saul. *Nazi Germany and the Jews.* Vol. I, *The Years of Persecution, 1933-1939.* New York: Harper Perennial, 1998.

———. *The Years of Extermination: Nazi Germany and the Jews, 1939-1945.* New York: Harper Perennial, 2008.

Gilbert, Martin. *The Routledge Atlas of the Holocaust.* Abingdon-on-Thames, UK: Routledge, 2009.

Hilberg, Raul. *The Destruction of the European Jews.* Chicago: Quadrangle Books, 1961.

Kater, Michael. *The Twisted Muse: Musicians and Their Music in the Third Reich.* Oxford: Oxford University Press, 1997.

Leff, Laurel. *Buried by The Times.* New York: Cambridge University Press, 2006.

Lipstadt, Deborah E. *Beyond Belief: The American Press and the Coming of the Holocaust 1933–1945.* New York: Touchstone, 1986.

MacDonogh, Giles. *1938: Hitler's Gamble.* New York: Basic Books Inc., 2011.

Margolick, David. *Beyond Glory: Joe Louis vs. Max Schmeling.* New York: Knopf, 2005.

McWilliams, Carey. *A Mask for Privilege: Anti-Semitism in America.* Charleston, SC: Nabu Press, 2011.

Olson, Lynne. *Those Angry Days: Roosevelt, Lindbergh, and America's Fight Over World War II, 1939-1941.* New York: Random House Trade Paperbacks, 2014.

Stember, Charles Herbert, and others. *Jews in the Mind of America [Opinion Research Surveys, October 1941 and June 1945.]* New York: Basic Books, 1966.

Weiss, John. *The Ideology of Death: Why the Holocaust Happened in Germany.* Chicago: Ivan R. Dee Publishing, 1997.

Wyman, David. *Paper Walls.* New York: Pantheon Books, 1985.

CHAPTERS IN EDITED BOOKS

Arndt, Ino, and Heinz Boberach. "Deutches Reich." In *Dimension des Völkermords: Die Zahl der Jüdischen Opfer des Nationalsozialismus*, ed. Wolfgang Benz. Munich: Oldenbourg, 1991.

Glaser, Hermann. "Film." In *Enzyklopädie des Nationalsozialismus*, eds. Benz, Graml, and Weiss. Stuttgart: dtv (Deutscher Taschenbuch Verlag), 1997.

Heim, Susanne. "'Deutschland muss ihnen ein Land ohne Zukunft sein': Die Zwangsmigration der Juden 1933–1938." In *Arbeitsmigration und Flucht: Vertreibung und Arbetiskräfteregulierung im Zwischenkriegseuropa (Beitrage zur*

Nationalsozialistischen Gesundheits- und Sozialpolitik 11). Berlin: Verlag der Buchläden, 1993.

Maurer, Trude. Part IV: "From Everyday Life to a State of Emergency: Jews in Weimar and Nazi Germany." In *Jewish Daily Life in Germany 1618-1945*, edited by Marion Kaplan, 271–373. New York: Oxford University Press, 2005.

Strauss, Herbert. "Jewish Emigration from Germany, Part I." In *Leo Baeck Institute Year Book*, 1980.

COLLECTIONS OF DOCUMENTS

Das Sonderrecht für die Juden im NS-Staat. Ed. Joseph Walk. Heidelberg: Müller Juristischer Verlag, 1981.

SD [Sicherheitsdienst—Security Service—intelligence service of Nazi SS] Section II 112 [Jewish section], 15.6.1939, SD-Hauptamt, microfilm MA 554. Institut für Zeitgeschichte, , Munich.

JOURNALS, NEWSPAPERS, MAGAZINES, AND PAMPHLETS

Aronson, Tim. "A Personal History of the Marburg Newspaper Conference." *Wiesbadener Kurier—Wiesbadener Verlag GmbH*, October 22, 1945.

Bankier, David. "Jewish Society Through Nazi Eyes 1933–1936." *Holocaust and Genocide Studies* 6, no. 2 (1991).

Dawson, James P. "Louis Defeats Schmeling by a Knockout in First." *New York Times*, June 23, 1938.

"Five Soldiers Get Citizenship Thru New Law." *Denver Post*, June 13, 1942.

Frankfurter Zeitung, March 31, 1933, in *Dokumente zur Geschichte der Frankfurter Juden 1933-1945*, 22ff, edited by Kommission zur Erforschung der Geschichte der Frankfurter Juden, Frankfurt (1963).

inside.mag, Special Edition of the Axel Springer AG Staff Magazine. "Farewell to Ernst Cramer, 28 January 1913 – 19 January 2010." January 2010.

Kutzik, Alfred J. "Kristallnacht Was the Name the Nazis Gave It." *New York Times*, November 25, 1988. https://www.nytimes.com/1988/11/25/opinion/l-kristallnacht-was-the-name-the-nazis-gave-it-681188.html.

"Labor Democracy is Bar to Fascism, Lewis Says Here." *New York Times*, March 16, 1937. https://timesmachine.nytimes.com/timesmachine/1937/03/16/118964747.html?pageNumber=1.

Lichtblau, Eric (reporter for the *New York Times* and visiting fellow at the United States Holocaust Memorial Museum). "The Holocaust Just Got More Shocking." *New York Times*, March 1, 2013.

Lindbergh, Charles A. "Aviation, Geography, and Race." *Reader's Digest*, November 1939, Volume 5.

Lippman, Paul. Letter to the editor. "In World War II, Many Jewish GI.'s Left Religion Off Dog Tags." *New York Times*, June 22, 1994. https://timesmachine.nytimes.com/timesmachine/1994/06/22/470333.html?pageNumber=20

Males, Rabbi Akiva. "Jewish GIs and Their Dog-Tags." *Hakirah Press*. Last edited 2013. www.hakirah.org/Vol15Males.pdf.

Smale, Alison. "A Holocaust Survivor Tells of Auschwitz at 18 and, Again, at 90." *New York Times,* March 13, 2015.

Thomas, Louisa. "America First, for Charles Lindbergh and Donald Trump." *The New Yorker*, July 24, 2016. https://www.newyorker.com/news/news-desk/america-first-for-charles-lindbergh-and-donald-trump.

Time Magazine. "Adolph Hitler, Man of the Year." January 2, 1939. http://content.time.com/time/covers/0,16641,19390102,00.html.

Time Magazine. "Adolph Hitler: Man of the Year, 1938." January 2, 1939. http://content.time.com/time/magazine/article/0,9171,760539,00.html.

Time Magazine. "The Presidency: Tenth of June." June 17, 1940. http://content.time.com/time/subscriber/article/0,33009,789854-2,00.html.

Whitman, Alden. "Lindbergh Says U.S. 'Lost' World War II." *New York Times*, August 30, 1970. https://archive.nytimes.com/www.nytimes.com/books/98/09/27/specials/lindbergh-lost.html?_r=1&oref=slogin.

OTHER

Bauer, Christian, dir. *The Ritchie Boys: A Film by Christian Bauer.* Tangram Productions, 2004.

Cunard White Star R.M.S. *Berengaria,* Southampton (via Cherbourg) to New York. Abstract of log, November, 1936.

WEBSITES

American Jewish Joint Distribution Committee Archives: New York. Jewish Transmigration Bureau Files and Index. "Jewish Transmigration Bureau Deposit Cards, 1939-1954 (JDC)." https://www.ancestry.com/search/collections/1355/.

Anti-Defamation League. Sources: Echoes and Reflections – Anti-Defamation League, USC Shoah Foundation, Yad Vashem, www.echoesandreflections.org. "Nazi Germany and Anti-Jewish Policy." https://www.adl.org/sites/default/files/documents/assets/pdf/education-outreach/nazi-germany-and-anti-jewish-policy.pdf.

Berenbaum, Michael. "Kristallnacht." *Encyclopedia Britannica*. Last edited February 13, 2020. https://www.britannica.com/event/Kristallnacht.

———. "Nürnberg Laws." *Encyclopedia Britannica*. Last edited May 13, 2020. https://www.britannica.com/topic/Nurnberg-Laws.

Chaplin, Charlie. Final speech from *The Great Dictator*.1940. https://www.charliechaplin.com/en/articles/29-the-final-speech-from-the-great-dictator-.

Claims Conference. "Saul Kagan, Architect of Holocaust Restitution." http://www.claimscon.org/about/history/saul-kagan/.

Constitutional Rights Foundation. "History Lesson 5: U.S. Immigration Policy and the Holocaust." http://crfimmigrationed.org/index.php/lessons-for-teachers/144-hl5.

Daemmig, Lara, and Marion Kaplan. "Juedischer Frauenbund (The League of Jewish Women)." *Jewish Women: A Comprehensive Historical Encyclopedia*. February 27, 2009. Jewish Women's Archive. http://jwa.org/encyclopedia/article/juedischer-frauenbund-league-of-jewish-women.

Eckhardt, Hanna. "Martha Wertheimer." From *Frankfurter Biographie 2*, 1996, for Frankfurter Personenlexikon. https://frankfurter-personenlexikon.de/node/1724.

Einstein, Albert. "Letter to Mrs. Franklin D. Roosevelt, July 26, 1941." Franklin D. Roosevelt Presidential Library and Museum: FDR's Papers as President: President's Personal File 7177. https://fdrlibrary.tumblr.com/post/141047307759/i-have-noted-with-great-satisfaction-that-you.

Encyclopedia Britannica. "America First Committee." *Encyclopedia Britannica*. Last edited March 28, 2019. http://www.britannica.com/EBchecked/topic/19247/America-First-Committee.

Federal Reserve History. "Recession of 1937-1938." Last edited November 22, 2013. https://www.federalreservehistory.org/essays/recession_of_1937_38.

German Missions in the United States, German Consulates General in the United States. "Restoration of German Citizenship – Article 116 par. 2 of the Basic Law (Grundgesetz)." https://www.germany.info/us-en/service/03-Citizenship/restoration-of-german-citizenship/925120.

Greene, Daniel, and Frank Newport. "American Public Opinion and the Holocaust." Last edited April 23, 2018. https://news.gallup.com/opinion/polling-matters/232949/american-public-opinion-holocaust.aspx.

Gruner, Wolf. "Poverty and Persecution: The Reichsvereinigung, the Jewish Population, and Anti-Jewish Policy in the Nazi State, 1939-1945." Yad Vashem, Shoah Resource Center, The International School for Holocaust Studies. https://www.yadvashem.org/odot_pdf/Microsoft%20Word%20-%203214.pdf.

Herder, Harry J., Jr. "Liberation of Buchenwald." Remember.org. http://www.remember.org/witness/herder.html.

Hitler, Adolf. "Speech at Berlin Sports Palace, January 30, 1941." Recorded by the Monitoring Service of the British Broadcasting Corporation, courtesy of the Research Project for Totalitarian Communication, New School for Social Research. http://www.ibiblio.org/pha/policy/1941/410130a.html.

Institut für Stadtgeschichte Frankfurt am Main. https://www.frankfurt1933-1945.de/nc/chronologie/.

International Boxing Hall of Fame. "Louis Destroys Schmeling in Rematch." Last edited 2000. http://www.ibhof.com/pages/archives/louisschmeling.html.

Jewish Telegraphic Agency. *Daily News Bulletin*, vol. II, no. 94, November 24, 1936. "2000 Books by Jews on New Nazi Blacklist." http://www.jta.org/1936/11/24/archive/2000-books-by-jews-on-new-nazi-blacklist.

———. *Daily News Bulletin*, vol. III, no. 4, August 4, 1937. "Weizmann Advises Partition Be Accepted As 20th Congress Opens in Zurich." https://www.jta.org/1937/08/04/archive/weizmann-advises-partition-be-accepted-as-20th-congress-opens-in-zurich.

Jewish Virtual Library, a Project of American-Israeli Cooperative Enterprise [Source: ibiblio] "Adolf Hitler: Speech at the Berlin Sports Palace (January 30, 1941)." http://www.jewishvirtuallibrary.org/jsource/Holocaust/hitler013041.html.

———. "Nuremberg Trial Defendants: Alfred Rosenberg." [Source: Nizkor; Nazi Conspiracy & Aggression, Volume II, Chapter XVI]. https://www.jewishvirtuallibrary.org/jsource/Holocaust/Rosenberg.html.

———. "The Holocaust: Timeline of Jewish Persecution (1932–1945)." [Source: Holocaust Memorial Center, Yad Vashem]. http://www.jewishvirtuallibrary.org/jsource/Holocaust/chron.html#37.

———. "The Holocaust: Timeline of Jewish Persecution (1932-1945)." www.jewishvirtuallibrary.org/jsource/Holocaust/chron.html#38.

———. "The Nazi Party: Hitler Youth." http://www.jewishvirtuallibrary.org/jsource/Holocaust/hitleryouth.html.

———. "The Nazi Party: Women of the Third Reich." George Duncan. https://www.jewishvirtuallibrary.org/women-of-the-third-reich.

———. "The Nuremberg Laws: Background & Overview." [Source: Jeremy Noakes and Geoffrey Pridham, "Documents on Nazism 1919-1945." Viking Press, 1974; The Nizkor Project]. https://www.jewishvirtuallibrary.org/jsource/Holocaust/nurlaws.html.

———. "U.S. Policy During WWII: U.S. Army & the Holocaust." http://www.jewishvirtuallibrary.org/jsource/Holocaust/usarmy_holo.html.

———. "Zionist Congress: Zionist Congresses During British Mandate (1923-1946)." [Source: Jewish Agency of Israel, 1997, 1998, 1999, 2000]. https://www.jewishvirtuallibrary.org/zionist-congresses-during-british-mandate-1923-1946.

———. "Zionism: World Zionist Organization (WZO)." [Source: Israeli Foreign Minister.] https://www.jewishvirtuallibrary.org/world-zionist-organization-wzo.

Ladwig-Winters, Simone. "The Attack on Berlin Department Stores (Warenhaeuser) after 1933." Yad Vashem, Shoah Resource Center, The International School for Holocaust Studies, http://www.yadvashem.org/odot_pdf/Microsoft%20Word%20-%205622.pdf.

Lindsay, James M. "TWE Remembers: Charles Lindbergh's Des Moines Speech." Council on Foreign Relations. September 11, 2012. https://www.cfr.org/blog/twe-remembers-charles-lindberghs-des-moines-speech.

———. "TWE Remembers: FDR's 'Stab in the Back' Speech." Council on Foreign Relations. June 10, 2013. http://blogs.cfr.org/lindsay/2013/06/10/twe-remembers-fdrs-stab-in-the-back-speech/.

Linfield, H. S. "Statistics of Jews – 1929." *American Jewish Year Book Vol. 34: Statistics of Jews and Jewish Organizations in the United States: An Historical Review of Ten Censuses, 1850-1937*. American Jewish Committee and Springer, 2008. http://www.ajcarchives.org/ajc_data/files/1930_1931_7_statistics.pdf.

NPR. "The Fight of the Century: Louis vs. Schmeling." NPR. http://www.npr.org/2006/11/25/6515548/the-fight-of-the-century-louis-vs-schmeling.

PBS. "Communication, News & Censorship." PBS. Last edited September, 2007. http://www.pbs.org/thewar/at_home_communication_news_censorship.htm.

———. "Ford's Anti-Semitism." PBS. https://www.pbs.org/wgbh/americanexperience/features/henryford-antisemitism/.

Reder, Hillary. "Max Beckmann." MoMA. https://www.moma.org/artists/429?locale=en.

Rees, Laurence. "Hitler's Invasion of Russia in World War Two." BBC. Last edited March 30, 2011. http://www.bbc.co.uk/history/worldwars/wwtwo/hitler_russia_invasion_01.shtml.

Roosevelt, Franklin D. "Fireside Chat, September 3, 1939." The American Presidency Project. https://www.presidency.ucsb.edu/documents/fireside-chat-13.

Steen, Jürgen. "Air War Damage as a Sensation." Institut für Stadtgeschichte Frankfurt am Main. Last edited January 1, 2003. https://www.frankfurt1933-1945.de/nc/beitraege/show/1/thematik/der-luftkrieg-1940-1942/artikel/luftkriegs-schaeden-als-sensation/.

United Nations. "1941: The Atlantic Charter." UN. https://www.un.org/en/sections/history-united-nations-charter/1941-atlantic-charter/index.html.

United States Holocaust Memorial Museum. "1937 Munich Exhibition of Degenerate Art." https://www.ushmm.org/collections/the-museums

-collections/collections-highlights/julien-bryan/nazi-germany-1937/1937-munich-exhibition-of-degenerate-art.

———. "Anti-Jewish Legislation in Prewar Germany." https://encyclopedia.ushmm.org/content/en/article/anti-jewish-legislation-in-prewar-germany.

———. "Auschwitz." Last edited March 16, 2015. https://encyclopedia.ushmm.org/content/en/article/auschwitz.

———. "Buchenwald." http://www.ushmm.org/wlc/en/article.php?ModuleId=10005198.

———. "Concentration Camps, 1933-39." Last edited June 27, 2019. http://www.ushmm.org/wlc/en/article.php?ModuleId=10005263.

———. "Dachau." Last edited December 5, 2006. http://www.ushmm.org/wlc/en/article.php?ModuleId=10005214.

———. "'Degenerate' Art." Last edited June 8, 2020. https://encyclopedia.ushmm.org/content/en/article/degenerate-art-1.

———. "The Evian Conference." http://www.ushmm.org/outreach/en/article.php?ModuleId=10007698.

———. "Franklin Delano Roosevelt." http://www.ushmm.org/wlc/en/article.php?ModuleId=10007411.

———. "Jewish Businesses – Atonement Fee." *Reichsgesetzblatt.* https://www.ushmm.org/information/exhibitions/online-exhibitions/special-focus/kristallnacht/jewish-businesses/atonement-fee.

———. "Jewish Refugees from the German Reich, 1933-1939." http://www.ushmm.org/exhibition/st-louis/teach/supread2.htm.

———. "Killing Centers: An Overview." https://encyclopedia.ushmm.org/content/en/article/killing-centers-an-overview.

———. "Law Justice, and the Holocaust — Part I: Documents Relating to the Transition from Democracy to Dictatorship." Last edited 2009. Translated from *Reichsgesetzblatt* I, 1933, p. 83. https://www.ushmm.org/m/pdfs/20091123-ljh-dictatorship.pdf.

———. "Nazi Party Platform." Last edited October 15, 2020. https://encyclopedia.ushmm.org/content/en/article/nazi-party-platform.

———. "Synagogues." https://www.ushmm.org/information/exhibitions/online-exhibitions/special-focus/kristallnacht/synagogues.

———. "Timeline of Events, 1938, Evian Conference." http://www.ushmm.org/learn/timeline-of-events/1933-1938/evian-conference.

———. "Timeline of Events, 1938, German Jews' Passports Declared Invalid." http://www.ushmm.org/learn/timeline-of-events/1933-1938/reich-ministry-of-the-interior-invalidates-all-german-passports-held-by-jew.

———. "Timeline of Events, 1942–1945." http://www.ushmm.org/learn/timeline-of-events/1942-1945.

———. "Timeline of Events, 1942-1945: D-Day." http://www.ushmm.org/learn/timeline-of-events/1942-1945/d-day.

———. UCLA Film and Television Archive. "Mussolini Meets with Hitler in Germany." http://www.ushmm.org/wlc/en/media_fi.php?MediaId=200.

———. "War Refugee Board: Background and Establishment." https://encyclopedia.ushmm.org/content/en/article/war-refugee-board-background-and-establishment.

———. "Warsaw." http://www.ushmm.org/wlc/en/article.php?ModuleId=10005069.

University of Virginia Miller Center. Presidential Speeches Franklin D. Roosevelt Presidency. "June 10, 1940: 'Stab in the Back' Speech." https://millercenter.org/the-presidency/presidential-speeches/june-10-1940-stab-back-speech.

———. "October 5, 1937: Quarantine Speech." https://millercenter.org/the-presidency/presidential-speeches/october-5-1937-quarantine-speech.

US Department of State. "Peace and War: United States Foreign Policy, 1931-1941." Publication 1983. Washington, DC: U.S., Government Printing Office, 1943. https://www.mtholyoke.edu/acad/intrel/interwar/fdr11.htm.

USC Shoah Foundation, Center for Initiatives in Jewish Education, IWitness. "Unit One: The World Before." https://iwitness.usc.edu/SFI/Documents/CIJE/Curriculum/Unit%201.pdf.

World Jewish Congress. "Germany Recognizes 1936 High Jump Record by Jewish Woman." Last edited November 25, 2009. https://www.worldjewishcongress.org/en/news/germany-recognizes-1936-high-jump-record-by-jewish-woman?print=true.

Yad Vashem, Shoah Resource Center, The International School for Holocaust Studies. Extract of the Speech by Hitler, January 30, 1939." [Source: *The Speeches of Adolf Hitler*, I. Edited by N.H. Baynes, London, 1942]. https://www.yadvashem.org/odot_pdf/Microsoft%20Word%20-%201988.pdf.

———. "Frankfurt am Main." http://www.yadvashem.org/odot_pdf/Microsoft%20Word%20-%205861.pdf.

———. "The Establishment of the Reichsvereinigung, July 1939." [Source: *Documents on the Holocaust, Selected Sources on the Destruction of Germany and Austria, Poland, and the Soviet Union.*"Edited by Y. Arad, Y. Gutman, and A. Margaliot – Yad Vashem, 1981]. http://www.yadvashem.org/odot_pdf/Microsoft%20Word%20-%205389.pdf.

Yale Law School. The Avalon Project. "The British War Blue Book: Reichstag Speech, February 20, 1938." http://avalon.law.yale.edu/wwii/blbk05.asp. [full page accessed in 2015 is no longer accessible]

———. "Nazi Conspiracy and Aggression Volume 2 Chapter XVI Part 4: Wilhelm Keitel." http://avalon.law.yale.edu/imt/chap16_part04.asp.

ARCHIVES

Arolson Archives in Bad Arolson Germany. Record Number 1202255 1202227 4 1.1.22.1/0003A/0028 65: Jews from Frankfurt Murdered in Lodz. Accessed at the United States Holocaust Memorial Museum Digital Collection. August 18, 2015.

Hessian State Archives. In Wiesbaden, Germany. Files of documents of Norbert and Julie Baum and of the Norbert Harff Company. Accessed beginning in February 2014.

Institut für Stadtgeschichte, Frankfurt am Main. Accessed beginning in 2010.

Jewish Museum Frankfurt Archives. Accessed beginning in 2010.

Polish State Archives. In Lodz, series: Head of the Jewish Council of Elders, signature*:* Name lists of foreign Jews brought into the ghetto, number 997. Accessed through the Radegast Station Division of the Museum of Independence Traditions in Lodz on July 21, 2020.

Polish State Archives. RG 05.008M.0009.00000257 (Record Group 05.008M, Reel 9, page 257): Lodz Ghetto Hospital Death Records. Accessed at the United States Holocaust Memorial Museum Archives in October, 2009.

Yad Vashem. Central Database of Shoah Victims' Names. "List of Jews from Dresden Who Perished During the Holocaust." Item ID 7710741. Accessed on September 15, 2020. https://yvng.yadvashem.org/nameDetails.html?language=en&itemId=7710741&ind=1.